BRAND® NEW THEOLOGY

To (Dr.) Dianne Marie McGee, my mother,
who was my best teacher and always administered life's
toughest qualifying exams. Not only was she beautiful, smart,
and prophetic—she dared to dream a bigger dream for
her daughters than she dreamed for herself.

BRAND® NEW THEOLOGY

The Wal-Martization of T.D. Jakes and the New Black Church

PAULA L. MCGEE

ORBIS BOOKS
Maryknoll, New York

ORBIS BOOKS
Maryknoll, New York 10545

Founded in 1970, Orbis Books endeavors to publish works that enlighten the mind, nourish the spirit, and challenge the conscience. The publishing arm of the Maryknoll Fathers and Brothers, Orbis seeks to explore the global dimensions of the Christian faith and mission, to invite dialogue with diverse cultures and religious traditions, and to serve the cause of reconciliation and peace. The books published reflect the views of their authors and do not represent the official position of the Maryknoll Society. To learn more about Maryknoll and Orbis Books, please visit our website at www.maryknollsociety.org.

Library of Congress Cataloging-in-Publication Data

Names: McGee, Paula L., 1962- author.
Title: Brand? new theology : the Wal-Martization of T.D. Jakes and the new Black church / Paula L. McGee.
Description: Maryknoll : Orbis Books, 2017. | Includes bibliographical references and index.
Identifiers: LCCN 2016040041 (print) | LCCN 2016053982 (ebook) | ISBN 9781626982277 (pbk.) | ISBN 9781608336920 (ebook)
Subjects: LCSH: Jakes, T. D. | African American Pentecostal churches. | African American Pentecostals—Biography. | Pentecostal churches—United States. | Pentecostals, Black—United States. | Blacks—United States—Religion.
Classification: LCC BX8762.5.Z8 J355 2017 (print) | LCC BX8762.5.Z8 (ebook) | DDC 289.9/4092 [B] —dc23
LC record available at https://lccn.loc.gov/2016040041

Contents

Acknowledgments

This project at times was overwhelmingly painful. Unexpectedly, it violently ventured into too many of my tender places. I am thankful, however, for the many prayers and conversations with preachers, scholars, professors, and classmates. I am especially grateful to the CGU Writing Center and the dissertation boot camps. I would like especially to thank my friend Paula McGhee, with the "h," who partnered with me and vigilantly became a sponsor, when the dissertation process felt like I needed a twelve-step program.

Cara Pfeiffer made real the text from Scripture about those "who have entertained angels unaware." She appeared at the very end of the process and worked diligently to get the final dissertation submission completed. Most important, I would like to thank my Ph.D. "dream team," to pull a basketball metaphor from my past life. Rosemary, Zayn, Dr. Phil, and Dr. Baldwin. Your work was definitely interdisciplinary and revolutionary. I look forward to the work that we will do in the future.

I am thankful for Robert Ellsberg at Orbis Books for very graciously helping me to craft the right formation for the book version of my dissertation. I also am thankful for the students and my colleagues at Memphis Theological Seminary, who provided a place for me to use my gifts for *scholarship*, *piety*, and *justice*.

Thank God! This station and season on my journey has come to an end as another begins. I place my Ph.D. and the words of my first book on the altar. We anxiously await with tip-toe anticipation, to see what God will do with *Brand® New Theology* and Reverend Doctor Paula—author.

Preface

In this work I converse with some scholars more than others because their pioneering contributions unlocked new pathways and new academic discourses. Authors like Shayne Lee with his work on T.D. Jakes and Milmon Harrison's *Righteous Riches* were food for the soul. Kate Bowler's *Blessed: A History of the American Prosperity Gospel* arrived after I finished my dissertation but was a welcome addition to the prosperity canon. Marla Frederick's *Between Sundays* is an impeccable treatise. *Colored Television* adds to the many colors of her body of work. Marla writes as an anthropologist but tells her stories like a woman of faith. Mara Einstein's *Brands of Faith* gave me permission to tell the story of my own brands. Finally, Paul Gifford's critical commentary on prosperity Pentecostalism, especially in Africa, is mentioned in almost every chapter.

One of the challenges of a truly interdisciplinary and transdisciplinary project is that you must teach scholars the terminology and philosophy of their neighboring scholars—and you must teach them well. As a result, the dissertation overflowed with footnotes. Long explanatory notes filled the bottom of almost three hundred formatted pages. I have reduced the number of pages and also updated much of the work. A long bibliography remains to direct future scholars into the conversation and acts as the final benediction for scholarly worship with confession, repentance, and celebration.

I give myself permission to write as me—a religious woman of color and scholar—not beholden to sexist, racist, androcentric, and patriarchal language. Women's Studies and Cultural Studies provide the framework to dance on the pages with many clever words and symbols. [Brackets] encompass the words that replace God as "Him," and the phrases that historically decided to speak only to brothers and the brotherhood. Most times, the words are changed to [God], [him or her]. Some statements remain intact because the alteration changes the author's intent or style. Elisabeth Schüssler Fiorenza strategically uses an "*" for G*d and the*logy; however, for such a lengthy project the insertions are too cumbersome for a friendly read. My invitation to the womanist, feminist, queer, *resisting readers* illumines the challenge and reminds the faithful that regardless of our vigilance, the literary voice of the white straight male American Christian still oppresses and silences many. At a minimum, I converse with those writers and scholars who want to be like Moses, who, according to the writer of Hebrews, refused to be known as the [child] of Pharaoh's daughter. Instead he chose to suffer with the people of God. Maybe we too, by faith, can choose to suffer with the people of our god/desses and refuse those words that seek to control us and our stories.

Foreword

I met Paula L. McGee when she was a graduate student in the Department of Religious Studies at Vanderbilt University back in the early 1990s. I was an associate professor of religious studies there at the time, and also an emerging Martin Luther King, Jr., scholar-activist. I invited Paula to deliver a lecture on black women in ministry in my introductory course on the history of the Black Church. I was impressed with how she helped students to better understand the failure of communities of faith to address both white privilege and black male privilege. Paula had a clear grasp of African American religious studies and an ability to enlighten and effectively challenge undergraduates and other students around the social-justice history and traditions of the Black Church. I now know that this was part of an amazing journey that led to *Brand® New Theology: The Wal-Martization of T.D. Jakes and the New Black Church*.

Paula's claims about televangelism and megachurches were not so clear to me back in the 1990s, even as I served as an examiner for her qualifying examinations and as a member of her dissertation committee. In any case, her recent research on the New Black Church, prosperity preachers, and theologies of prosperity draws on years of teaching, preaching, and activism in the Black Church. Her work is advancing the conversation regarding the African American religious experience to a new level of vitality and sophistication.

Reverend McGee is mindful that today's Black Church in particular is an increasingly elusive phenomenon, and that there are different opinions about its strengths and weaknesses. She has been part of the continuing scholarly conversation in which some scholars speak of the decentering of the Black Church and its declining prophetic energies and influence, and others suggest a deepening and pronounced identity crisis. Others proclaim the death of what was once a proud and richly meaningful and/or relevant institution. Dr. McGee simply provides yet another piece to that puzzle that is the Black Church and African American religion. Consequently, she establishes her place among that cadre of scholars who can properly claim special authority in this regard.

Unquestionably, Paula McGee has become a leading authority on the Black Church–New Black Church dichotomy and phenomena, and the interesting and often diverging leadership models. She writes from an insider perspective, having preached for Noel Jones and Frederick Price, the godfather of black Word of Faith. As a result, she shares with readers the intimacies of this new kind of pastor–parishioner relationship of the New Black Church.

In this timely and provocative volume, Dr. McGee focuses on the pastor/CEO leadership and the parishioner/consumer of "the New Black Church," which she describes as "a combination of televangelism and the super-megachurch movements." Highly interested in the ideological significations, she treats Martin Luther King, Jr., as "the icon of the Black Church," which she defines as "a refuge model with preachers' continuing discourses on race and social justice," and Bishop T.D. Jakes, the pastor of The Potter's House in Dallas, Texas, as "the quintessential representative of the New Black Church."

Bishop Jakes and The Potter's House are a case study. In bold terms, she concludes that The Potter's House and Jakes's success with the Woman Thou Art Loosed (WTAL) brand, based on Luke 13:12, amounts to "the Wal-Martization of African American religion." Jakes "is considered to be the Sam Walton of the New Black Church." He and other television preachers are pastoring super-megachurches with one congregation in numerous locations, and they make up the core of the New Black Church phenomenon. According to Dr. McGee, these preachers exploit "the traditions of uplift, lively worship, and the ideological power of the institution and the power of black preachers as the spokespersons and linkage figures *for* and *to* the community." Clearly, Bishop Jakes and the New Black Church are synonymous with the kind of personal-enrichment themes and materialistic ingredients that are antithetical, at least on some levels, to the communitarian ethic and the spiritual traditions of traditional black churches.

Dr. McGee challenges black churches and religious scholars with a clarion call to take the preacher and churches of this new model more seriously. As she notes, millions of black folk read the books of Bishop Jakes and other super-megachurch pastors, attend their churches, and tune in during their radio and television broadcasts. These faithful followers celebrate preachers like T.D. Jakes. The congregants are repeating and living out the God-talk of these popular preachers. The theologies of the New Black Church are popular *folk* theologies or *lived religion,* and much more accessible and malleable than academic theologies.

Her ideological critique underscores what is apparently "a paradigm shift in post–civil rights America." Bishop Jakes and other pastor-CEOs are offering theologies that promise "liberation within the confines of capitalism." Unlike academic liberation theologians, who have critiqued capitalism for its perpetuation of inequalities, these preachers offer "an individual economic salvation" to African Americans who are very comfortable with their middle-class lifestyle and their pursuit of the American dream. Far removed from the stories of suffering and struggle that marked the era of Jim Crow, these black Christians welcome the branding and this new theology. In the process, she adds, "the preferential option for the poor" is lost and buried beneath the brands and a plethora of branded spiritual products. The religious experiences of these churches have become the products of a big box spiritual Wal-Mart.

Bishop Jakes and other super-megachurch pastors are turning the biblical narratives of the Exodus and the cross event into "branded stories" that guarantee congregants health, wealth, and prosperity. These stories have not only become expressions of prosperity theology; Dr. McGee concludes that the brands act as *theological norms*, and the branded products and religious experiences are the *medium* in which consumers encounter the *contextual theology* of each preacher.

Dr. Paula McGee is particularly concerned, and understandably so, with the ways in which the New Black Church model of ministry and its theologies actually undermine the liberation and empowerment of women. Women who attend and participate in Bishop Jakes's Woman Thou Art Loosed (WTAL) conferences are, in her words, "socially constructing their collective and individual branded identities as *loosed* women." Although deeply conscious of why so many women feel empowered by "the preached branded biblical stories," whose messages "are entertaining, intoxicating, and even cathartic," nonetheless, McGee contends that "Bishop Jakes is not really liberating women." His "theology of prosperity and biblical brands do not offer a systematic critique of capitalism." In this context, patriarchal structures are preserved, male privilege reinforced, and "individual economic salvation" encouraged "within an oppressive system."

Jakes's magnetic personality, his amazing power and charisma, and his dynamic and engaging preaching style are all acknowledged. Dr. McGee can appreciate why he is "America's preacher," and why he is praised by the likes of President Barack Obama and Oprah Winfrey. Yet, the New Black Church model for McGee is not sustainable. Bishop Jakes and other popular preachers are not really "empowering their followers." Instead, Jakes is basically empowering women and his followers to stay loyal to his brand. Her conclusion is that the liberation promised by the prosperity preachers is, at best, "only a pseudo liberation." The majority of women who volunteer at his church and send monthly donations will more than likely never have access to Jakes's celebrity status and his affluent lifestyle. Most African American women will not have an entrée to perform the ultimate trope of empire—the celebrity CEO.

Dr. McGee extends a rallying cry to academics, and especially black academics, "to offer more than a caricature or homily" concerning these popular church leaders and their approaches to ministry and mission. Her final word is a reminder that the call of the prophet, especially in the Black Church, is "to speak truth to power."

Brand® New Theology is clearly one of the most important books written on the Black Church and African American religion since the civil rights movement of the 1950s and '60s. It is an intriguing and well-documented treatment of some of the most dramatic changes occurring in African American religious life and culture. This book gives an accurate account of the wider cultural significance and impact of the current Black Church. *Brand® New Theology* answers so many questions about what is happening *with* and *to* African Americans in the worlds of televangelism and mega- and super-megachurches. Moreover, it advances the conversation among black and womanist theologians and black pastors concerning the present and future directions of the Black Church and, more specifically, about its public role today and tomorrow.

Lewis V. Baldwin
Emeritus Professor of Religious Studies
Vanderbilt University
July 10, 2016

T.D. Jakes and
the New Black Church

*Oprah is a big brand. Tyler is a big brand. Jakes is that next
big brand.* —Darrell Miller,
entertainment attorney for Bishop Jakes

Theodore Dexter Jakes is the popular international televangelist
and the senior pastor of The Potter's House—a super-megachurch
in Dallas, Texas, one church in four locations.[1] On any day of the
week, you may see a woman buying one of the thousands of Bishop
T.D. Jakes's products. She might even be one of the women who
has followed him and his ministry since his early Pentecostal roots
in Charleston, West Virginia. These humble beginnings are often
overshadowed by his enormous celebrity, fortune, and fame. Most
notably, he is the preacher/pastor who travels with Oprah Winfrey for her Lifeclasses. Oprah participated in Bishop's Jakes's 2013
Megafest. He also has a multimillion-dollar, nine-motion-picture
deal with Sony Pictures that in some ways surpasses the success of
familiar black directors such as Tyler Perry and Spike Lee.

Jakes is far removed from his Pentecostal storefront days in the
second poorest state in the Union. Those days were before he moved

---

1. The official name of T.D. Jakes's church is now The Potter's House of
Dallas. Throughout the book I will simply use "The Potter's House."

his entire ministry with fifty families to build a megachurch in Dallas, Texas.[2] Jakes is now a global brand and an icon of the New Black Church. President Barack Obama invited T.D. Jakes to deliver the morning sermon at his historic presidential inauguration. In an interview Obama stated: "I am fortunate to count myself among the countless Americans whose lives have been touched by the ministry of Bishop T.D. Jakes. . . . [He] has made us better as individuals [and] more compassionate, and move loving in this country."[3] Oprah considers T.D. Jakes to be "the best preacher in the nation," and he now appears regularly with her on her network (OWN)— just one more indication of the power of his brand and his ability to reach broad audiences. T.D. Jakes is ambitious. He now hosts his own daytime television talk show.[4] His goal is to one day expand his brand to be as popular as the big name brands that we recognize immediately with just one name: Oprah, Mike, Tiger, and Tyler.[5]

Millions of women, the majority of them African American, are faithful ministry partners, sending a minimum of thirty dollars a month to Bishop Jakes. They also make up the majority of active members in his super-megachurch, where they cheerfully give their tithes and volunteer their time. Moreover, these women are his best customers, buying each new book and crowding into movie theaters to see his latest movie. Most of these women, however, never question his theology, nor do they seem to be concerned about his financial empire and personal wealth. Actually, most of them see him as their liberator—the preacher/pastor who has empowered them to overcome their deepest hurts and traumas. Bishop T.D. Jakes, in the last forty years, has successfully branded himself as a *liberator of women*. Women believe that Jakes is just like Jesus—when, according to the Gospel of Luke, he healed the infirmed woman with the

---

2. Shayne Lee, *T.D. Jakes: America's New Preacher* (New York: New York University Press, 2005), 71.

3. Matthew Faraci, "The Bishop's Life," *Variety* 330, no. 7 (December 2015): 119.

4. Faraci, "The Bishop's Life," 120.

5. Carolyn M. Brown, "Sowing Seeds of Prosperity," *Black Enterprise* 44, no. 8 (April 2014): 60.

words: "Woman thou art loosed." Jakes has successfully convinced women all over the world that they need *to be loosed*, and they need *to be loosed* by him.

This book is about the "brand® new theology" of the New Black Church, with particular focus on the branding and contextual theology of Bishop Jakes and his most popular brand, Woman Thou Art Loosed (WTAL). I argue that his success with the WTAL brand and The Potter's House is a vivid example of the Wal-Martization of African American Religion. In this context, I see T.D. Jakes as the Sam Walton of the New Black Church.

This case study of Jakes is the scaffolding of an ideological critique of the New Black Church model of ministry.[6] The churches represented in this model are mainly independent churches founded or redeveloped in the 1980s and 1990s.[7] A large majority are considered Word of Faith or word churches.[8] The New Black Church is the result of televangelism and the mega/super-megachurch movements.[9] The churches and their pastors represent a definite paradigm

---

6. For examples of case study research, see Bruce L. Berg, *Qualitative Research Methods for the Social Sciences* (Boston, MA: Pearson Press, 2004), 4.

7. Many of the New Black Churches were founded by their pastors. Others were originally older black churches that were redeveloped and reorganized into New Black Churches.

8. For examples and definitions of Word of Faith and word churches, see Milmon F. Harrison, *Righteous Riches: The Word of Faith Movement in Contemporary African American Religion* (New York: Oxford University Press, 2005).

9. The term "megachurch" usually refers to churches with two thousand or more Sunday morning worshipers. However, I am using the term "super-megachurch" to reference churches that boast memberships of ten thousand members or more. The language is similar to the difference between a Wal-Mart and a Super Wal-Mart. Because of the marketing nature and combination of television and local church ministries, the actual membership numbers are difficult to verify empirically. Additionally, the number of members and the size of the churches serve as part of the branding. Kate Bowler states, "In 1970, megachurches numbered 50. By 1990, the total swelled to 310" (101). She also argues that "throughout the 1980s, prosperity theology rose with a new vitality in African American churches" (111). See Kate Bowler, *Blessed: A History of the American Prosperity Gospel* (New York: Oxford University Press, 2013). Tamelyn Tucker-Worgs quotes Scott

shift from what has traditionally been recognized and understood as the Black Church.[10] Bishop Jakes is now the pastor of a church with more than 30,000 members. He is also the CEO of an international television and conference ministry and several for-profit businesses.[11] Jakes has become "the broker with the power to make or break others' careers, or at least enhance them by giving them an appearance at a well-attended conference."[12] Almost single-handedly, he has launched the careers of several women televangelists and megachurch pastors.[13] Without a doubt, he is a celebrity and a multimillionaire. His financial empire is estimated to be worth $400 million.[14] His personal net worth is reported to be about $18 million or at least 200 times the average income of his members in the Dallas community.[15] He is a pastor/CEO.

"Pastor" and "entrepreneur/CEO" are both cultural signifiers

Thumma and Dave Travis as the experts on megachurches and super-megachurches. They "claim that in 2005 there were about 1,250 megachurches in the United States (up from 50 in 1970)." Tucker-Worgs identifies 149 black megachurches. See Tamelyn N. Tucker-Worgs, *The Black Megachurch: Theology, Gender, and the Politics of Public Engagement* (Waco, TX: Baylor University Press, 2011), 24.

10. Archie Smith, Jr., *The Relational Self: Ethics & Therapy from a Black Church Perspective* (Nashville, TN: Abingdon Press, 1982).

11. The not-for-profit is T.D. Jakes Ministries, while TDJ Enterprises is the for-profit entity.

12. Sarah Posner, *God's Profits: Faith, Fraud, and the Republican Crusade for Values Voters* (Sausalito, CA: PoliPoint Press, 2008), 58.

13. Speaking at a WTAL Conference is great exposure for women preachers. However, Paula White and Juanita Bynum are two televangelists and megachurch pastors who have benefitted greatly from their relationships with Jakes. Marla Frederick-McGlathery, "But It's Bible," in *African American Women and Television Preachers in Women and Religion in the African Diaspora: Knowledge, Power, and Performance*, ed. R. Marie Griffith and Barbara Dianne Savage (Baltimore, MD: Johns Hopkins University Press, 2006), 277.

14. Faraci, "The Bishop's Life," 119; Brown, "Sowing Seeds of Prosperity," 56. *Variety* magazine lists the income at 400 billion. I assume that is a typographical error, and the correct amount is 400 million.

15. "8 Black Pastors Whose Net Worth is 200 Times Greater than Folks in Their Local Communities," http://atlantablackstar.com (July 6, 2014).

that carry weight in American secular and Black Church mythologies of success, and represent leadership roles of two important organizations in American culture—the church and the corporation. How Jakes describes and brands himself is a blend of what many consider to be two different worldviews with different values—one sacred and one secular. Remarkably, Bishop T.D. Jakes is the only black preacher who is compared to Billy Graham, on the one hand,[16] and to Donald Trump and Michael Dell, on the other.[17] Forbes.com describes Jakes and The Potter's House as "Christian Capitalism: Megachurches and Megabusinesses."[18] For Jakes, and other New Black Church pastors, African American worship and its components, testimony, prayer, song, and sermon—so critical to the religious identity of black churches and their members—are also products to be packaged, marketed, and sold. Unashamed of his success, Jakes proudly touts the trinkets of American financial success: a Bentley, a private jet, expensive suits, and a mansion.[19] He expects to live as comfortably as any secular CEO. With over forty books to his credit, he has a team of marketers, publicists, and agents who guarantee that his image and brand will continue to be profitable and expand. He now boasts about his global brand.

Choosing Jakes as a case study and representative of New Black Church pastors and their churches is very much like choosing Sam Walton and Wal-Mart to study CEOs and American businesses. It is inappropriate to study Sam Walton and Wal-Mart if you are trying to describe the average American business and CEO. But, from an ideological perspective, we can comfortably argue that no CEO and

---

16. David Van Biema, "Spirit Raiser: America's Best," *Time* 158, no. 12 (September 17, 2001): 52-56; Shayne Lee and Phillip Luke Sinitiere, *Holy Mavericks: Evangelical Innovators and the Spiritual Marketplace* (New York: New York University Press, 2009), 61-62.

17. Lee, *T.D. Jakes*, 83.

18. Luisa Kroll, "Christian Capitalism: Megachurches, Megabusinesses," http://www.forbes.com (September 17, 2003).

19. Jonathan L. Walton, *Watch This! The Ethics and Aesthetics of Black Televangelism* (New York: New York University Press, 2009), 117; Lee, *T.D. Jakes*, 109-10.

company has changed the way Americans do business more than Sam Walton and Wal-Mart. The same applies for T.D. Jakes with T.D. Jakes Ministries and The Potter's House. Jakes is the quintessential example of a successful pastor in the New Black Church. Moreover, it is no surprise that Wal-Mart's growth and expansion in the 1980s and '90s coincided with the expansion of black megachurches.[20] Today, Wal-Mart is not only the largest corporation in America but in the world—the "template industry," setting the bar for its competitors."[21]

Wal-Mart is for this generation what General Motors (GM) was for previous generations. Just as the GM model of business and its CEO differ from the Wal-Mart model, the same differences exist for black churches and their pastors. Martin Luther King, Jr., and Dexter Avenue are the iconic representation for the Black Church refuge model of the GM generation. King's view of the church was "as a refuge, as a voice for the voiceless, as the conscience of the state and as the chief symbol of the beloved community."[22] Bishop T.D. Jakes, instead, is an example of a pastor in the New Black Church. An exceptional orator with a distinctive black preaching aesthetic, Jakes "tactically blends biblical teaching with psychological theories, folk wisdom, pop culture, and American idealism."[23] Jakes is a black man, who, like Sam Walton, represents something very American. The complexity of this Americanness, combined with a black preacher and Black Church aesthetic and identity, is what makes him and the New Black Church such an interesting phenomenon.

---

20. Wal-Mart Stores, Inc., grew not only in stature from a mere "276 stores to 1528, but also in sales from 1.2 to 26 billion dollars." Justin R. Watkins, "Always Low Prices, Always at a Cost: A Call to Arms Against the Wal-Martization of America," *J. Marshall Law Review* 40 (2006–2007): 274.

21. Watkins, "Always Low Prices, 274.

22. Lewis V. Baldwin, *The Voice of Conscience: The Church in the Mind of Martin Luther King, Jr.* (New York: Oxford University Press, 2010), 225.

23. Shayne Lee and Phillip Luke Sinitiere, *Holy Mavericks; Evangelical Innovators and the Spiritual Marketplace* (New York: New York University Press, 2009), 4.

In past generations a black preacher who fit so comfortably within the image of what it means to be a successful American would be unimaginable.[24] However, in the current economic and social configurations of America, with the socioreligious identities of African Americans (especially for African American Protestants), a figure like T.D. Jakes as a black preacher not only exists, but flourishes—with a host of Black Church pastors who aspire to be just like him.[25] He is often branded as a celebrity and a twenty-first-century example of a successful minister. More important, as the icon of faith, with a global brand, he promotes himself as a successful Christian. He is comfortable with his success as both a pastor and an entrepreneur.[26]

Bishop T.D. Jakes and New Black Church pastors signal a larger shift on the world landscape of religion. Several religious scholars and theologians argue that in America, the market and capitalism are functioning more and more like a religion and an expression of faith. David Loy writes that "the Market is becoming the first truly world religion, binding all corners of the globe more and more tightly into a world view and set of values whose religious role we overlook because we insist on seeing them as 'secular.'"[27] Harvey Cox echoes Loy, affirming that "the market is construed not as a creation of culture . . . but, as the 'natural' way things happen." For Cox, this means that "a global market culture . . . is generating an identifiable value-laden, 'religious' worldview."[28] Philosopher

---

24. Lee and Sinitiere, *Holy Mavericks*, 55.

25. John Blake writes that Jakes has "spawned a new generation of imitators. The religious landscape is now full of Junior Jakeses." John Blake, "Therapy and Theology: Atlanta's Megafest Shows Many Sides of T.D. Jakes Ministry," *Atlanta Journal-Constitution,* June 23, 2004, home edition.

26. Walton, *Watch This!,* 116.

27. David Loy, "The Religion of the Market," *Journal of the American Academy of Religion* 65, no. 2 (Summer 1997): 275.

28. Harvey Cox, "Mammon and the Culture of the Market: A Socio-Theological Critique," in *Meaning and Modernity: Religion, Polity, and Self,* ed. Richard Madsen, William M. Sullivan, and Steven M. Tipton (Berkeley, CA: University of California Press, 2002), 124. See also Cox's "The Market as God," in Robert Ellsberg, ed., *A Harvey Cox Reader* (Maryknoll, NY: Orbis Books, 2016), 283-91.

and theologian John Cobb uses the term "economism." He defines economism as "that organization of society that is intentionally in the service of economic growth. All other values, including national sovereignty, are subordinated to this end, with the sincere expectation that sufficient prosperity will enable the world to meet its noneconomic needs as well."[29] In their book *Selling Spirituality,* Jeremy Carrette and Richard King define these cultural realities as the "growing power of corporate capitalism and consumerism as the defining ideology of our time."[30]

> We now see how corporate capitalism begins to operate according to the traditional role of religious institutions. . . . Capitalism in effect is the new religion of the masses—the new opium of the people—and neoliberalism is the theological orthodoxy that is facilitating its spread. [31]

Bishop Jakes and the preachers of the New Black Church are selling spirituality, and their brands are the secular sacred stories that promote neoliberalism and its orthodoxy. The branded identities of the churches, pastors, parishioners, and conference participants are an illustration of not only Wal-Martization, but the global impact of capitalism on our personal and public spiritual lives.

Brand® New Churches and Brand® New Preachers

Mara Einstein, a marketing specialist, in her book *Brands of Faith,* defines "brands" as "commodity products that have been given a name, an identifying icon or logo, and usually a tagline as a means to differentiate them from other products."[32] She asserts that in our contemporary society "religion is a product, no different from any

---

29. John Cobb, "Economic Aspects of Social and Environmental Violence," *Buddhist and Christian Studies* 22 (2002): 4.

30. Jeremy Carrette and Richard King, *Selling Spirituality: The Silent Takeover of Religion* (New York: Routledge, 2005), 17.

31. Ibid., 138.

32. Mara Einstein, *Brands of Faith: Marketing Religion in a Commercial Age* (New York: Routledge, 2008), 12.

other commodity sold in the consumer marketplace."[33] Brands do several things for producers and consumers. They create financial value for the producer or owner of the brand, and the value created for consumers encourages them to keep buying the brand. Brands also create important relationships between employees and other stakeholders.[34] Eventually, a great brand becomes "a part of culture." Michael Jordan and what he accomplished with Nike is an example of a brand becoming "a cultural icon."[35]

Marketers and media specialists use storytelling to create "much of our shared knowledge about ourselves and our culture."[36] I like James Twitchell's simplification of the term "branding." He says that we brand people and things by "storifying" them.[37] Furthermore, "In the modern world almost all consumer goods are marketed via stories."[38] The main goal of branding is to create a story about a product that elicits an emotion from the consumer.[39] The story "is told in many ways, such as through advertising, packaging, endorsements, PR, word of mouth, [and] logos."[40]

Ultimately, whether branding churches, people, or things, branding is about the social construction of identity.[41] Brands now take the place of traditions by giving the public and consumers the ideas they will live by. Our religious and spiritual identities are narrative in nature. More than ever, people are using brands to create a religious identity.

Black Protestants are especially tied to stories—for example, the scriptural stories that define Jesus Christ, the didactic parables of

---

33. Ibid., 4.

34. Ibid., 71

35. Ibid.

36. James B. Twitchell, *Branded Nation: The Marketing of Megachurch, College, Inc., and Museumworld* (New York: Simon & Schuster, 2004), 2.

37. Ibid., 36.

38. Ibid., 4.

39. James B. Twitchell, *Shopping for God: How Christianity Went from in Your Heart to in Your Face* (New York: Simon & Schuster, 2007), 74.

40. Ibid.

41. Phil Cooke, *Branding Faith: Why Some Churches and Non-profits Impact Culture and Others Don't* (Ventura, CA: Regal Publishing, 2008), 26.

Jesus of Nazareth, and the epistles of Paul and his missionary travels. Evangelical Christians proudly share their conversion stories of when they gave their lives to Jesus. Preachers have a call story of how God chose them with the enormous task of preaching the gospel. Furthermore, Pentecostal and charismatic believers keep a ready testimony of how God has made a way out of no way. The songs of Zion—from the spirituals, hymns, to rap music—all tell the stories about a God who provides for God's people. More important, black Christians are inextricably tied to the Exodus story, which tells the story of a God who delivers an oppressed people from slavery.

Congregants or people of faith "no longer practice their faith within the confines of a church or synagogue, but instead get their spiritual fulfillment through interacting with religious products and events."[42] Popular preachers use branding to create "faith brands" and "brand communities." Faith brands are "spiritual products that have been given popular meaning and awareness through marketing."[43] Brand communities are "a specialized, non-geographically bound community, based on a structured set of social relations among admirers of the brand."[44] Furthermore, faith brands have the same power as other brands, in that they "communicate to other people who we are . . . [and] we use brands for identity creation."[45] We often identify ourselves by using a brand. New Black Church pastors such as Bishop Jakes create many faith brands and religious brand communities.

The women who follow Jakes are connected to him by his most popular brand—Woman Thou Art Loosed. At the WTAL conferences they are socially constructing for themselves a brand community, and a branded identity as Loosed Women. The phrase "Woman, thou art loosed!" is adapted from Luke 13:11-13 KJV.[46]

---

42. Einstein, *Brands of Faith*, 60.

43. Ibid., 93.

44. A. M. Muniz and T. C. Guinn, "Brand Community," *Journal of Consumer Research* 27, no. 4 (March 2001): 412.

45. Einstein, *Brands of Faith*, 13.

46. "And he was teaching in one of the synagogues on the Sabbath. And behold there was a woman which had a spirit of infirmity eighteen years and

The brand began in 1992 as a six-week Sunday school lesson and a sermon given by Jakes when he pastored a small church in West Virginia.[47] The WTAL brand expanded into a myriad of products, including a nonfiction book that sold millions of copies, a novel, annual conferences (with a record-breaking 83,500 women in attendance at the Georgia Dome), a stage play, and a 2004 motion picture that not only had box office success but also sold over a million DVDs.[48] Jakes was able to leverage the WTAL movie success into a nine-picture, first-look deal with Sony Pictures.[49]

Theologically, Jakes asserts that God can liberate women from their oppression and from personal traumas like domestic violence and rape. Jakes takes the story of an unnamed woman with an eighteen-year infirmity who is healed by Jesus in the synagogue, and teaches the story in a Bible study. He then preaches several sermons, starts local conferences, and self-publishes a book—all based on the same text. In so doing, he not only successfully creates a brand, but the faith brand—WTAL.[50] Ultimately, he brands himself as the one whom God, through the Holy Spirit, has divinely ordained and anointed to share this message of liberation. Simply put, God has called and anointed him *to loose women*. After branding himself to both the biblical story and WTAL, he convinces women of all ranks that they need the brand, and that they need to purchase all of the branded products and religious experiences. In essence, Jakes's brand message for black women is: Women need *to be loosed* and they need *to be loosed by him*.

---

was bowed together, and could in no wise life up herself. And when Jesus saw her, he called her to him and said unto her, Woman, thou art loosed from thine infirmity. And he laid his hands on her, and immediately she was made straight, and glorified God" (Luke 13:10-13, KJV).

47. Walton, *Watch This!*, 106; Lee, *T.D. Jakes*, 67. T.D. Jakes moved his family and fifty families from West Virginia to Dallas, Texas, to found The Potter's House in 1996.

48. Lee, *T.D. Jakes*, 82.

49. Tatiana Siegel, "Author Jakes Lands Inspiring Deal with SPE," *The Hollywood Reporter* 394, no. 1 (April 18, 2006): 4.

50. Einstein, *Brands of Faith*, 93.

T.D. Jakes, like other New Black Church pastors, uses God-talk within a religious community to make claims about God and the world. Jakes theologizes with a large community of African American women; for me, and for the purposes of this book, that makes him and other New Black Church pastors—theologians. Moreover, I identify Bishop Jakes as a prosperity theologian, or "theologian of prosperity."[51] Bishop Jakes interprets Scripture and the rites of the Christian Church and provides his followers with prescriptions for liberation. Therefore, I believe it is also legitimate to reflect on his message in relation to other contemporary models of liberation theology. Just as the ideological perspectives of the New Black Church are nothing like the Black Church refuge model, it becomes clear that Jakes is nothing like the liberation theologians who challenged the status quo and the ideological problems of capitalism. Jakes is a true capitalist and deeply supportive of the neoliberal ideology of a post-1980s America.

Prosperity gospel(s) are primarily associated with Word of Faith or the faith movement.[52] The Potter's House is not a Word of Faith church or directly part of the faith movement. As a result, Jakes is not always identified as a prosperity theologian.[53] He differs from Word of Faith because he has what some scholars identify as a "blues sensibility."[54] Jakes and many other preachers do not fit these categories because there really is no clear definition of theologies of prosperity outside of Word of Faith.

---

51. Although the terms "prosperity theologian" and "theologian of prosperity" can be synonymous, I prefer "theologian of prosperity" and "theologies of prosperity."

52. Harrison, *Righteous Riches*; Stephanie Y. Mitchem, *Name It and Claim It? Prosperity Preaching in the Black Church* (Cleveland, OH: Pilgrim Press, 2007); Marla Frederick, *Between Sundays: Black Women and Everyday Struggles of Faith* (Berkeley: University of California Press, 2003), 146.

53. Walton, *Watch This!*, 117; Anthony Pinn, *The Black Church since the Civil Rights Movement*, 139. Shayne Lee changes his position from his early book, *T.D. Jakes*. Lee writes, "More recently Jakes has been critical of the excesses of prosperity theology." See Lee and Sinitiere, *Holy Mavericks*, 59.

54. Stacy C. Boyd, *Black Men Worshipping: Intersecting Anxieties of Race, Gender, and Christian Embodiment* (New York: Palgrave Macmillan, 2011), 74.

In our culture, however, there is an expanding acceptance of theologies of prosperity—the worldview and the related ritual practices of seed-faith giving and positive confession. A much broader definition is needed. The definition must include Word of Faith, but it must also include the practices of pastors and congregants from mainstream churches. I suggest a more expansive approach and definition for prosperity preachers and theologies of prosperity: *Prosperity preachers interpret Scripture and use rituals such as seed–faith giving and positive confession to create contextual theologies that justify their personal economic empires. They affirm that it is God's will and a believer's right to obtain prosperity, or health and wealth.*

The theologies that T.D. Jakes and other New Black Church pastors teach and practice are not academic, ivory-tower theologies. Theologies of prosperity are *folk* theologies, which are not intended to be "systematic" or "scholarly theology." They are "deliberately devotional, motivational, and inspirational."[55] Because of this non-academic, motivational, and popular appeal, their force and influence are greater than academic theologies that are at least in dialogue with, and open to, scholarly critique.[56]

When comparing the ethos of black churches of the New Black Church that emerge in the 1980s and 1990s with traditional churches of the Black Church—some stark differences appear.[57] A *Wall Street Journal* article asserts that "African-American churches have struggled with how to inspire constituents who have been moving into the middle class and away from social-justice issues."[58] This reality is a result of "the rise of black 'megachurches,' huge, middle-

---

55. Joe E. Barnhart, "Prosperity Gospel: A New Folk Theology," in *Religious Television,* ed. Robert Abelman and Stewart M. Hoover (Norwood, NJ: Ablex Publishing Corporation, 1990), 159.

56. Barnhart writes that "big time television charismatics appear to have avoided testing out their new theology in scholarly give-and-take exchanges." Barnhart, "Prosperity Gospel," 160. The same applies for many Black Church pastors. Feminist, mujerista, black, and womanist theologies are all theologies that seek legitimacy in the academy. However, because they are written by academic theologians they are open for critique and further scholarship.

57. Harrison, *Righteous Riches,* 150.

58. Lisa Miller, "Prophet Motives: Grammy Nomination, Book Deal, TV

class congregations whose pastors preach a 'prosperity gospel'—an optimistic message that glorifies personal and economic success while shunning the role of victim."[59] These churches are much more commercialized.

With their global brands, New Black Church pastors exploit the liberation themes and economic ethos of the Black Church and rework the familiar historic stories and myths for their own capitalist purposes. Through their teaching and preaching, they tell a different story—a story and mythology that make sense to many African Americans in a post–civil rights, post–baby boomer, post-Reaganomics America. This different story rings true for them because it resonates with the values of an overall expanding American global capitalist culture. New Black Church pastors, such as Jakes, have interpreted and translated the mythology of black religion for a new generation of African Americans—a generation steeped in neoliberalism and a culture of advanced capitalism.

African Americans, who are far removed from the stories and sufferings of slavery and Jim Crow, appreciate what they consider to be the liberating stories of these preachers. Branding for this generation is normal. The branded stories of success are commonplace and expected from their pastor.[60] Black congregants of the New Black Church are very comfortable with their American middle-class existence. Prosperity preachers reframe the culturally significant Exodus narrative and the story of Jesus of Nazareth. The pastors sacralize the familiar American secular myths of Horatio Alger[61] and exceptionalism.[62] These

---

Spots—A Holy Empire Is Born," *Wall Street Journal,* August 21, 1998, eastern edition, A1.

59. Ibid.

60. Einstein, *Brands of Faith,* 120-121.

61. For the Horatio Alger myth also identified as the self-made man/woman, see Richard Weiss, *The American Myth of Success from Horatio Alger to Norman Vincent Peale* (New York: Basic Books, 1969). For references to the New Black Church and the mythology, see Robert M. Franklin, *Crisis in the Village: Restoring Hope in African American Communities* (Minneapolis, MN: Fortress Press, 2007), 118; and Walton, *Watch This!*, 179-183.

62. For the exceptionalism myth, see Godfrey Hodgson, *The Myth of American Exceptionalism* (New Haven: Yale University Press, 2009).

secular myths with tales of Manifest Destiny and rags-to-riches stories are given divine importance and framed as God's will.[63] The pastors of the New Black Church often present their personal testimonies of the call to ministry as Horatio Alger stories. The exceptionalism is no longer the ideology of America being the "city on a hill" and Manifest Destiny.[64] It is now the ideology represented by the branded identities of Loosed Women, God's Leading Ladies, and World Changers[65]— black Christian consumers who participate in the New Black Church and consider themselves to be "blessed," "anointed," and proudly living out their individual financial and economic destinies. When they declare that "the wealth of wicked is laid up for the righteous!" they are now identifying themselves as the chosen people of God, positioned to treat those who are richer, more powerful, even their oppressors as "the Other." The God of the New Black Church—especially Word of Faith—is redistributing the world's wealth from the hands of sinners into the bank accounts of God's anointed.[66]

Whereas the traditional churches of the Black Church have been described as supporting "the liberation of the self and the liberation of the community,"[67] the New Black Church stresses prosperity for "the individual over community."[68] Furthermore, these churches are rarely critical of America and advanced capitalism,[69] and they do not

---

63. For references to the New Black Church and the mythology, see Robert Franklin, *Crisis in the Village*, 118; and Walton, *Watch This!*, 179-83.

64. The most famous example is John Winthrop's sermon "A Model of Christian Charity," 1630, where he states that America will be like a "city on a hill," from the New Testament text Matthew 5:14. Also see Anders Stephanson, *Manifest Destiny: American Expansionism and the Empire of Right* (New York: Hill and Wang, 1995).

65. Loosed Women refers to the women who participate in the WTAL conferences and buy the related products. God's Leading Ladies is another brand created by T.D. Jakes. World Changers is the branded identity of the members of Creflo Dollar's church in College Park, GA.

66. Harrison, *Righteous Riches*, 148.

67. James H. Evans Jr., *We Have Been Believers: An African American Systematic Theology* (Minneapolis: Fortress Press, 1992), 135.

68. Mitchem, *Name It and Claim It?*, 108.

69. Lee and Sinitiere, *Holy Mavericks*, 74.

advocate the virtues of delayed gratification and sublimation. The pastors promote economic and material liberation in the here and now—immediate gratification—by encouraging middle- and upper-class aspirations of wealth as a goal in itself. The congregants are very comfortable with America and its dream. With a sense of entitlement, they claim a God-given right to pursue the dream and to reap all of its financial and material benefits.[70]

The best way to describe what has happened to Jakes and the many black Christians that populate these churches is to use a familiar brand, the institution, and the institutionalization of the brand. My choice of terms is "Wal-Martization." The theoretical metaphor adequately describes the cultural differences between the Black Church and the New Black Church.

My Story as a Preacher and Scholar in the New Black Church[71]

Choosing to write about T.D. Jakes is as much a personal endeavor as it is an academic one. What has happened over the last thirty years with T.D. Jakes as a pastor/entrepreneur, and with WTAL as a brand, is a perfect example of what I am describing as "the Wal-Martization of African American religion." I strategically chose Jakes and this brand as a case study so that the focus is not solely on a model of ministry and the churches of the New Black Church. This book takes an intimate look at the relationship that plays out for African American churchwomen and their pastor in post–civil rights

---

70. Harrison, "Prosperity in African American Religion," in *Righteous Riches,* 131-46; Lee, "A Message of Prosperity," in *T.D. Jakes,* 98-122; Mitchem, *Name It and Claim It?,* 49.

71. Ordinarily, this personal and biographical information would not be included in the body of an academic or scholarly work. It would be placed in the preface and not the actual book. However, it is precisely the voice of a preacher, scholar, parishioner, and consumer that is often masked or not considered in the discourse about the Black Church. The various levels of power that vocations and social history garner in the various communities of meaning (church, academy, and popular audiences), are important to any ideological critique.

America. The relationship between parishioner and pastor extends far beyond just brick-and-mortar edifices and local congregations to include women who are connected by mass communication, global networks, media, and a host of products. Many pastors, like Jakes, strategically take advantage of their pastoral relationship and the fact that women expect their church to be a therapeutic refuge and "safe space" to address personal pain and struggles. Jakes and other pastors are able to capitalize financially in a "faith industry"[72]—a global consumer market of self-help spiritual products designed and marketed specifically to meet the psychological and social needs of African American women. As Shayne Lee argues, Jakes is successful because he quickly understood "that his capacity for soothing women's pains and troubles could yield considerable dividends."[73] Jakes was able to corner a market that not only translated "into a worldwide ministry," but also translated into "millions in revenue."[74]

My life story and vocational aspirations as a public theologian, preacher, and a scholar of African American religion inform this work. In many respects, because of my relationship with several New Black Church pastors and congregants, I am also an *insider* and a *primary source* for this investigation. When I lived in Atlanta as a seminary student, I was briefly a member of Eddie Long's church—New Birth in Lithonia, Georgia.[75] (This was before Eddie Long was a celebrity, and before his sex scandal.[76]) New Birth was a megachurch, but not yet a super-megachurch. I have known Bishop Noel Jones since he pastored a small Apostolic church in Longview,

72. Lee and Sinitiere, *Holy Mavericks*, 63.

73. Lee, *T.D. Jakes*, 124.

74. Ibid.

75. Eddie Long pastors New Birth Missionary Baptist Church in Lithonia, GA. He also has a television ministry and conference ministry. See http://www.newbirth.org/about/bishop_eddie_long.

76. In September 2010 four young men filed a lawsuit accusing Eddie Long of coercing them into improper sexual relationships when they were members of his church. See Sheila M. Poole, Megan Matteucci, and Katie Leslie, "Lawsuits Accuse Bishop Long of Sexual Coercion; Long 'Adamantly Denies,'" *Atlanta Journal-Constitution*, September 21, 2010, http://www.ajc.com.

Texas—long before he became a celebrity,[77] and before he became a global brand and one of the preachers featured in the Reality TV show *Preachers of LA*.[78] In fact, at the time, I was more of a celebrity as an All-American basketball player. My sister and I were known as the McGee Twins. We were featured in *Sports Illustrated* and twice on the cover of *Jet*—which is the *Time* magazine for working-class black folk. Noel Jones's sister Grace Jones was the celebrity in his family. This history makes me too close to be the supposedly objective and value-neutral scholar. I come from a family of celebrity professional athletes with public lives and a family of women who love Bishop T.D. Jakes and his ministries.

I agree with feminist theory, which "has insisted that scholarship is not done from a disembodied, value-neutral position or a 'god's eye view,' but is always perspectival and socio-politically situated."[79] Objectivity is usually about the subjectivity of men or other powerful groups who simply exercise their authority and power to impose their worldview and values on others. In order to counter this position of dominance, as a committed feminist/womanist, "I am obliged to reveal my concrete story within the framework of the social forces I have lived in."[80]

As womanist theologian Kelly Brown Douglas reminds us, "We are to value the perspectives of the 'least of these'"—what she identifies as "the underside."[81] Honoring those perspectives requires that

---

77. Bishop Noel Jones now pastors City of Refuge in Los Angeles, CA, and is often a guest speaker for T.D. Jakes's conferences. Similar to Eddie Long and T.D. Jakes, he has a television ministry and travels internationally. See http://noeljonesministries.org.

78. *Preachers of LA* is a reality show on the Oxygen network. See http://www.oxygen.com.

79. Elisabeth Schüssler Fiorenza, "Method in Women's Studies in Religion: A Critical Feminist Hermeneutics," in *Methodology in Religious Studies: The Interface with Women's Studies*, ed. Arvind Sharma (New York: State University of New York Press, 2002), 207.

80. Ada María Isasi-Díaz, *Mujerista Theology: A Theology for the Twenty-first Century* (Maryknoll, NY: Orbis Books, 1996), 3.

81. Kelly Brown Douglas, "Marginalized People, Liberating Perspectives: A Womanist Approach to Biblical Interpretation," in *I Found God in Me: A*

COVER STORY

Twins With The Same Looks But Different Lifestyles

ketball player while sister Paula is an ordained minister.

The McGee twins gained national attention in the early 1980s when they won back-to-back NCAA basketball championships at the University of Southern California (USC). People look at the twins and assume they're in sync in every aspect of life.

But the McGees are very much opposite. In addition to having very different professions, their personal lives are very different. Pamela

6-Foot-3 Twins Tower In Talent For USC Cagers

Pamela and Paula McGee are both 24, 6-foot-3 and 180 pounds. But that's just about where all the similarities with the well-known twins end. Pamela is a professional bas-

▸ *Pamela and Paula appeared on the cover of the May 7, 1984 issue of Jet (above). They have remained close as sisters although they have chosen different careers.*

Figure 1. 1982 cover and 1997 cover of *Jet* magazine of the McGee Twins of USC. Source: "Twins with the Same Looks but Different Lifestyles [Pamela and Paula McGee cover story]," *Jet* (July 21, 1997), https://www.highbeam.com.

we name our own points of privilege in order to recognize that our vantage point may indeed not be the best vantage point. Such a naming then frees us to appreciate the perspectives of those on the underside.[82]

I enter this investigation as a scholar of African American religion and a preacher (not a pastor) in the Black Church and the New Black Church. I am also a consumer. I am an African American woman who bought the book, attended Jakes's WTAL conferences, and saw the movie he produced that bears the same name (*Woman Thou Art Loosed*). Having occupied both the position of producer and consumer provides a unique lens through which to view the phenomenon of black super-megachurches, the preachers, the brands, and the subsequent power relationships.

Womanist Biblical Hermeneutics Reader, ed. Mitzi J. Smith (Eugene, OR: Cascade Books, 2015), 83.

82. Ibid., 85.

Wal-Martization is a fitting term for describing the capitalistic dynamics of the New Black Church reality, namely, the social construction of identities expressed in the representations of the institution, the preacher as CEO and brand, and the parishioner as consumer. Furthermore, the branding and storytelling at each level are important for understanding the identities of African American churchwomen in the twenty-first century. Ultimately, to understand the crucial differences between the New Black Church and the Black Church we first must understand the branding and how the super-megachurches in the New Black Church function as institutions, and how the television and conference ministries resemble revival-style crusades. More important, we must recognize the for-profit nature of these ministries with multimillion-dollar revenues from movies, books, Bibles, and other products.

Stylistically, the New Black Church is very similar to the Black Church with its rich tradition of gospel music, dynamic preaching, and a community of black people assembled for a common purpose. However, at other times, it resembles the revivals of a Billy Graham crusade. In most cases, however, these churches are a combination of both. As a result, the New Black Church often appears as a spiritual Wal-Mart—a one-stop, big box shopping experience with celebrity preachers attempting to meet the needs of religious consumers by providing a variety of well-packaged, well-marketed spiritual products.

The catalyst for my interest in the New Black Church and what scholars and the media have identified as "prosperity theology" was my own national ministry (Paula McGee Ministries), a 501c3 not-for-profit corporation, with a small governing board. I created several products: conferences, lunch-time Bible studies, T-shirts, bookmarks, and a website. I had also written several articles and published sermons that became the beginning of two faith brands: Accepting Your Greatness and Divine Divas. At the time, I saw no contradiction or any problem with branding and marketing as a significant component of the ministry.

Traveling and preaching around the country, I was often invited to churches that meet my criteria of both the Black Church and the New Black Church. At times, I was concerned. At other times, I was

Figure 2. Brands and logos for
Paula McGee Ministries, Inc.

close to embarrassed by my association with many of the churches
of the New Black Church. I was academically trained at the Interdenominational Theological Center in Atlanta, Georgia, where my
mentors had often painted a picture of these churches and their pastors (especially Word of Faith)[83] as not worthy of even a visit—unless
of course, my purpose was to observe and bring back a scathing
scholarly critique.

After leaving ITC, I attended Vanderbilt University and finished
another master's degree, this time in Hebrew Bible. My first full-
time position was as the Dean of Chapel at Fisk University. At Fisk
we invited "The Godfather of Faith"—Dr. Frederick K. C. Price[84]—
as a speaker for a series of lectures. During that time I met his wife
and daughters. With that introduction, I was often invited to preach
and teach at their national women's conferences. Betty Price did not
know my basketball history and wanted to mentor me into the prosperity world. However, after a presentation on anger at Crenshaw
Christian Center, I didn't line up with the theology. I also used lan-

---

83. Word of Faith is the name given to non-denominational churches
that are a part of the faith movement and usually associated with prosperity
theology.

84. Lee, *T.D. Jakes*, 103; Harrison, *Righteous Riches*, 134.

Figure 3. 2004 Crenshaw Christian Center Women's Conference. Paula McGee is the center photo. Several prominent Word of Faith women were speakers: Dr. Betty Price, wife of Fredrick K. C. Price (large picture upper left); Pastor Taffi Dollar, wife of Creflo Dollar (top row, upper right); and Dr. Bridget Hilliard, wife of I. V. Hilliard (bottom row, second picture from the left).

guage that they felt was inappropriate for a Woman of God. As a result, I was uninvited as a keynote speaker and no longer included in the very closed circles of Word of Faith.

What I learned through these experiences astonished me. Before visiting these churches, I could not imagine that anyone could actually believe, with authenticity, the faith claims of Word of Faith. How could anyone believe that praying and confessing scripture could cure cancer or make you rich? The women that I encountered believed these propositions with conviction, and sometimes even to their own detriment.

Receiving more and more invitations to preach, I personally struggled with the combination of ministry and business. Attempting to respond to invitations from a marketplace of individuals and churches challenged me to examine my own ethics and definitions of the *sacred* and *secular*. Where was I supposed to draw the line between business and ministry, or was there even a line to be drawn? Was there a contradiction in making a lot of money and doing ministry? Was the "bottom line" the final determination for my choices of churches and speaking invitations? Discerning which church invitations to accept became a challenge, especially when the Word of Faith churches (New Black Church) often paid ten to twenty times the honorarium of traditional churches (Black Church). Was it ethical to eliminate the smaller churches with the smaller honorarium when I felt just as compelled to speak to the women and parishioners attending those churches? Also, from a holistic stewardship standpoint, the constant travel made it difficult for me to maintain my physical health and to sustain significant personal relationships.

One of the most revealing moments happened when I accepted an invitation from a traditional church to speak as the lecturer for a three-day revival with a young thirty-something pastor/evangelist. Each night he would preach a sermon after my lecture. He was an amazing preacher. I compared his oratorical giftedness to that of Malcolm X and Martin Luther King, Jr. We had several heartfelt conversations, but the discussion that surprised me and became a catalyst for my own scholarship and vocational discernment was his definition and vision for a successful ministry. I shared with him how impressed I was with his wonderful prophetic gift and that I saw a great future in ministry for him. He agreed with my assessment of his gifts. However, I quickly realized that his vision for a successful ministry was very different from my own. For him, the measurement and cultural signifier of success was a corporate plane. "One day I will own a plane," he declared. These words became the epiphany, the anecdotal research moment, that hauntingly jarred me into understanding that something had happened—something had changed—there had been a paradigm shift. What it meant to be a preacher and to minister, or to pastor black people, had changed in some very profound ways. Those few days with him and with the women in Word of Faith churches prompted me to return to the academy to cultivate more academic skills and tools. After several months of prayer and consultations with friends, I chose Claremont

Graduate University, which offers one of only two Ph.D. programs in the country in Women's Studies and Religion.[85]

Claremont is also the home of the Peter F. Drucker and Masatoshi Ito School of Management. Peter Drucker said in a 1998 *Forbes* magazine article that "pastoral megachurches are the most significant social phenomenon in American society in the last 30 years." Drucker's commentary on why these churches were succeeding over traditional churches was "because they asked, 'What is value?' to a nonchurchgoer and came up with answers the older churches had neglected. They have found that value to the *consumer* [emphasis mine] of church services is very different from what churches traditionally were supplying."[86] Drucker was not specifically looking at black megachurches. He was mainly referencing the white megachurches that have been identified as "seeker churches"—the Bill Hybels/Willow Creek and Rick Warren/Saddleback versions.[87] However, his observations became the foundation for my concerns about the changing face of religion, especially African American religion. No one raised the question of whether treating people as *consumers* was problematic for the overall Christian understanding of making disciples, and whether this fit with each church's identity within the universal church—what Christians theologically identify as the Body of Christ.

At the time I was entering Claremont, many of my friends and many black churches were reading Rick Warren's *The Purpose-Driven Life* and *The Purpose-Driven Church*.[88] More and more people were following televangelists: T.D. Jakes, Creflo Dollar, Joyce Meyer, and Fred Price. What did it mean culturally for Peter

---

85. Other Ph.D. programs exist in Women's Studies. However, there are only two programs that concentrate on Women's Studies in Religion. The second program is at Harvard University.

86. Peter F. Drucker, "Managements New Paradigms (Cover Story)," *Forbes* 162, no. 7 (October 5, 1998): 152-77.

87. For details and a brief description of the churches and history of Bill Hybels at Willow Creek and Rick Warren at Saddleback, see Einstein, *Brands of Faith*, 103-7.

88. Rick Warren, *The Purpose-Driven Life* (Grand Rapids, MI: Zondervan, 2002); Rick Warren, *The Purpose-Driven Church: Growth Without Compromising Your Message and Your Mission* (Grand Rapids, MI: Zondervan, 1995).

Drucker, a business guru and scholar, to consider churches and pastors as the exemplary model of business success? What are the ramifications when the Great Commission of making disciples becomes making consumers?

African Americans were talking about T.D. Jakes in the way that a previous generation spoke of Martin Luther King, Jr. Moreover, King's daughter had even proclaimed that prosperity preacher Eddie Long was her father's successor; she was convinced that he would carry King's social justice agenda forward because of Long's controversial position on homosexuality.[89] Many New Black Church preachers were gaining greater prominence. Jakes was gaining more and more exposure with T.D. Jakes Ministries and his WTAL conferences.

More important, my existential financial concerns were always present in choosing to pursue yet one more expensive graduate degree, especially in Women's Studies and Religion. Both fields garner no guarantees for economic success. My working-class, blue-collar background, and being the first in my family to receive a bachelor's degree, also informs my worldview and approach. I grew up in Flint, Michigan, the struggling car-industry city most famously explored in the films of activist filmmaker Michael Moore.[90]

After I finished my Ph.D., I returned to Flint. Unable to secure a tenure-track position, I worked part-time as an adjunct professor, editor, and guest teacher in local high schools. I was living in Flint, when the water crisis happened with lead-pipe contamination. While in Flint, I visited Triumph Church–Flint. Based on 2012 data, Triumph is the "fasting growing evangelical church in the United States."[91] The majority of the satellites are in the Detroit area,

---

89. Walton, *Watch This!*, 139.

90. Michael Moore has done several independent films that mention Flint, Michigan. However, the film that made Flint a setting for most of his films is *Roger and Me*. The 1989 film is about Michael Moore attempting to confront General Motor's CEO, Roger Smith, to explain the cultural devastation of the city after massive downsizing.

91. Jan Stievermann, Phillip Goff, and Detlef Junker, eds., *Religion and the Marketplace in the United States* (New York: Oxford University Press, 2014), 1.

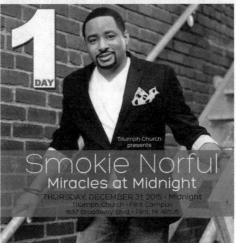

Figure 4. Logo for Triumph Church–Flint, Michigan, the fasting growing megachurch in the nation. An example of a New Black Church, a multisite church, which merged with a traditional church, North Star Missionary Baptist Church. The other photo is a flyer for Watch Night Service with gospel singer Smokie Norful.

but Triumph added an older traditional church in Flint to its cadre of churches. Only limited leadership remained from the local traditional church. Each Sunday, Triumph's associate ministers usually led worship in Flint. What was also unique is the number of celebrity gospel singers and preachers that were marketed and appeared at the services. Triumph is an example of a black super-megachurch in several locations. The pastor does not preach the prosperity gospel. But the church is another example of a black church that is run like a business and the pastor functions as a CEO. The church was very effective with marketing and public relations. Furthermore, each Sunday everything was run efficiently—from the security in the parking lot to the preaching in the pulpit, even the precision of the hour-long service.

The challenges and changes with local churches and other economic realities in Flint were a constant reminder that the city was no longer the thriving city that I knew as a child. My parents and the majority of my family members worked for General Motors. So I grew up fully immersed in the culture of the UAW (United Automobile Workers) and the labor movement.[92] In the 1970s Flint had one of the highest per capita incomes in the nation.

The Metropolitan Baptist Church in Flint, Michigan, is where I had my first exposure to black churches. I spent more days of my childhood than I can remember at Youth Mission, Youth Fellowship, Jr. Church, and Vacation Bible School. The church and its activities proved to be a safe place for my parents to send my sisters and me. The church of my childhood easily meets the criteria of the Black Church refuge model of ministry. It is a church that believed in caring for and nurturing children and young people. This is also the church where Jesse Jackson led a traditional march during the water crisis. Nonetheless, Metropolitan Baptist is a church that still does not allow women in ministry or in certain leadership positions. The complexity of this church and its impact on my life are why writing about black churches, with the categories established in the academy—even feminist, womanist, and postcolonial—is usually

---

92. For a history of UAW and the relationship to the Labor Movement, visit the website at http://www.uaw.org.

insufficient. In other words, inhibiting women's participation in the pulpit and in other key leadership positions qualifies this church as undeniably sexist and patriarchal. However, I still credit this church with instilling the cultural values that continue to frame my social justice ethos and commitment. The women that mentored me were never in formal positions of leadership, such as deacon, trustee, or pastor. Nevertheless, they were central to my spiritual formation and must be credited with having a lasting impact on my religious life. Furthermore, their contribution to my life ranks in ways that no male deacon or pastor could ever be able to claim.

Along with other women scholars, feminists, and womanists, my attempt is, as Evelyn Brooks Higginbotham states, "to rescue these women from invisibility."[93] In other words, I do not see these women as powerless and passive participants. Instead, I know them to be the true protagonists in the stories of American black churches and faith communities. I continue to write and preach as a small down payment toward a tremendous debt that I owe.

The Scope of This Book

This book investigates the theology of Bishop T.D. Jakes to provide a glimpse into the theology of the New Black Church.[94] More important, the project offers a theological research method for future academic theologians to study the theology of popular preachers like Jakes. These preachers and their theologies must be named in order to place them in conversation with academic theologies, church leaders, and religious scholars. I unapologetically take the theology or God-talk of these preachers seriously, as well as the theology embedded in the many branded products that they produce and sell.

---

93. Evelyn Brooks Higginbotham, *Righteous Discontent: The Women's Movement in the Black Baptist Church, 1880–1920* (Cambridge, MA: Harvard University Press, 1993), 2.

94. The correct statement would be the "theologies" of the New Black Church. In other words, "theology" may communicate a monolithic view of the God-talk presented by the many preachers and in the thousands of products. However, I am using "theology" in the singular, because I do believe that the ideology is singular.

I am committed to the early philosophical commitments of liberation theology—to reread scripture, to give voice to the poor, to allow
people to speak *for themselves* and *not for them*. I do not have to agree
with a theology to present it or to study its impact.[95]

Pastors in the New Black Church *brand* all elements of worship
and church participation through television, media, and marketing.
Moreover, they "self-brand."[96] No preacher brands more effectively
with African American churchwomen than Bishop T.D. Jakes. To
understand the theology of preachers like T.D. Jakes, who not only
produce many brands but are brands themselves, I investigate the
stories or their churches and personal histories to identify the meaning making and social construction of collective and individual
identities. This meaning making in the New Black Church happens
with the churches, the pastors, the participants in the annual conferences and with the women as a group.

Women say that Jakes tells their story—especially the stories
about issues like domestic violence and sexual abuse—stories that
are usually seen as taboo and silenced in other churches.[97] He tells
these stories through his branding. When black women purchase
a book, go to the movie, or attend a WTAL Conference, they are
expressing to others who they are. They are Loosed Women. During
these conferences the women preachers and the congregants are constructing a counternarrative to the negative identities promulgated
about black women by the dominant culture as well as the negative
portrayals that happen at their home churches. What I am suggesting is that the branding of black churches and the worship experiences like The Potter's House, and WTAL international conferences

---

95. Paula L. McGee, "Pastor or CEO?," *The National Baptist Voice (NBV)*
5, no. 3 (Summer 2006): 64-65.

96. A personal brand "is the perception or emotion, maintained by somebody other than you." See *Brands of Faith*, 59.

97. Marla Frederick-McGlathery, "'But It's Bible': African American
Women and Television Preachers," in *Women and Religion in the African
Diaspora: Knowledge, Power, and Performance*, ed. R. Marie Griffith and
Barbara Dianne Savage (Baltimore, MD: Johns Hopkins University Press,
2006), 266-92.

are central to religious identity formation for African American women. It is important, however, to note that Jakes profits from his relationship with these women and the telling of their story. This is where theology, ethics, and culture converge: What does this relationship, which is wedged somewhere between pastor/parishioner and CEO/customer, mean for African Americans—especially African American women—and their relationship to their God, their church, their pastor, and each other?

In the next chapter, I outline the historical and ideological differences between the Black Church and the New Black Church. In Chapter 2, I provide a detailed definition of prosperity preachers and theologies of prosperity. Whereas most scholars consider prosperity churches to be only Word of Faith, my definition includes more mainstream churches because the ideology and ritual practices of seed-faith giving and positive confession are now much more prevalent in mainstream denominational churches. I also explain how these theologies are very similar to *the gospel of wealth*. Prosperity preachers offer an economic salvation to congregants with prescriptions of liberation from economic and physical suffering. As a result, theologies of prosperity represent a type of theodicy and even theology of "liberation." Unlike traditional liberation theologies, which interrogate and challenge social structures, the theologies of prosperity offer solutions within the orbit of capitalism. Instead of a preferential option for the poor, they offer a preferential option for the rich, which ultimately blames the victims for their own poverty. In Chapter 3, I use James McClendon's theological method of biography as theology to study Bishop Jakes. McClendon argues that the narrative approach of telling the faith stories and exposing the images that define the person under study is a viable theological method. Like most theologians of prosperity, the key life metaphors of T.D. Jakes are *pastor* and *CEO*. Both vocations are why he is able to exploit the mythologies of Horatio Alger and American exceptionalism. He is able to capitalize on the power of being a black pastor and the secular influence of a CEO. In Chapter 4, I use Bishop Jakes's most popular brand of WTAL to demonstrate that brands are theology and act as theological norms. Regardless of the brand, New Black Church preachers create a contextual theology that targets a particular audience. I use qualitative research methods (case study and participant observation) to examine the religious experiences and theological practices of T.D. Jakes and the women who follow him. I examine several of the WTAL products: the first 1993 Azusa WTAL sermon, the nonfiction book, the movie, and a live Woman Thou Art Loosed conference (in person and on CD). I also draw on the material I received when I became an Aaron's Army monthly ministry partner.

In my Conclusion, after my in-depth study of T.D. Jakes and the WTAL brand, I explain how the *process* and *ideology* of Wal-Martization accounts for the continuous expansion of these churches and the influence of their preachers. I also conclude that the New Black Church model of ministry is not a good model for African American churches nor for the women who attend these churches. These churches and their pastors fit comfortably within the culture of advanced capitalism, and they actually promote a preferential option for the rich, which implicitly blames the poor for their poverty. The churches of the New Black Church and their pastors promote a theology that is much more about brand loyalty than the gospel and spiritual healing. Finally, I close the book with an invitation to other religious scholars and theologians to include popular preachers like T.D. Jakes and this new theology in their theological discourses about black churches and black women. The future of liberation theology and what we have come to know and love as the Black Church depend on it.

1

The Black Church vs. the New Black Church

The terminology of Black Church and even New Black Church is no longer adequate for the more nuanced discussions of African American religion and theology. The terminology is left over from an earlier generation of religious and theological discourse. As such, most contemporary scholars who use the term Black Church provide at least a footnote, and, at other times, a detailed explanation stating that African American religion is not monolithic.[1] Scholars have a long list of debates and complaints. Harvard professor of African Studies and Religion Eddie Glaude posted an essay on The Huffington Post with the title "The Black Church Is Dead."[2] His goal was

---

1. Hans A. Baer and Merrill Singer write that "while this concept [Black Church] may have a certain heuristic value, it is misleading in its implication that the religious experience among blacks has been uniform or monolithic." Hans A. Baer and Merrill Singer, *African American Religion: Varieties of Protest and Accommodation,* 1st ed. (Knoxville, TN: University of Tennessee Press, 1992), xv. Marla Frederick writes, "Black presence in majority black, yet white-pastored churches, participation in multicultured communities of faith, and the growing numbers of black churches in white denominations complicate the narrow definition." Marla Frederick, *Between Sundays: Black Women and Everyday Struggles of Faith* (Berkeley: University of California Press, 2003), 89.

2. Eddie Glaude, Jr., "The Black Church Is Dead," http://www.huffingtonpost.com (February 24, 2010). Also see Anthea Butler, Jonathan Walton, et al., "The Black Church Is Dead—Long Live the Black Church," updated with response (March 9, 2010) http://www.religiondispatches.org.

to challenge people to think about how we categorize black religion. Barbara Dianne Savage states, "Despite common usage, *there is no such thing as the 'black church'* [emphasis mine]. It is an illusion and a metaphor that has taken on a life of its own, implying existence of a powerful entity with organized power, but the promise of that also leaves it vulnerable to unrealistic expectations."[3] Yet, like other personal accounts, her book shows how the critiques still point us back to the power that these institutions still hold for African Americans. Her book begins with her acknowledgment of the influence of "the sacred space of a country church in Virginia,"[4] and ends with her admission that "black churches are still the strongest and most ubiquitous of black institutions."[5]

These definitional and descriptive challenges are outlined by Hans Baer and Merrill Singer in their text *African American Religion: Varieties of Protest and Accommodation*. The authors explain that religious diversity has always existed for African Americans, but this fact has not been acknowledged in the scholarship.[6] They list three compelling reasons: First, they show that throughout history, little or no attention from media, education, and the social sciences has been given to African American religion. The second reason is that the majority of institutions and their subsequent writers did not produce adequate images for the totality of African American life. Finally, and definitely important for any study of the Black Church, is the fact that until this century, most African American intellectuals were preachers who felt compelled to offer a response to the negative images presented by the dominant culture. These intellectuals and writers wanted to present "unity and communality."[7] "As a

---

3. Barbara Dianne Savage, *Your Spirits Walk beside Us: The Politics of Black Religion* (Cambridge: Belknap Press of Harvard University Press, 2008), 9.

4. Ibid., 1.

5. Ibid., 283.

6. Baer and Singer, *African American Religion*, xv. For a further explanation of the terminology and its use, see C. Eric Lincoln and Lawrence Mamiya, *The Black Church in the African American Experience* (Durham, NC: University of North Carolina Press, 1990), 1.

7. Baer and Singer, *African American Religion*, xv.

consequence, the myriad expressions of African American religiosity have been compressed in scholarly understanding into a number of major types and a few peripheral and largely unattended variants, a pattern that can be seen in the tendency to equate African American religion with the 'Black Church.'"[8]

Historian Evelyn Higginbotham focuses on the lives of black Baptist women from 1880 to 1920. Writing against the grain of earlier studies, she affirms that these important institutions represent "a complex body of shifting cultural, ideological, and political significations."[9] The ideological representations and significations of black churches are critical to any discourse or historical narrative. Academics may continue to fight about the specific jargon and which religious institutions make up the black religious canon. However, in the real world, Mother Emanuel AME Church in Charleston, South Carolina, was a traditional Black Church—and the alleged shooter who killed nine black people was clearly able to identify the church and its members as such.[10]

I avoid the definitional dilemma by focusing on "models of ministry." This terminology speaks to the claims of Christian identity, which is always determined to some degree by how each self-identified Christian community defines words such as church, pastor, revelation, conversion, and member or disciple. Using the word "model" as a typology allows me to explore the community's understanding of these relationships and to counter the idea of one distinguishable institution with a monovocality and a singular identity. A certain amount of variance is inevitable whenever we reference an entity

---

8. Ibid.

9. Evelyn Brooks Higginbotham, *Righteous Discontent: The Women's Movement in the Black Baptist Church, 1880–1920* (Cambridge, MA: Harvard University Press, 1993), 16.

10. Mother Emanuel was targeted by a white male. Reports state that he targeted the church because he knew that it was a historic black church. For an academic treatment of the massacre, see Chad Williams, Kidada E. Williams, and Keisha N. Blain, eds., *Charleston Syllabus: Readings on Race, Racism, and Racial Violence* (Athens, GA: University of Georgia Press, 2016).

as diverse and complex as the people, preachers, and institutions of what we affectionately name as the Black Church.

Historically, most religious scholars and theologians have simply used the term "Black Church." I intentionally include and honor the foundational works and scholarly pioneers that use the term.[11] Many possibilities and configurations of contemporary African American churches exist. The Black Church[12] and the New Black Church,[13] however, are the most prevalent models that the majority of contemporary religious and theological scholars reference.

Televangelist and prosperity theologian Eddie Long, in popular discourse, and Black Church historian and King scholar Lewis

---

11. For a list of sources that use the terminology of "Black Church," see Dolores C. Leffall, *The Black Church: An Annotated Bibliography* (Washington, DC: Minority Research Center, 1973); other examples include C. Eric Lincoln, *The Black Church since Frazier* (New York: Schocken Books, 1974); Peter J. Paris, *The Social Teaching of the Black Churches* (Philadelphia: Fortress Press, 1985); Lincoln and Mamiya, *The Black Church in the African American Experience*; Anthony Pinn, *The Black Church in the Post-Civil Rights Era* (Maryknoll, NY: Orbis Books, 2002).

12. Throughout this book, I will use "the Black Church" to identify the traditional model. However, when I am quoting other scholars, it does not necessarily refer to the traditional model. Whenever possible, I will make a note. These issues are difficult to address because the use of the term does tend to create a monolithic view of the many kinds of churches in which African Americans make up the majority of their membership. I am using the terminology of new as in "neo-Black Church" in the way that neo-Pentecostalism is similar to yet different from Pentecostalism.

13. The term "New Black Church" is taken from Shayne Lee. See the chapter, "The New Black Church," in Shayne Lee, *T.D Jakes: America's Preacher* (New York: New York University Press, 2005), 158-77. Marc Lamont Hill identifies "the New Black Church" as follows: "the current configuration of mainline black Christianity, . . . which has taken its current shape over the past two decades is the progeny of the civil rights movements but can be distinguished by its increased materialism, questionable theology, and dubious politics." Marc Lamont Hill, "The Barbershop Notebooks: 'I Bling Because I'm Happy,'" http://www.popmatters.com (August 5, 2005),

Baldwin in academic discourse are two perfect examples. Long, in a statement to the *Atlanta Journal-Constitution,* states,

> We're not just a church, we're an international corporation. We're not just a bumbling bunch of preachers who can't talk and all we're doing is baptizing babies. I deal with the White House. I deal with Tony Blair. I deal with presidents around the world. I pastor a multimillion dollar congregation. You got to put me on a different scale than the little black preacher sitting over there that supposed to be just getting by because the people are suffering.[14]

Lewis Baldwin argues for Martin Luther King's "model of prophetic witness and mission, not the entrepreneurial spirituality of today's mega preachers." He critiques the megachurch phenomenon as "elitist, capitalistic, and materialistic."[15] Please note, however, that both Baldwin and Long inscribe the same two models: the New Black Church as the black megachurch with the CEO/pastor teaching a prosperity gospel, and the Black Church as the small church with a prophetic pastor, teaching what scholars consider to be the social gospel. Furthermore, Baldwin shows in his book that Martin Luther King, Jr., as a preacher/pastor with the work he accomplished at Dexter Avenue or Ebenezer during the civil rights movement is the iconic example for the Black Church refuge model.[16] For this generation, T.D. Jakes, as a celebrity pastor/entrepreneur of The Potter's House (one church in four locations) with his many brands and for-profit ventures, claims that same iconic status for the New Black Church.

Both preachers represent their historical context in their approach to church leadership as pastors and national celebrities. As icons of

---

14. John Blake, "Bishop's Charity Generous to Bishop: New Birth's Long Received 3 Million," *Atlanta Journal-Constitution*, August 28, 2005.

15. Lewis V. Baldwin, *The Voice of Conscience: The Church in the Mind of Martin Luther King, Jr.* (New York: Oxford University Press, 2010), 237.

16. Ibid., 68-69.

faith they reveal a certain worldview, ethos, and sociocultural identity in relation to the black Christians of their time. Both King and Jakes were featured on the cover of *Time* magazine—a testament to their cultural reach.[17] However, for Jakes the cover reads: "Is This the Next Billy Graham?" Jakes is identified as:

> One of religion's most prodigious polymaths. His books, starting with his breakthrough inspirational volume *Woman Thou Art Loosed!* have sold millions. His 26,000-member Potter's House megachurch in South Dallas drew George W. Bush and Al Gore prior to the 2000 election. Jakes is a Grammy-nominated gospel singer and has a deal with Hallmark for a line of "Loose Your Spirit" inspirational greeting cards. He preaches regularly to millions on both Black Entertainment Television and the Trinity Broadcasting Network.[18]

King was featured as the Man of the Year, and *Time* magazine referred to him as the

> symbol of a revolution. In 1963, the centennial of the Emancipation Proclamation, that coalition of conscience ineradicably changed the course of U.S. life. The U.S. Negro, shedding thousands of fears that have encumbered his generations, made 1963 the year of his outcry for equality.[19]

The covers illustrate the social-justice focus of some preachers like King in the Black Church, and the commercialization and individualism of preachers in the New Black Church.

---

17. Martin Luther King, Jr., and Bishop T.D. Jakes were featured on the cover of *Time* more than once. However, the point is made with the one cover as evidence.

18. David Van Biema, "Spirit Raiser: America's Best," *Time*, September 17, 2001, 52.

19. "Man of the Year: Never Again Where He Was," *Time*, January 3, 1964, 13-27.

The preparation for ministry and spiritual leadership also speaks volumes about who King and Jakes are as black leaders. King prepared for ministry by attending Morehouse College, seminary at Crozer Theological Seminary, and he received a Ph.D. from Boston University.[20] Bishop Jakes has a GED, one year of college at Virginia Tech, and a master's and doctorate of ministry from Friends International Christian University (FICU)—an unaccredited correspondence school.[21] King left the pastorate to lead the Southern Christian Leadership Conference (SCLC) and to actively participate in the civil rights movement. [22] Although Jakes travels around the world as an evangelist, he continues to pastor The Potter's House and act as senior pastor for the three satellite churches. The covers and captions of *Time* magazine of these two important black men dramatically point to the ideological differences between the Black Church and the New Black Church.

"Black Church" is the overall encompassing heuristic that most scholars in a variety of fields continue to use. The classification of the New Black Church was first introduced by Marc Lamont Hill in an online post and by Shayne Lee in his book on Jakes.[23] The current terminology is not used in the way that C. Eric Lincoln described the Negro Church and the Black Church. Lincoln declared that the "Negro Church accepted death in order to be reborn. Out of the ashes of its funeral pyre there sprang the bold, strident, self-conscious phoenix that is the contemporary Black Church."[24] The two models are not sequential steps on a Black Church history timeline. Instead, they stand side by side in the current history of African American religion. The New Black Church model is *new,* simply to emphasize that its pastors exploit many

---

20. Baldwin, *The Voice of Conscience*, 13.

21. Jonathan L. Walton, *Watch This: The Ethics and Aesthetics of Black Televangelism* (New York: New York University Press, 2009), 105. Jakes also has a doctor of ministry degree in religious studies from Friends International Christian University (FICU). See http://www.ficu.edu/alumni/Jakes.html.

22. Baldwin, *The Voice of Conscience*, 119.

23. Shayne Lee, *T.D. Jakes*, 158-77; Hill, "The Barbershop Notebooks."

24. Lincoln, *The Black Church since Frazier*, 105-6.

of the *old* traditions of the Black Church.[25] New Black Church pastors strategically manipulate the mythological power of the institution, as well as the rhetorical power that preachers continue to possess as the spokespersons of the community.[26] The prosperity preachers capitalize on the history of the uplift ideology[27] of black churches by resembling the Black Church and persuading parishioners to believe that they are providing not only a liberating truth but a better truth than that of other traditional black churches.[28] With the power of the institution, the preacher, and the right rhetoric these preachers continue to create new brands and brand communities.

Congregations in the New Black Church are very different from the traditional congregations that make up the Black Church. The faith communities are a mixture of local congregants, brand communities, television viewers, and consumers. Although research shows declining membership for African Americans attending denominational churches, black churches as a whole continue to play a significant role in African American religion and thought and African American Protestant Christian identity formation.[29]

---

25. Stacy Boyd, *Black Men Worshipping: Intersecting Anxieties of Race, Gender, and Christian Embodiment* (New York: Palgrave Macmillan, 2011), 76.

26. Charles Hamilton, *The Black Preacher in America* (New York: Morrow, 1972), 118.

27. Melissa Harris-Lacewell, "From Liberation to Mutual Fund: Political Consequences of Differing Conceptions of Christ in the African American Church," in *From Pews to Polling Places: Faith and Politics in the American Religious Mosaic*, ed. J. Matthew Wilson (Washington, D.C.: Georgetown University Press, 2007), 147.

28. Milmon F. Harrison, *Righteous Riches: The Word of Faith Movement in Contemporary African American Religion* (New York: Oxford University Press, 2005), 153.

29. See Dale P. Andrews, *Practical Theology for Black Churches: Bridging Black Theology and African American Folk Religion* (Louisville, KY: Westminster John Knox Press, 2002), 40-49; Michael Battle, *The Black Church in America: African American Spirituality* (Malden, MA: Blackwell Publishing, 2006); Paris, *The Social Teaching of the Black Churches*; Lee Butler, *Liberating*

As social institutions, black churches have been the most economically independent and the only institutions where African Americans have exercised leadership and power away from the purview of white control.[30] In this "surrogate world"[31] or "a nation within a nation,"[32] African Americans have claimed a unique kind of spirituality[33] and have understood the church as a place for prophetic preaching against racism and other injustices.[34] "For many people, the Black Church became a way out, the forum in which each week's mountain of frustrations and tragedies are eliminated from one's consciousness, a holy place of peace in a world of utter madness and dark decay,"[35] as historian and social critic Manning Marable expressed it in *Blackwater*. When "there were the conservative tendencies within black faith [that] reach for a Spirit which liberates the soul, but *not* the body . . . the radical consciousness within black faith was concerned with the immediate conditions of black people." This meant "if the rituals of the church conveyed a message of long tolerance of suffering and acceptance of secular oppression, *blackwater* [emphasis mine] was the impetus toward political activism

Our Dignity, Saving Our Souls (St. Louis: Chalice Press, 2006); and Cornel West, *Prophecy Deliverance! An Afro-American Revolutionary Christianity* (Philadelphia: Westminster Press, 1982), 15.

30. Lincoln and Mamiya, *The Black Church in the African American Experience*, 241; Katie Cannon, *Katie's Canon: Womanism and the Soul of the Black Community* (New York: Continuum, 1995), 115.

31. Paris, *The Social Teaching of the Black Churches*, 1-25.

32. E. Franklin Frazier, *The Negro Church in America* (New York: Schocken Books, 1963), 44.

33. Calvin E. Bruce, "Black Spirituality, Language and Faith," *Religious Education* 71, no. 4 (July-August 1976): 363-76.

34. David Howard-Pitney, "'To Form a More Perfect Union': African Americans and American Civil Religion," in *New Day Begun; African American Churches and Civic Culture in Post-Civil Rights America*, ed. Drew Smith (Durham, NC: Duke University Press, 2003), 93.

35. Manning Marable, *Blackwater: Historical Studies in Race, Class Consciousness, and Revolution* (Niwot, CO; University Press of Colorado, 1981/1993), 43.

and the use of religious rhetoric to promote the destruction of the white status quo."[36]

The prevalence of white supremacy meant that African Americans had to respond to a negative identity forced on them by the dominant culture.[37] The community as a whole has often struggled with a kind of cultural identity crisis. In his book about spirituality and the religious practices of the Black Church, Michael Battle writes that the

> struggle over human identity for African American Christian spirituality has been to make such a dominant understanding of negative identity obsolete, through mutual and integral practices of what is now understood as the Black Church. In other words, the Black Church did not emerge because it wanted to; instead, it emerged out of the necessity to redefine African American identity—especially in the peculiar context of European identities.[38]

He is clear that spirituality plays a critical role in the identity formation of black people. The Black Church was the home of this unique spirituality and provided the emotional space and place to create a sense of community. [39]

Both the Black Church and the New Black Church continue in some form of uplift ideology, but they differ in profound ways. The ideological differences are similar to what Marable argues has happened to black America as a whole. Writing in 2009, he says: "We are in the midst of a major ideological realignment within black America with the demarcation of potentially antagonistic and confrontational formations and groups that will battle for the future of our people."[40] Both models possess preachers, pastors, public figures,

---

36. Marable, *Blackwater*, 40–41.

37. Paris, *The Social Teaching of the Black Churches*, 30.

38. Battle, *The Black Church in America*, 28.

39. Flora Wilson Bridges, *Resurrection Song: African American Spirituality* (Maryknoll, NY: Orbis Books, 2001), 5.

40. Manning Marable, *Beyond Black and White: Transforming African American Politics*, 2nd ed. (New York: Verso, 2009), 213. Marable is speaking

and theologians who are battling for the future of a people, and for these important religious and sociocultural institutions that we continue to identify as *black churches.*

Cultural anthropologist Marla Frederick has studied black churches and the faith of black women extensively. She does not use the exact terminology of Black Church and New Black Church, but she argues that contemporary black churches are pulled between "two different traditions" or "two polarities," resulting from the fact that black churches historically have been both *prophetic* and *priestly.*[41] The Black Church, she says, "reflects the church's more radical history of critiquing political and economic institutions and systems that repress social and economic progress." The New Black Church "reflects the more conservative integrationist approach to social problems, as it encourages radical changes solely in the individual desiring to advance swiftly in the American mainstream."[42] Two models articulate the ideological foundations that speak to the religious practices and worldview of millions of black Christians.

A New Relationship between the Pastor/Preacher and the People

Historically, because the Black Church has been considered a refuge for black people, preachers have possessed an iconic presence in the larger African American community. Charles Hamilton in "the first in-depth portrait of black America's preachers,"[43] writes: "There has developed over several centuries a very close, almost familial tie between the black preacher and his people. They have come to rely heavily on each other, and they have come to know the strengths and weaknesses of each other."[44] For W. E. B. DuBois, writing at the turn of the twentieth century in *The Souls of Black Folk,* "The

---

about the ideological differences between what he calls "inclusionist scholars" and "Afrocentric scholars." The same can be said about the differences between those that represent the Black Church and the New Black Church.

41. Frederick, *Between Sundays*, 142.
42. Ibid.
43. Charles Hamilton, *The Black Preacher in America,* cover.
44. Ibid., 25.

preacher is the most unique personality developed by the Negro on American soil. A leader, a politician, an orator, a 'boss,' an intriguer, and idealist."[45] Focusing on the South, regardless of whether every individual attended Sunday services, DuBois writes that "practically every American Negro is a church member. . . . Practically, a pro-scribed people must have a social centre, and that centre for this people is the Negro church."[46]

The black preacher was responsible for black worship—the sacred time when the community assembled to speak with one another and their God. According to Harold Trulear, African American wor-ship "mediates meaning through symbol and ritual." Through "tes-timony, prayer, song, and sermon" black people with the preacher socially construct a "communal religious identity" and a "religious worldview."[47] Usually the most educated person in the community, the preacher helped African Americans make many of the difficult life transitions. The preacher/pastor was "the linkage figure"[48] who helped black people transition from slavery to freedom or from the South to the urban ghettos of the North during the Great Migra-tion.[49] As the metaphoric Moses of black people, the preacher was intricately tied to the congregants. Henry Mitchell affirms that this special orator was "ear deep in the condition of the people."[50] The lives of people and preacher were "intimately close together—so close together that the themes which invade the consciousness of the one also invade the other." [51]The black preacher embraced the racial identity of himself and his people.

---

45. W. E. B. DuBois, *The Souls of Black Folk* (New York: Signet Classic, 1969/1903), 211.

46. Ibid.

47. Harold Dean Trulear, "The Lord Will Make a Way Somehow: Black Worship and the Afro-American Story," *Journal of the Interdenominational Theological Center* 13, no. 1 (Fall 1985): 87-88.

48. Hamilton, *The Black Preacher*, 35-36.

49. Ibid.

50. Henry H. Mitchell, *Black Preaching: The Recovery of a Powerful Art* (Nashville, TN: Abingdon Press, 1990), 6.

51. Ibid.

Unlike the pastors of the Black Church, New Black Church pastors have substituted a *racial identity* with a *branded consumer*,[52] or more precisely, a *celebrity identity*."[53] New Black Church pastors with majority African American leadership and congregants seldom identify their churches as "black." Instead, they prefer the moniker of multiculturalism,[54] which provides a broader base for the many brands and products.[55]

Most Black Church pastors only served one congregation. Bishop T.D. Jakes and other preachers embrace the franchise or multisite model of one church in many locations. In addition, they seek to build relationships through social media and products with brand community members, television viewers, and ministry partners. New Black preachers often claim the ecclesial and vocational title of "Bishop," which is also part of their brand. As bishops they oversee

---

52. For an explanation of "branded identity," see Mara Einstein, *Brands of Faith: Marketing Religion in a Commercial Age* (New York: Routledge, 2008), 72-74.

53. In a previous work on Sheryl Swoopes, a famous women's basketball player, I define *celebrity identity* and the relationship to identity formation in the global marketplace. I write: "Sheryl Swoopes has a *branded celebrity identity* [emphasis mine] that gives her what I am calling a 'capitalist or economic identity.' This identity is expressed by [Swoopes's] ability to brand herself and be marketable. Her ability to sell herself, her name, and her image as a product is critical to the discourse. 'Celebrity' as an identity is new to theological discourse, but important in understanding the new ways that collective and individual identities are socially constructed in the global marketplace (57)". See "Feminist Theology, Identity, and Discourse: A Closer Look at the 'Coming Out' of Sheryl Swoopes," *Feminist Theology* 19, no. 1 (2006): 54-72. Also see Einstein, *Brands of Faith*, 122. For specific information on celebrity preachers, see Lee, *T.D. Jakes*, 168-72. For celebrity in general, see P. David Marshall, *Celebrity and Power: Fame in Contemporary Culture* (Minneapolis: University of Minnesota Press, 1997).

54. For a discussion on the New Black Church's position on race relations and multiculturalism, see Frederick, *Between Sundays*, 153-59. Also see Lee, *T.D. Jakes;* and Stephanie Y. Mitchem, *Name It and Claim It? Prosperity Preaching in the Black Church* (Cleveland, OH: Pilgrim Press, 2007), 108.

55. Einstein, *Brands of Faith*, 121.

or act as a "pastor of pastors" for various ministerial fellowships and networks.[56] The local pastors who follow preachers like Jakes have their own churches with their own brands. Subsequently, the brands and the theology of pastors in the New Black Church are impacting faith communities around the world.

Through their local churches, media, and conference/television ministries, New Black Church pastors commodify almost every aspect of worship and religious experience. A live worship service is often edited and packaged into a variety of consumable goods. One brand can consist of movies, music CDs, books, devotionals, Bibles, and a variety of other products. Churches, pastors, sermons, testimonies, scriptures, music, and worship can all be branded. "The spiritual marketplace"[57] gives the preachers of the New Black Church unprecedented access to black consumers, who because they benefit from many of the civil rights advancements have substantial financial resources.[58] The pastors market their own vision of faith to a wide variety of religious consumers. Shayne Lee describes them best: "These celebrity preachers are CEOs of international ministries

---

56. According to Hubert Morken in 2001, T.D. Jakes leads the Pater Alliance, which has over 231 churches and pastors from 13 denominations. Hubert Morken, "Bishop T.D. Jakes: A Ministry of Empowerment," in *Religious Leaders and Faith-Based Politics: Ten Profiles*, ed. Jo Renee Formicola and Hubert Morken (Lanham, MD: Rowman & Littlefield, 2001), 25-52 (29).

57. Wade Clark Roof, *The Spiritual Marketplace: Baby Boomers and the Remaking of American Religion* (Princeton, NJ: Princeton University Press, 1999), 80.

58. There is not adequate space to develop an argument around key issues such as integration, affirmative action, slavery, Jim Crow, and others that have affected the earning potential of African Americans. As more African Americans make up the middle class and have gained some wealth, their buying power and access to services, events, and products have also expanded in ways that were not available in a segregated America. There have been other prosperity preachers and megachurches in the past. However, we must acknowledge the many market changes in the culture such as television, the Internet, and print media. There are discussions about Father Divine and Reverend Ike. While both men accumulated wealth, however, they did not have access and exposure to mainstream outlets now available to the preachers of the New Black Church.

that reach millions of people through television, radio, and Internet, and by satellite technology, and their churches have resources rivaling denominations. These pastors take advantage of our media age by marketing their books, videos, and tapes to secure personal fortunes."[59]

T.D. Jakes and other super-megachurch pastors are "creative religious entrepreneurs," who have reframed the mythology and ethos of the traditional Black Church. They have taken the *old* meanings of black suffering and struggle and created *new* meanings for a younger generation of American Americans. The members of this younger generation seek to be major players in the American dream. They are negotiating their personal economic visions of middle-class American success with the past stories of struggle.

Each preacher in the New Black Church creates his/her own celebrity identity through well-developed marketing and public relations.[60] In the global marketplace, celebrity transcends the conventional identity markers of race, gender, and class. New Black Church pastors are able to leverage their celebrity and gain more rhetorical and world-making power to socially construct both collective and individual religious/theological identities.[61] Identified as both pastors and CEOs, these preachers have epistemic privilege, authority, and social capital that blurs—more than ever—the sacred and secular, and the public and private. The pastors have unprecedented access and status in the religious world, as well as in the secular and corporate world.

---

59. Lee, *T.D. Jakes*, 159.

60. Walton, *Watch This!*, 5.

61. In respect to subjectivity in the global marketplace, when I say that the branded identity, or celebrity identity, transcends traditional identity markers of race, gender, and class, I am suggesting that celebrity allows access to resources, privilege, and discourse that may not ordinarily be available because of race, gender, and class. However, this does not imply that within the identity category of celebrity there are no hierarchical relationships based on race, gender, and class. Within the ranks of celebrity there will be greater access and privilege based on race, gender, and class.

A New Theology and a New Prosperity

The theology of the New Black Church may be what concerns many academic theologians and religious Black Church scholars the most.[62] Traditional churches of the Black Church model are often critical of the theology represented in the super-megachurches of the New Black Church. The pastors of the New Black Church present similar criticisms of traditional churches.[63] Preachers and scholars who identify with the Black Church model[64] do not like the *new* definitions for prosperity, salvation, and liberation, and excessive branding in the New Black Church. James Cone, the father of black theology, refused to even sit on the podium at a seminary graduation because of a New Black Church pastor. Cone felt it necessary to take a stand, not against the preacher but against the preacher's theology.[65] Robert Franklin, in his book *Crisis in the Village*, outlines a host of problems. The prosperity gospel, however, tops his list. He goes so far as to say that the New Black Church's prosperity theology may be the "single greatest threat to the historical legacy and core values of the contemporary black church tradition."[66] The idea that the theology of these churches poses a threat to a historical legacy and its values exemplifies the antagonistic relationship that exists between churches and pastors who represent the Black Church and New Black Church.[67] "The New Black Church has a fondness for challenging everything

---

62. Religion and Ethics Newsweekly, "The Prosperity Gospel," episode 1051, August 17, 2007, http://www.pbs.org.

63. Harrison, *Righteous Riches*, 149.

64. James H. Evans, Jr., *We Have Been Believers: An African American Systematic Theology* (Minneapolis, MN: Fortress Press, 1992).

65. Mitchem, *Name It and Claim It?*, 48.

66. Robert M. Franklin, *Crisis in the Village: Restoring Hope in African American Communities* (Minneapolis, MN: Fortress Press, 2007), 112.

67. Benjamin K. Watts, "Social Justice and Church Growth in the African-American Church," in *Why Liberal Churches Are Growing*, ed. Martyn Percy and Ian Markham (New York: T&T Clark International, 2006), 96. Lawrence Mamiya, *River of Struggle, River of Freedom: Trends among Black Churches and Black Pastoral Leadership; Pulpit and Pew Research on Pastoral Leadership Reports* (Durham, NC: Duke Divinity School), 12-14.

it perceives as wrong with Grandma's religion and positions itself as the antipode to the old religious establishment,"[68] is how Lee articulates the differences.

New Black Church pastors not only offer salvation from sin, but they offer their congregants an *economic* and *secular* salvation—a Promised Land of financial blessings and rewards. Whereas the preachers of the Black Church, have been accused by scholars of being other worldly—not so for the preachers of the New Black Church. Without a doubt, these preachers are definitely this worldly. They promote and support a liberation and material salvation very much in the here and now. Their theology is defined as what many scholars pejoratively identify as *prosperity theology, prosperity gospel,* or the *gospel of prosperity.* I use what I think is a more accurate description—"theologies of prosperity."[69]

Not all the churches represented by the New Black Church preach this form of theology and gospel. At a minimum, many churches, because of their size and the need to fund their ministries, participate in some of the rituals and practices, such as seed-faith giving, which are often associated with these theologies.[70] Television ministries and super-megachurches are very expensive and unsustainable without continuous cash flow. The ministries are centered on the charismatic leadership and personality of the preacher. As a result, they are difficult to sustain. The late Robert Schuller's television ministry, the *Hour of Power* from the Crystal Cathedral, is just one example. Schuller was not African American, but he was successful with books and television for many years.[71] After he retired, his son,

68. Lee, *T.D. Jakes*, 162.

69. Stephanie Mitchem also uses the terminology "theologies of prosperity" (*Name It and Claim It*, x).

70. Barnhart writes that "when televangelists elect to go on television daily, they wittingly or unwittingly commit themselves to becoming disciples of the Gospel of Prosperity. The financial needs of the daily program virtually require that they embrace the new folk-theology." Joe E. Barnhart, "Prosperity Gospel: A New Folk Theology," in *Religious Television*, ed. Robert Abelman and Stewart M. Hoover (Norwood, NJ: Ablex Publishing Corporation, 1990), 162.

71. See Douglass J. Swanson, "The Beginning of the End of Robert H.

daughter, and grandson were unable to maintain the following to support the expensive ministry and the maintenance of the beautiful Crystal Cathedral. A similar fate often befalls these mega-ministries; with the passing of a charismatic minister, the followers often respond like other secular fans and consumers—they find another personality to follow.

New Black churches are Pentecostal, neo-Pentecostal, evangelical, charismatic, sanctified, and fundamentalist.[72] They are difficult to define because definitions or descriptions like Pentecostal, neo-Pentecostal, or charismatic vary worldwide, both historically and geographically.[73] Additionally, the pastors and adherents in

---

Schuller's Crystal Cathedral Ministry: A Towering Failure in Crisis Management as Reflected Through Media Narratives of Financial Crisis, Family Conflict, and Follower Dissent," *Social Science Journal* 49, no. 4 (December 2012): 485-93.

72. Stephen Hunt explains how the theologies of the faith movement are both Pentecostal and fundamentalist: "It shares with other Pentecostal groups an emphasis on the 'second baptism' (of the spirit), the charismata (glossolalia, prophecy, words of knowledge, etc.), and revivalism. It also tends to be fundamentalist in that it places great stress on preaching the uncompromised word of God and through prophetic revelation, it claims a greater articulation of the divine 'truth' of the 'End times.'" See B. Bannon, *The Health and Wealth Gospel* (Downers Grove, IL: InterVarsity Press, 1987), 44. For definitions and the histories of charismatics, Pentecostals, and fundamentalists, see Simon Coleman, *The Globalisation of Charismatic Christianity: Spreading the Gospel of Prosperity* (Cambridge, UK: Cambridge University Press, 2000), 20-25; Paul Gifford, "Prosperity: A New and Foreign Element in African Christianity," *Religion* 20 (1990): 373-74. Also see Gifford's distinctions within the Religious Right in *The New Crusaders: Christianity and the New Right in Southern Africa* (London: Pluto Press, 1991), 3-5. For how these categories play out among televangelists, see Jeffrey K. Hadden and Anson Shupe, *Televangelism: Power and Politics on God's Frontier* (New York: Henry Holt and Company, 1988), 79-81. For general definitions of evangelical, Pentecostal, and fundamentalist, see Randall Balmer, "A Word about Words," in *Mine Eyes Have Seen the Glory: A Journey into the Evangelical Subculture in America*, 3rd ed. (New York: Oxford University Press, 2000), xv-xvi.

73. Steven Brouwer, Paul Gifford, and Susan D. Rose, *Exporting the American Gospel: Global Christian Fundamentalism* (New York: Routledge, 1996), 29, 266; Harrison, *Righteous Riches*, 14. In Nigeria, Deji Isaac Ayegboyin

these churches rarely use this social-scientific vocabulary to describe themselves.[74] A general inclusive term would be that these churches and their pastors practice what R. Andrew Chesnut calls "pneumacentric" or "spirit-centered" religion or religiosity.[75] In other words, the pastors and adherents in these churches, as Lee and Sinitiere suggest, place an emphasis "on the power of the Holy Spirit for healing, prophetic utterances, vibrant worship and music, and prosperity."[76]

Like the academy as a whole, black and womanist academic theologians have written very little about these preachers.[77] Jonathan Walton contends that when they do write about these popular preachers, the preachers "are too easily deemed anomalous, aberrant, and/or nonblack when measured against black theology's

defines two different groups. Charismatic Pentecostals are those influenced by Classical Pentecostals who "focused on holiness and righteousness as its hallmark" (72). The second group he identifies are New Pentecostals, the term used for prosperity preachers. He also footnotes that some of the preachers prefer the term New Pentecostals to distance themselves from Neo-Pentecostal churches in America. Deji Isaac Ayeboyin, "A Rethinking of Prosperity Teaching in The New Pentecostal Churches in Nigeria," *Black Theology* 4, no. 1 (2006): 73n9. Also, for the differences between Charismatic and New Pentecostals in Ghana, Africa, see Paul Gifford, *Ghana's New Christianity: Pentecostalism in a Globalizing African Economy* (Bloomington, IN: Indiana University Press, 2004), 23, 26.

74. Coleman, *The Globalisation of Charismatic Christianity*, 5. Also see James Barr, "The Problem of Fundamentalism Today," in *Explorations of Theology* 7, ed. James Barr (London: SCM Press, 1980), 67-68.

75. For a definition of pneumacentric religion, see R. Andrew Chesnut, "Pragmatic Consumers and Practical Products: The Success of Pneumacentric Religion among Women in Latin America's New Religious Economy," *Review of Religious Research* 45, no. 1 (September 2003): 20-31.

76. Shayne Lee and Phillip Luke Sinitiere, *Holy Mavericks: Evangelical Innovators and the Spiritual Marketplace* (New York: New York University Press, 2009), 63.

77. Theologians may mention prosperity preachers; however, currently there are no *theological* complete works by academically trained theologians that specifically look at the history and theology of these preachers. The closest would be Stephanie Mitchem's text, *Name It and Claim It*. For a discussion of womanist and feminist perspectives on T.D. Jakes, see Lee, *T.D. Jakes*, 125.

constructed norms."[78] Both womanist and black theologians affirm their allegiance to black churches and with the poor.[79] However, the challenge remains that most African American Christians, including those who are poor, are usually unfamiliar with the God-talk and worldview of academic liberation theologians.[80]

Prosperity preachers such as Creflo Dollar, Fred Price, Eddie Long, Paula White, and T.D. Jakes have limited or no academic training.[81] Yet, this has not prevented them from gaining entrée into the lives of black Christians across the globe.[82] Many African Americans are not only familiar with their theologies, but they are actually repeating and attempting to live out the God-talk of these popular preachers.[83] The rituals, religious practices, and worldview reinforced by their theologies are changing the face of African American religion. The

---

78. Walton, *Watch This!*, 32.

79. James H. Cone, *For My People: Black Theology and the Black Church, Where Have We Been and Where Are We Going?* (Maryknoll, NY: Orbis Books, 1984); Delores S. Williams, *Sisters in the Wilderness: The Challenge of Womanist God-talk* (Maryknoll, NY: Orbis Books, 1993), xiv-xv.

80. Harris-Lacewell, "From Liberation to Mutual Fund," 140; Cecil W. Cone, *The Identity Crisis in Black Theology* (Nashville, TN: AMEC, 1975); Katie G. Cannon, "Structured Academic Amnesia: As if the Womanist Story Never Happened," in *Deeper Shades of Purple: Womanism in Religion and Society*, ed. Stacey Floyd-Thomas (New York: New York University Press, 2006), 19-28.

81. I should clarify that I am privileging accredited seminaries. Many prosperity preachers have been trained in Bible institutes, colleges, or schools. Some also have nonreligious degrees. However, many of the schools do not have accreditation supported by the Department of Education. According to Jonathan Walton, T.D. Jakes has a GED and completed one year at West Virginia State College (Walton, *Watch This!*, 105). T.D. Jakes also has a doctor of ministry degree in Religious Studies from Friends International Christian University (FICU); see http://www.ficu.edu/alumni/Jakes.html. My point is that the degrees or credentials of these prosperity preachers would not qualify for admission or acceptance into the seminaries and institutions to which academically trained theologians give epistemic privilege.

82. Walton, *Watch This!*, 214.

83. Harris-Lacewell, "From Liberation to Mutual Fund," 142, 147.

serious scholar of religion cannot ignore this reality. Consequently, any viable critique requires that these prosperity preachers be taken seriously and treated as contemporary theologians. These preachers differ from academic theologians, but they have a certain praxis and offer what their congregants consider as spiritual prescriptions for salvation and a kind of liberation.

The men and women of the New Black Church are encouraged to get into *the Word* to find their own answers to life's problems.[84] Parishioners are offered (through church bookstores, websites, television, and direct mail) a variety of products to help them develop their faith. For the majority of people, who are exposed to a myriad of prosperity products in various mediums, the sermon continues to be the primary vehicle for dissemination of the New Black Church prosperity message.[85] The rhetorical influence of preaching and the Sunday service are where most followers receive their theology. According to homiletics scholar Olin Moyd, "preaching is still the most sacred element of the liturgy," and it is the "medium for communicating, elucidating, and illuminating God's revelation for God's people."[86] Therefore the words shared in a sermon have greater power than what is presented in any other faith medium or product.

The sermon is also the most important theological moment in the Black Church. The sermon creates a liberation ethos that supports the ability to delay gratification. Worship, sermons, songs, and testimonies are opportunities to reinforce and communicate this ethos. Biblical texts like the Exodus narrative and New Testament texts

---

84. Gifford, "Prosperity: A New and Foreign Element," 379.

85. Because of the position that the sermon has in the Protestant worship experience, and the rhetoric or persuasive power of preaching, the sermon continues to be the primary vehicle for disseminating theology. However, the worship service is only one of many mediums. The sermon can be reproduced in a television broadcast and also in book form. "Woman Thou Art Loosed" is an example of one sermon reproduced into many other products.

86. Olin P. Moyd, *The Sacred Art: Preaching and Theology in the African American Tradition* (Valley Forge, PA: Judson Press, 1995), 10-11.

that present Jesus as co-sufferer and liberator are foundational to how churches live out and practice this ethos.[87]

The Exodus narrative allowed slaves to identify with Israel. They saw themselves with "a communal identity as special, divinely favored people."[88] The most famous example of the Exodus story that supports this ethos is Martin Luther King, Jr.'s, speech when he evocatively told the community, "I've seen the Promised Land. And I may not get there with you. But . . . we as a people will get to the Promised Land."[89]

The New Black Church, however, stresses prosperity for "the individual over community."[90] The pastors promote economic and material liberation in the here and now—not through the transformation of social structures but by encouraging middle- and upper-class aspirations and wealth as a goal in itself. The parishioners of the New Black Church are very comfortable with America and its dream. With a sense of entitlement, they claim a God-given right to pursue the dream and to reap all of its financial and material benefits.[91] A philosophy of economic exceptionalism is how Harrison describes the people who populate these super-megachurches. He writes that the churches believe in a divine "redistribution of wealth

---

87. Lewis V. Baldwin, "Revisiting the 'All-Comprehending Institution': Historical Reflections on the Public Roles of Black Churches," in *New Day Begun: African American Churches and Civic Culture in Post-Civil Rights America*, ed. R. Drew Smith (Durham, NC: Duke University Press, 2003), 15-38 (17); Christopher Buck, *Religious Myths and Visions of America: How Minority Faiths Redefined America's World Role* (Westport, CT: Praeger, 2009), 40-44.

88. Albert J. Raboteau, "African Americans, Exodus, and the American Israel," in *Fire in the Bones: Reflections on African American Religious History* (Boston: Beacon Press, 1995), 34.

89. Raboteau, "African Americans," 35.

90. Mitchem, *Name It and Claim It?*, 108.

91. Harrison, "Prosperity in African American Religion," in Milmon F. Harrison, *Righteous Riches: The Word of Faith Movement in Contemporary African American Religion* (New York: Oxford University Press, 2005), 131-46; Lee, "A Message of Prosperity," in *America's New Preacher*, 98-122. Mitchem, *Name It and Claim It?*, 49.

out of the hands of 'sinners' into the hands of born-again Christians, while preserving the [capitalist] system intact . . . those believers who have prospered within the existing economic system have the reassurance that it is God's will."[92] The Promised Land in the New Black Church is about individual salvation and individual prosperity.[93]

Jesus is no longer the co-sufferer of the Black Church. Jesus is a corporate CEO responsible for twelve staff (his disciples).[94] In many New Black Churches—especially Word of Faith churches—almost every reference to suffering, including symbols like the cross, has been removed. Many African Americans are attracted to these churches because they can "seek material advancement [and] also appreciate the message because it does not suggest that a Christ-like existence entails a vow of poverty. Rather, these churches argue that God desires all Christians to have material comfort and individual salvation."[95] This position provides a way for these Christians "to justify [their] upward mobility and middle class existence without feeling guilty."[96]

Theologian Jacqueline Grant explains in her foundational text on womanist theology, *White Women's Christ and Black Women's Jesus*, that for African American women and African Americans as a whole, "'Jesus was all things.' Chief among these however was the belief in Jesus as the *divine co-sufferer* who empowered them in situations of oppression…. Jesus means freedom from the sociopsychological, psychocultural, economic and political oppression."[97] She

---

92. Harrison, *Righteous Riches*, 150.

93. Savage, *Your Spirits Walk Beside Us*, 274.

94. Harrison, *Righteous Riches*, 12. Shayne Lee gives a specific example about T.D. Jakes. He writes, "Jakes contended that soldiers gambled for Jesus Christ's cloak while he was on the cross, so he must have had great wealth, and therefore Christ's followers should emulate him by being wealthy." Lee, *T.D. Jakes*, 109.

95. Pinn, *The Black Church in the Post-Civil Rights Era*, 138.

96. Ibid.

97. Jacqueline Grant, *White Women's Christ and Black Women's Jesus: Feminist Christology and Womanist Response* (Atlanta: Scholars Press, 1989), 212-15 [emphasis mine].

affirms that African Americans believed that "Jesus identified with the lowly of his day, [therefore] he now identifies with the lowly of this day."[98]

Bishop Jakes speaks often about the suffering of black people—especially black women.[99] However, like other pastors in the New Black Church, he promulgates this very different ethos and mythology and is fully immersed in the prosperity worldview with all of its capitalist values.

98. Grant, *White Women's Christ*, 215.
99. Lee and Sinitiere, *Holy Mavericks*, 70-71.

2

Prosperity Theology, the New Black Church, and T.D. Jakes

Any investigation of the New Black Church is incomplete without an adequate discussion of the "prosperity gospel," "prosperity theology"—or what I think is a more accurate description, "theologies of prosperity."[1] Not all the churches in the New Black Church preach this form of theology and gospel. However, many churches because of their size and the amount of capital needed to fund their ministries, participate in many of the rituals and fund-raising practices associated with these theologies.[2] Although many scholars from a variety of disciplines are concerned about the impact of the American prosperity gospel, there is not one clear and concise definition that identifies prosperity preachers and theologies of prosperity.

Preachers like Bishop T.D. Jakes with their many brands create contextual theologies that help black parishioners negotiate what it means to be black and American—or the double consciousness and

---

1. Stephanie Mitchem also uses the terminology "theologies of prosperity." Stephanie Y. Mitchem, *Name It and Claim It? Prosperity Preaching in the Black Church* (Cleveland, OH: Pilgrim Press, 2007), x.

2. Barnhart writes that "when televangelists elect to go on television daily, they wittingly or unwittingly commit themselves to becoming disciples of the Gospel of Prosperity. The financial needs of the daily program virtually require that they embrace the new folk-theology." Joe E. Barnhart, "Prosperity Gospel: A New Folk Theology," in *Religious Television*, ed. Robert Abelman and Stewart M. Hoover (Norwood, NJ: Ablex Publishing Corporation, 1990), 162.

the problem of the color line that DuBois framed with the question: "How does it feel to be a problem?"[3] The prosperity gospel with its prescriptions for health and wealth attempt to help African Americans negotiate their racial and financial identities or the "income line"—as a response to the critical white gaze of the dominant culture.[4] In other words, although race continues to be a challenge, capitalism positions those who are poor and those not prospering within the system as the problem. Donald Trump winning the 2017 presidential campaign is substantial evidence that not much has changed in terms of race, gender, and class. Mary Ann Tolbert asserts:

> The hegemonic North American cultural values continue to privilege one who is male, white, of Anglo/European descent, educated, middle-to-upper-class (with attendant economic standing), heterosexual, married, healthy, physically fit, Christian/Protestant, youngish, slim, attractive, and so on.
>
> From television serial to advertisements, the dominant ideology of the attractive, successful, wealthy white male as the one in control whom we should all admire and trust is constantly reinforced. No matter how hard we try, some of us by definition will never be able to attain this hegemonic image, and that underscores its constructed nature and the

---

3. In *The Souls of Black Folk* (New York: Signet Classic, 1969/1903), W. E. B. DuBois writes, "One ever feels his twoness, — an American, a Negro; two souls, two thoughts, two unreconciled strivings; two warring ideals in one dark body, whose strength alone keeps it from being torn asunder" (2). In similar fashion, DuBois testifies how he personally experiences the daily challenges of white supremacy and racism. "Between me and the other world there is an unasked question: unasked by some because of feelings of delicacy; by others because of the difficulty in rightly framing it; all, nevertheless, flutter around it. They approach me in a half-hesitant sort of way, eye me curiously or compassionately, and, then instead of saying it directly, How does it feel to be a problem? I answer seldom a word" (1).

4. Marla Frederick, *Colored Television: American Religion Gone Global* (Stanford, CA: Stanford University Press, 2016), 90-92.

intent of those who construct it to preserve power and prestige in the hands of only a few.[5]

The theological propositions of prosperity preachers offer answers for a new generation about how to achieve American success in the midst of ever-changing complexity of American culture. Harrison concludes that theologies of prosperity offer "a sense of personal, individual *empowerment* to those who have been left out of the mainstream of economic and social life, making it attractive to the poor who don't want to stay poor in America and elsewhere."[6]

The preachers of the New Black Church often present themselves as innovative and different from traditional churches. However, they are not really creating anything *new*; the prosperity gospel resonates with an *old* secular American ideology called the gospel of wealth. Additionally, in speaking to the question of how their parishioners may overcome poverty and sickness, the prosperity preachers offer a form of theodicy—the area of theology that attempts to reconcile the existence of evil and suffering with a loving and all-powerful God. In addressing questions of health and wealth, they are essentially answering the question, with a twenty-first-century twist: "Why the rich are prosperous and healthy, while others, even Christians, are not?"[7]

Bishop Jakes and other preachers promise a kind of liberation to black consumers who are now finally able to exercise their middle-class purchasing power. Many of these consumers do not have a problem with worship through a television or movie screen, religiosity from the pages of a book, or a spiritual gathering in the Georgia Dome. According to Mara Einstein, "Many people no longer practice their faith within the confines of a church or synagogue, but instead get their spiritual fulfillment through interacting with

---

5. Mary Ann Tolbert, "Reading for Liberation," in *Reading from This Place: Social Location and Biblical Interpretation in the United States,* ed. Fernando Segovia and Mary Ann Tolbert (Minneapolis: Fortress, 1995), 263.

6. Milmon F. Harrison, *Righteous Riches: The Word of Faith Movement in Contemporary African American Religion* (New York: Oxford Press, 2005), 159.

7. Ibid., 151.

religious products and events, such as books, movies, and rock concerts."[8] African Americans in the New Black Church are a part of these trends. Subsequently, they have a different understanding of their spiritual and religious identities.

My intentional use of the term "theology" instead of the more commonly used term "gospel" is to underscore that it is no longer just a gospel. Without a doubt, it is now a *theology*. As Kate Bowler states, "millions of American Christians . . . see money, health, and good fortune as divine."[9] Academic theologians and religious scholars have often struggled with an artificial demarcation between the faith of elites and the faith of the masses. As a result, prosperity theology gets categorized as a popular or folk theology. It does not meet the ivory-tower criteria of the academy. As a popular theology, "it is communicated directly to the laypeople in their own language"[10] in large stadiums, the living rooms of television viewers, movie theaters, books, and church pulpits. Prosperity preachers like Bishop Jakes now have a substantial number of books, sermons, and products that cover almost every aspect and subject of a believer's life.[11] Moreover, because the theology is contextual, the plural "theologies" is a better description to represent the global, racial, geographical, and ecclesial differences that exist from preacher to preacher and church to church.[12]

North American preachers and televangelists like Jakes have many imitators.[13] Preachers from around the world are often emulating an

---

8. Mara Einstein, *Brands of Faith: Marketing Religion in a Commercial Age* (New York: Routledge, 2008), 60.

9. Kate Bowler, *Blessed: A History of the American Prosperity Gospel* (New York: Oxford University Press, 2013), 7.

10. Barnhart, "Prosperity Gospel," 159.

11. Deji Isaac Ayeboyin, "A Rethinking of Prosperity Teaching in the New Pentecostal Churches in Nigeria," *Black Theology* 4, no. 1 (2006): 73.

12. Harrison, *Righteous Riches*, 158. Jonathan Walton also advises that we should not impose "a fictitious uniformity on the widely theological, ecclesial, and social views of African American televangelists and megachurch pastors." Jonathan L. Walton, *Watch This! The Ethics and Aesthetics of Black Televangelism* (New York: New York University, 2009), 12-13.

13. Paul Gifford documents that T.D. Jakes had over one million people

American version of a successful neo-Pentecostal church and pastor. They seek to duplicate the "modern building, a large ever-growing congregation, a charismatic pastor . . . and plenty of funds."[14] This form of Christianity changes with the market. Therefore theologies of prosperity are "constantly mutating."[15] The churches and preachers are "represented by hundreds of independent ministries which might depart, to one degree or another, in both practice and doctrine, from the core teachings."[16] The foundational "doctrines of health and wealth are discernible in whatever the cultural context in which they are adopted."[17] The pastors and churches in the New Black Church also differ from one another because of the variety of brands.

Each brand has a particular target audience. Most televangelists have their unique niche or focus. For example, Benny Hinn is known as the miracle healing preacher;[18] Joel Osteen is the smiling preacher, and Mike Murdock the wisdom preacher.[19] T.D. Jakes has several niches; the one that has made him successful, however, is the healer and liberator of women.

New Black Church pastors and Bishop Jakes are always creating new brands with new contextual theologies to satisfy the needs of their target audiences and the millions of consumers. In fact, Jakes has changed his position or been less vocal on earlier proclamations

---

to attend three events in Nairobi in 2005. Because of his success, many pastors imitate the American success that Jakes presents. Paul Gifford, "Expecting Miracles: The Prosperity Gospel in Africa," *Christian Century* 124, no. 14 (July 10, 2007): 24.

14. Stephen Hunt describes the leadership as charismatic in a "Weberian sense" of charismatic leadership. Stephen Hunt, "'Winning Ways:' Globalisation and the Impact of the Health and Wealth Gospel," *Journal of Contemporary Religion* 15 no. 3 (2000): 337. Also see Harvey Cox, *Fire from Heaven: The Rise of Pentecostal Spirituality and the Reshaping of Religion in the Twenty-first Century* (Reading, MA: Addison-Wesley, 1995), 272.

15. Gifford, "Expecting Miracles," 21.

16. Ibid.

17. Hunt, "'Winning Ways,'" 343.

18. Bowler, *Blessed,* 141.

19. For information on Benny Hinn, see Bowler, *Blessed*, 137. For Mike Murdock, one of his most popular books is Mike Murdock, *Wisdom: God's Golden Key to Success* (Fort Worth, TX: Wisdom Center, 2005).

that might prove to be controversial or might hurt his brand.[20] Subsequently, with the number of churches, preachers, and brands, each preacher and church is unique. Therefore, the theology of Jakes as the pastor of The Potter's House in Dallas is not like that of Eddie Long in Georgia, or Pastor David Oyedepo in Lagos, Nigeria, who has several satellite churches and a 50,400-seat super-megachurch.[21]

The largest group of prosperity practitioners are the preachers and parishioners of Word of Faith churches. I agree with Harrison, who writes specifically about black Word of Faith churches, that "it is becoming increasingly difficult to distinguish Faith Message teachings and practices from those commonly associated with some of the denominational churches."[22] Furthermore, "for believers in the United States and in a host of nations abroad, the belief that it is God's will for them to be healthy and wealthy and to enjoy all the best this present world has to offer before they die and go to heaven serves as the core of their understanding of their relationship to the sacred."[23] The Pew Forum on Religion and Public Life conducted an international survey of ten countries on Pentecostalism. The survey documented that the majority of Christians believed that "God will grant good health and material prosperity" and "relief from sickness to those who have enough faith."[24] Black Christians are now interested in answering the question from the cover of *Time* magazine: "Does God Want You to Be Rich?"[25]

20. Shayne Lee and Phillip Luke Sinitiere, *Holy Mavericks: Evangelical Innovators and the Spiritual Marketplace* (New York: New York University Press, 2009), 67.

21. In 2000, Gifford records that David Oyedepo's church, Winners' Chapel, could be found in 38 African countries with 400 branches in Nigeria. Paul Gifford, *Ghana's New Christianity: Pentecostalism in a Globalizing African Economy* (Bloomington, IN: Indiana University Press, 2004), 56.

22. Harrison, *Righteous Riches*, 160.

23. Ibid., 19.

24. The Pew Forum on Religion and Public Life, *Spirit and Power: A 10-Country Survey of Pentecostals* (Washington D.C.: Pew Forum on Religion and Public Life), 31, http://www.pewforum.org.

25. David Van Biema and Jeff Chu, "Does God Want You to Be Rich?," *Time,* September 18, 2006, 48-56.

These popular and contextual theologies are what early Catholic liberation theologians Leonardo and Clodovis Boff and academic theologian Katheryn Tanner define as "theologies of the people." In other words, they are "theologies of ordinary people, who run the gamut of degrees of marginalization according to their distance from the legitimation that the complex intersection of a number of different factors such as ordination, academic degree, or privileged social location might confer."[26] Theologies of the people are about hearing "the problems brought by the people, and listen[ing] to the theology being done *by* and *in* the community."[27]

Similar to other prosperity theologians around the world, New Black Church pastors present "a thoroughly contextualized Christianity that directly addresses pressing needs."[28] Whether it is the African American women attending The Potter's House or a WTAL Conference, evangelical Christians in the Bible Belt, or poor people in Two-Thirds World countries, these theologies speak to the needs of those who feel marginalized—not just the marginalization from the usual categories of race, gender, and class oppression. The congregants often call on their pastors for deliverance and healing from demonic and cosmic evil—at other times, liberation from the threat of secularization and humanism.[29]

Prosperity churches and fellowships are all over the world, but the official birthplace of prosperity theology or Word of Faith is the United States.[30] Both internationally and locally, television, print

---

26. Katheryn Tanner uses the term "theologies of the people." See Kathryn Tanner, "Theology and Popular Culture," in *Changing Conversations: Religious Reflections & Cultural Analysis*, ed. Dwight N. Hopkins and Sheila Greeve Davaney (New York: Routledge, 1996), 101.

27. Leonardo Boff and Clodovis Boff, *Introducing Liberation Theology*, trans. Paul Burns (Maryknoll, NY: Orbis Books, 1986), 20 [emphasis mine].

28. Gifford, "Expecting Miracles," 24.

29. Gifford, *Ghana's New Christianity*, 61. For a discussion on the fundamentalist versions of theologies of prosperity that focus on spiritual warfare to fight evil forces, demons, communism, Islam, and secular humanism, see Steve Brouwer, Paul Gifford, and Susan D. Rose, *Exporting the American Gospel: Global Christian Fundamentalism* (New York: Routledge, 1996), 198.

30. The faith movement is attributed to Kenneth E. Hagin, Sr., in Tulsa,

media, Bible schools, conferences and crusades create a demand for the services and products of prosperity preachers. North American preachers, especially the pastors of the New Black Church, are in high demand.[31] Their theologies are malleable and uniquely indigenous to each cultural context and community.[32] As a result, the churches and theologies are responsive to market demands and have expanded exponentially throughout the world.

Three basic points characterize most of these theologies. Harrison states that followers embrace "the principle of knowing who you are in Christ; the practice of positive confession (and positive mental attitude); and a worldview that emphasizes material prosperity and physical health as the divine right of every Christian."[33] These theologies perceive the death of Jesus on the cross or the atonement of Jesus as providing several "victories for true believers: Deliverance of the soul from sin and hell, deliverance of the body from Satan and disease, and deliverance from poverty and economic hardship in this life."[34] Believers are taught that contemporary Christians should expect and are entitled to the blessings of Abraham (financial, spiritual, and physical) that are guaranteed in the Abrahamic Covenant of the Old Testament.[35] The Bible is treated as "a record of covenants, prom-

---

OK. Tulsa is a part of the area of the United States that is often called the Bible Belt. Bowler also identifies the birthplace as America. Bowler, *Blessed*, 4.

31. Brouwer, Gifford, and Rose point to Kenneth Hagin's Rhema Bible Institute as responsible for "exporting the faith to all parts of the world." Brouwer, Gifford, and Rose, *Exporting the American Gospel,* 26. Also see Asoneh Ukah, "African Christianities: Features, Promises and Problems," *Working Paper* 79, 13n51, http://www.ifeas.uni-mainz.de.

32. Andrew Perriman, ed., *Faith, Health and Prosperity: A Report on "Word of Faith" and "Positive Confession" Theologies by ACUTE (Evangelical Alliance Commission on Unity and Truth among Evangelicals),* (Carlisle, Cumbria UK: Paternoster Press, 2003), 6; Gifford, *Ghana's New Christianity,* 61.

33. Harrison, *Righteous Riches*, 8.

34. Barnhart, "Prosperity Gospel," 159.

35. Ken L. Sarles, "A Theological Evaluation of the Prosperity Gospel," *Bibliotheca Sacra* 143, no. 572 (October–December 1986): 334. Prosperity preachers interpret the New Testament text Galatians 3:14 ("In order that in Christ Jesus the blessing of Abraham might come to the Gentiles") to support

ises, pledges, and commitments between God and [God's] people."[36] When congregants put these principles into practice, "The believer claims a divine promise [usually in a Scripture verse], demands God to do what [God] has promised, then gives thanks for receiving it. Faith is [then] released through prayer to activate God to do something."[37]

Theologies of prosperity and the preachers are quite diverse and should not be considered as monolithic and static. Instead, it is better to place them on a continuum that allows for the variation from the crudest to the most subtle.[38] Bowler classifies the theologies into "hard prosperity" and "soft prosperity."[39] The variance is expressed as "hard prosperity hammered giving and receiving into rigid rules,"[40] [and] "drew a straight line between life circumstances and a believer's faith. Faith operated as a perfect law, and any irregularities meant that the believer did not play by the rules."[41] She explains that the theologies on this end of the continuum "emphasized [the] contractual nature, describing God as unable to 'multiply back' blessings except to those who give correctly."[42] Soft prosperity are the contextual theologies that are "therapeutic and down-to-earth Christian self-improvement,"[43] which "developed a smooth new language and style of persuasion.

---

their position that the blessings of the Abrahamic covenant are now available to contemporary Christians.

36. Gifford, "Expecting Miracles," 20.

37. George E. Hummel, *The Prosperity Gospel: Health and Wealth and the Faith Movement* (Downers Grove, IL: InterVarsity Press, 1991), 13.

38. Melissa Harris-Lacewell, "From Liberation to Mutual Fund: Political Consequences of Differing Conceptions of Christ in the African American Church," in *From Pews to Polling Places: Faith and Politics in the American Religious Mosaic*, ed. J. Matthew Wilson (Washington, D.C.: Georgetown University Press, 2007), 131-60 (140).

39. Bowler states, *"Hard prosperity* judges people's faith by their immediate circumstances, while *soft prosperity* appraises believers with a gentler, more roundabout, assessment." Bowler, *Blessed*, 7-8.

40. Ibid., 98.

41. Ibid., 97.

42. Ibid., 99.

43. Ibid., 78.

. . . It was therapeutic and emotive, a way of speaking . . . [with] a sweeter and secular tone."[44]

The worldview of prosperity practitioners is about individual salvation and believers achieving their individual personal wealth and health. Paul Gifford highlights the rugged individualism of these theologies, and what the individual congregant is taught about social responsibility. In discussing Word of Faith churches, he explains that believers do not see a need to help people who are not Christian. Similar to many of the congregants in New Black Churches, congregants feel no social responsibility to deal with issues of social justice and political issues: "There is no wider social responsibility in this Christianity . . . [because] only Christians matter. Christians will have jobs, food, and education and be successful. Non-Christians will not have these, neither should they . . . because the fruits of Jesus' sacrifice belong only to believers." Moreover, "the Christian's sole duty to deprived unbelievers is merely to convert them so that they can prosper miraculously as well."[45] This position is usually the response of extreme prosperity preachers and believers.

Bishop Jakes is much more subtle in his approach. He promotes Christians as having favor and being blessed because of their faith. He is very similar to the majority of Word of Faith preachers in that his lack of commitment to communal social justice fuels the passivity of Christians. Instead of inviting congregants to fight for political and social justice like many black preachers of the past, Jakes lifts up following God's Word as the ultimate strategy for success. However, Jakes's hermeneutic for following God's Word rarely includes social activism.[46]

Prosperity, Word Churches, and Preaching the Word

Prosperity preachers are always encouraging believers to get into *the Word* so that they can equip themselves to find their own answers

---

44. Ibid., 125.

45. Paul Gifford, "Christian Fundamentalism and Development," *Review of African Political Economy* 52: 14.

46. Lee and Sinitiere, *Holy Mavericks*, 59.

to life's problems.[47] The gospel is often presented in a democratic fashion that works equally for everyone. Word of Faith specifically "teaches that this sort of knowledge is available to all believers: the expectation is that God will clarify the meaning of Scripture, confirm the truth of Word of Faith teaching, and guide people in their daily lives through the rather commonplace experience of revelation."[48] The Word of God is what empowers the believer. The pastors promise and at other times *guarantee* that congregants can—with absolute certainty—possess the critical tools to be rich and prosperous.[49] Accordingly, a wide variety of products are presented to parishioners through church bookstores, websites, television, and direct mail. Each person is encouraged to develop and build their faith. Although the members are exposed to a myriad of prosperity products in various mediums—especially in black churches—the sermon continues to be the primary vehicle for dissemination of the prosperity message.[50]

Preaching has unmatched rhetorical influence. The words that are shared in a sermon are more powerful than what is presented in any other faith medium or prosperity production. Moyd explains that "preaching is still the most sacred element of the liturgy." The sermon is the "medium for communicating, elucidating, and illuminating God's revelation for God's people."[51] Each preacher builds what homiletics scholar David Buttrick describes as "a faith-world, in consciousness, made from images, metaphors, illustrations and

---

47. Paul Gifford, "Prosperity: A New and Foreign Element in African Christianity," *Religion* 20 (1990): 379.

48. Perriman, ed., *Faith, Health and Prosperity*, 31.

49. Harrison, *Righteous Riches*, 9.

50. Because of the position that the sermon has in the Protestant worship experience, and the rhetoric or persuasive power of preaching, the sermon continues to be the primary vehicle for disseminating theology. However, the worship service is only one of many mediums. The sermon can be reproduced in a television broadcast and also in book form. "Woman Thou Art Loosed" is an example of one sermon being reproduced into many other products.

51. Olin P. Moyd, *The Sacred Art: Preaching and Theology in the African American Tradition* (Valley Forge, PA: Judson Press, 1995), 10-11.

examples."[52] Preachers actually teach their "congregations to interpret experience in the light of scripture and scripture in view of
experience."[53] How the preacher "names God with the world will
tend to determine how people understand scripture, its meaning,
message, and application to life."[54] During each worship experience
the preacher-as-creator[55] within the communal call and response of
black preaching is constructing a local or contextual theology.[56] For
example, at funerals the community is offered a theological position
on death; at weddings, they are given theological reflections about
love and whom God deems worthy of the sacred union.

In the traditional churches of the Black Church, one pericope,
story, or text from Scripture is expounded upon. In the so-called
"word churches,"[57] preachers pride themselves on "teaching."[58] A
very common image in the New Black Church is that of the prosperity preacher standing in front of the congregation with members searching through their highlighted Bibles to follow the verses

52. David G. Buttrick, *Homiletic Moves and Structures* (Philadelphia: Fortress Press, 1987), 168-69.

53. Ibid., 19.

54. Ibid.

55. Dolan Hubbard, *The Sermon and the African American Literary Imagination* (Columbia: University of Missouri Press, 1994), 4.

56. For discussions and definitions of *local* and *contextual* theologies, see
Stephen B. Bevans, *Models of Contextual Theology*, rev. and expanded. ed.
(Maryknoll, NY: Orbis Books, 2002); Robert J. Schreiter *Constructing Local
Theologies* (Maryknoll, NY, Orbis Books, 1985); Clemens Sedmak, *Doing
Local Theology: A Guide for Artisans of a New Humanity* (Maryknoll, NY, Orbis
Books, 2002).

57. Harrison describes a Word church as one in which "a church's minister
specializes in teaching, as opposed to preaching, what the Bible 'really' says,
the implication being that other churches do not do this" (*Righteous Riches*,
86). Robert Franklin writes that black word churches emerge "from the pre-
dominantly white evangelical community." Robert M. Franklin, *Another
Day's Journey: Black Churches Confronting the American Crisis* (Minneapolis,
MN: Fortress Press, 1997), 69.

58. Franklin, *Another Day's Journey*, 70. Harrison, *Righteous Riches*, 89;
Walton, *Watch This!*, 157.

expounded upon in the sermon.[59] In black word churches, like traditional black churches, there is still the *call and response* between congregation and preacher.[60] Yet, the presentation of the sermon intentionally resembles more of an organized lecture. Prosperity preachers want to present a middle-class decorum to make sure that they differentiate themselves from "the emotional hooping" of traditional black preachers and churches.[61]

The preachers pride themselves on being teachers and experts in the Word of God. Only a few scriptures, however, support their controversial worldview, ethos, rituals, and religious practices. The prosperity ethos includes the ethical expectations of both the believer and God. God is also required to respond ethically to the spiritual laws of the prosperity worldview. Many preachers argue that God is *obligated* to honor God's Word. Scripture, however, is the central scaffolding to explain and inculcate the rituals or religious practices of prayer, positive confession, and tithing/seed-faith giving.

Prosperity Scriptures

The sermons may include verses from all over the Bible, but prosperity preachers selectively use only a small number of verses to theologically substantiate their positions on health and wealth.[62] Their

---

59. Gifford, *Ghana's Charismatic Christianity*, 28.

60. Harrison, *Righteous Riches*, 102.

61. Harrison, *Righteous Riches*, 89, 157; Shayne Lee, *T.D. Jakes: America's New Preacher* (New York: New York University Press, 2005), 102.

62. Perriman, *Faith, Health and Prosperity*, 84. Paul Gifford identifies several biblical texts used by prosperity preachers: "Ps 35:27; Gen 13:2-17; Gen 14:22f.; Gen 17:5ff.; Gen 26:12ff., Gen 30:43; Gen 39:2f.; Exod 3:7f.; Deut 8:18; Deut 28:11; Isa 1:19; Josh 1:8; Deut 29:9; Isa 55:11; Ps 37:25f.; Prov 10:22; Prov 22:7; Prov 19:17; Luke 12:15; 12:21; Prov 28:13; Ps 1:3; Prov 13:22; Heb 11:6; Mark 4:19; Luke 6:38; 2 Cor 9:6; Prov 3:9f.; Mal 3:10ff.; Heb 7:8; 2 Cor 9:8-11; Eccles 11:1; 3 John 2; Matt 6:25-33; 1 Cor 13:3; Rom 13:7f.; 1 Tim 6:17ff.; Matt 6:19ff.; Luke 16:10ff.; Phil 4:19; Mark 10:29f.; Mark 4:23-29; 2 Chr 26:5; 31:21; 2 Kgs 18:7; Isa 48:15ff.; Deut 30:19f.; 2 Cor 8:9; Deut 28:1f.; Gal 3:13f.; Eph 4:28; Luke 7:23; Hag 2:7-9; Mark 4:20-25; Josh 1:5." Gifford, "Prosperity: A New and Foreign Element," 384n6.

use of the Bible is "classically fundamentalist," which means congregants are taught that "everything necessary is contained in the Bible."[63] Most pastors and churches are fundamentalists. As biblical scholar James Barr explains, "For fundamentalists, Scripture comes from God and is inspired in all its parts. It provides the basis for preaching and for practical impact upon personal life. The typical assertion of the evangelist is 'The Bible says' (not so often 'The Bible means')."[64] Because of this fundamentalist appropriation of Scripture, these preachers or leaders may actually have "greater influence in their constituency than bishops, theologians, or biblical scholars in non-fundamentalist Christianity."[65]

God, in the prosperity worldview, meets congregants in this world and provides them with the knowledge to obtain wealth and be healthy. In order to achieve this wealth and health believers must satisfy strict ethical requirements. The ethos and unique worldview are reinforced and authenticated in the rituals of prayer, tithing, and testimony. Stephen Hunt asserts that the worship experiences become a kind of "status confirmation ritual"[66] for adherents. The worship also creates a sense of belonging. By belonging to "the religious collective," the individual members of a church, for example, are able to "reflect the lifestyles and materialist orientations of its membership."[67] Generally speaking, this means that God has blessed the believers—especially the prosperity preachers—who present themselves as exemplars of prosperity. Hence, the preachers are the living brands for the prosperity worldview. In the case of T.D. Jakes, he is not just any brand, he is an international or global brand.[68] The preachers, their churches, and their product

---

63. Gifford, "Expecting Miracles," 20.

64. James Barr, "The Fundamentalist Understanding of Scripture," in *Conflicting Ways of Interpreting the Bible*, ed. Hans Küng and Jürgen Moltmann (New York: T. & T. Clark, 1980), 70.

65. Barr, "The Fundamentalist Understanding of Scripture," 73.

66. Stephen Hunt, "Dramatising the 'Health and Wealth Gospel': Belief and Practice of Neo-Pentecostal 'Faith Ministry,'" *Journal of Beliefs and Values: Studies in Religion and Education* 21, no. 1 (2000): 76.

67. Ibid.

68. Einstein, *Brands of Faith,* 122.

lines become the tangible proof for believers that the worldview and practices work. Thousands of people assembled together and ready to give their tithes and offerings reinforce the believer's expectation that God has blessed, and will continue to bless, those who are faithful. The most popular verses used to justify the prosperity worldview are the following:

> *Beloved, I pray that you may prosper in all things and be in health, just as your soul prospers.* (3 John 2 NKJV)

> *My God will supply every need of yours according to his riches in Christ Jesus.* (Philippians 4:19)

> *The wealth of the sinner is stored up for the righteous.* (Proverbs 13:22 NKJV)

> *It is [God] who gives you power to get wealth.* (Deuteronomy 8:18 NKJV)

In the prosperity worldview, Satan is the one that steals and keeps believers from health and wealth, and Jesus provides the abundance:

> *The thief does not come except to steal, and to kill, and to destroy. I [Jesus] have come that they may have life, and that they may have it more abundantly.* (John 10:10 NKJV)

The passages that justify tithing and giving are:

> *Bring all the tithes into the storehouse, . . . "If I will not open for you the windows of heaven and pour out for you such blessing that there will not be room enough to receive it"* (Malachi 3:10 NKJV)

> *Give and it will be given to you. . . .* (Luke 6:38 NKJV)

The most used verse that supports positive confession and prayer is:

> *Therefore I say to you, whatever things you ask when you pray, believe that you receive them, and you will have them.* (Mark 11: 23-24 NKJV)

It is not only the selection of scriptures but how they are inter-preted that is unique to these theologies.[69] The form of interpreta-tion used by the majority of prosperity preachers is often identified as proof-texting.[70] Proof-texting, positive confession, and seed-faith giving, with its extreme emphasis on tithing, have become synony-mous with theologies of prosperity.[71]

Proof-texting, Positive Confession, and Seed-faith Giving

Proof-texting is the form of biblical interpretation in which individ-ual texts or pericopes are extracted from their literary and historical context and used as proof for a particular position.[72] In other words, "taking a statement out of its original context to support a teach-ing we desire to affirm."[73] This type of interpretation is difficult to define adequately without a full history of biblical interpretation in mainline Christianity. However, Gifford articulates it well when he says that this form of interpretation "is the diametrical opposite of liberal Protestantism" and that "narratives are assumed to be his-torically factual . . . and there is a presumption that all texts agree and adhere."[74] The use of Scripture by prosperity preachers is often considered to be "seriously distorted, selective, and manipulative,"[75] and "purely subjective and arbitrary."[76] A couple of phrases or words

---

69. For an example of how prosperity preachers use biblical texts and stories to promote health and wealth, see Gifford, *Ghana's New Christianity*, 73-79.

70. Harrison, *Righteous Riches*, 8.

71. Gifford, "Expecting Miracles," 20.

72. Gordon D. Fee, *The Disease of the Health and Wealth Gospels* (Vancou-ver, BC: Regent College Publishing, 2006), 9-10; Harrison, *Righteous Riches*, 87.

73. Hummel, *The Prosperity Gospel*, 7.

74. Gifford, *Ghana's New Christianity*, 79.

75. The Lausanne Theology Working Group is an evangelical group of theologians that are committed to missions. "Lausanne Theology Working Group Statement on the Prosperity Gospel," 101, http://www.lausanne.org.

76. Fee, *The Disease of the Health and Wealth Gospels*, 9.

can frame an entire theological or philosophical argument. Many of the "doctrines are built around texts plucked from obscurity rather than central biblical arguments."[77] The verses chosen are rarely situated within the larger biblical canon for a more holistic biblical hermeneutic. Instead, preachers avoid "hundreds of texts that stand squarely in opposition to their teaching."[78]

For the extremists among prosperity preachers, "whatever you ask in prayer" is taken literally to mean "whatever you ask!" The believer can ask to be a millionaire with cars, money, and divine healing with the expectation that not only will God respond, but God is "obligated" to perform for those believers who have enough faith. The Word of Faith founder Kenneth Hagin is definitive about what God wants and will provide for true believers: "[God] wants [God's] children to eat the best, [God] wants them to wear the best clothing. [God] wants them to drive the best cars, and [God] wants them to have the best of everything."[79] "Above all prosper" is interpreted to mean that congregants have a divine right to achieve not only American prosperity but wealth and affluence, which is why these theologies are often identified as "prosperity" or "health and wealth" gospels.

Positive confession is based on an interpretation of the scripture Mark 11:23-24 KJV:

> Truly I tell you, if anyone says to this mountain, "Go, throw yourself into the sea," and does not doubt in their heart but believes that what they say will happen, it will be done for them. Therefore I tell you whatever things you ask when you pray, believe that you receive them, and you will have them.

---

77. Perriman, *Faith, Health and Prosperity*, 86.

78. Fee, *The Disease of the Health and Wealth Gospels*, 12.

79. Kenneth Hagin, *New Thresholds* (Tulsa: Faith Library, 1980), 54-55. Hagin's statement in the original uses the pronoun "He." For inclusive language purposes, I have inserted "God" in place of the pronoun "He." For New Thought origins, see Simon Coleman, *The Globalisation of Charismatic Christianity: Spreading the Gospel of Prosperity* (Cambridge, UK: Cambridge University Press, 2000), 42-47.

When believers fully understand the power they have from God, then they must *confess the Word* and think the right thoughts.

The positive confession and thinking good thoughts is why these theologies are often linked to New Thought. People such as Phineas Quimby and Essek William Kenyon are mentioned, along with the American positive-thinking movement that began in the nineteenth century.[80] Some writers suggest that Kenneth Hagin actually plagiarized Kenyon's writings.[81] Positive thinking is also attributed to cultural influences from books by American popular writers such as Napoleon Hill's *Think and Grow Rich* in the 1930s and Norman Vincent Peale's *The Power of Positive Thinking* written in 1952.[82]

Two realms—one spiritual and one material—are the backdrop for the prosperity worldview. The material realm is ruled by Satan.[83] Positive confession is what gives the confessor legitimate access to the spiritual or divine laws that produce miraculous answers to prayer.[84] For believers, "'the law of faith' in the spiritual realm is like 'the law of gravity' in the physical realm; whenever the law is set in motion it

---

80. Harrison, *Righteous Riches*, 134; Coleman, *The Globalisation of Charismatic Christianity*, 42-45; Hunt, "Dramatising 'Health and Wealth Gospel,'" 74; Perriman, *The Disease of the Health and Wealth Gospels*, 69; and Bowler, *Blessed*, 13-20.

81. Many scholars show that Hagin plagiarized much of his teachings from the works of Essek William Kenyon. For details on Kenneth Hagin and Kenyon, see D. R. McConnell, *A Different Gospel*, rev. ed. (Peabody, MA: Hendrickson Publishers, 1995), 3-14; Walton, *Watch This!*, 97; Paul Gifford, *Christianity and Politics in Doe's Liberia*, Cambridge Studies in Ideology and Religion (New York: Cambridge University Press, 1993), 146, 148; and Hummel, *The Prosperity Gospel*, 10-16.

82. Marla Frederick, *Between Sundays: Black Women and Everyday Struggles of Faith* (Berkeley: University of California Press, 2003), 146-47.

83. Hummel, *The Prosperity Gospel*, 10; R. Jackson, "Prosperity Theology and the Faith Movement," *Themelios* 15 (October 1989): 20.

84. Harrison, *Righteous Riches*, 10; Brouwer, Gifford, and Rose, *Exporting the American Gospel*, 193; Mitchem, *Name It and Claim It?*, 69; Perriman, *Faith, Health and Prosperity*, 33; and Tamelyn Tucker-Worgs, *The Black Megachurch: Theology, Gender, and the Politics of Public Engagement* (Waco, TX: Baylor University Press, 2011), 91.

[supposedly] works."[85] The extreme preachers often blame those who are in pain or without resources as not having enough faith.[86]

Seed-faith giving and *tithing* are the religious practices that are the most challenging aspect of these theologies and the worldview, mainly because of the way that believers are taught to use these practices in order to access and obtain wealth. This particular teaching is why many prosperity preachers are seen as charlatans. Moreover, it is during the offering of a worship service or the financial appeal of a broadcast that prosperity preachers can be quite manipulative and exploitive.

For the majority of Protestants and African American Christians, tithing as a ritual is not unusual or rare. Many Christians see God as the giver of all gifts. As an act of worship, giving a tithe (10 percent) of one's income to a church or ministry is returning a portion back to God to help do God's work on earth. This is based on an interpretation of the following Old Testament text: "Will anyone rob God?" (Malachi 3:8-10). Not giving tithes to a local church is sometimes considered as robbing God.[87] However, in Word of Faith and the majority of these related theologies, tithing is taken to a completely different level.[88] Tithing is considered as the minimum spiritual commitment for the believer if he or she expects to have access to God's blessings.[89] If believers do not tithe, then they cannot expect God to honor God's end of the bargain.

The idea of seed-giving, also called "seed faith," was made famous by Oral Roberts.[90] Christians are encouraged to plant spiritual seeds that function very much like natural seeds in that they produce a har-

---

85. Hummel, *The Prosperity Gospel*, 12.

86. Perriman, *Faith, Health and Prosperity*, 42.

87. For an excellent discussion on tithing in African American churches, see Frederick, "Financial Priorities," in *Between Sundays*, 166-85.

88. Mitchem, *Name It and Claim It?*, 80.

89. Bowler, *Blessed*, 128.

90. Brouwer, Gifford, and Rose, *Exploring the American Gospel*, 25. Paul Gifford also attributes the fundraising and seed-giving concept to A. A. Allen. See Gifford, *Ghana's New Christianity*, 62n27. Also see Oral Roberts, *Miracle of Seed Faith* (Tulsa, OK: Oral Roberts Evangelistic Association, 1970).

vest from God. Roberts emphasized that seed-faith giving was very different from what most Christians had been taught about tithing:

> In tithing you give one tenth AFTER you have made the income. In seed-giving . . . you give BEFORE the expected return. . . . Jesus wants to show you how your SEED-GIVING [all caps in original] makes possible two very necessary things: (1) that there may be "meat in [God's] house," . . . and (2) that [God] can take what you give and multiply back that there may be "meat in your house," or enough for your personal needs today.[91]

Seed-faith giving is not only supposed to bless the church but the giver as well. The ritual is presented to congregants as an opportunity to consummate a special contract with God that guarantees reciprocity from God for financial wealth and success. "Prosperity preachers claim that by making a contribution to a church or ministry, Christians are planting a seed to which God will respond with a supernatural harvest of financial blessings."[92] It is not rare for a television preacher to predict that the harvest will be a one hundred fold increase on the believer's initial investment.[93] In other words, as one prosperity preacher expresses, "You give $1 for the gospel's sake and $100 belongs to you. You give $10 and you receive $1000. Give $1000 and receive $100,000."[94]

Many of the financial exchanges are framed in an evangelistic appeal in the form of a request for an offering, ministry partnership, or a financial gift. Additionally, most of the consumer products exchanged in these churches are rarely directly sold just as products. Steve Bruce explains:

> The pitch is not a straightforward commercial transaction. The theme is always one of an exchange of *gifts*. God has

---

91. Roberts, *Miracle of Seed Faith,* 27-29.
92. Lee, *T.D. Jakes: America's Preacher,* 111.
93. Brouwer, Gifford, and Rose, *Exporting the Gospel,* 197-98.
94. Gloria Copeland, *God's Will Is Prosperity* (Fort Worth, TX: Kenneth Copeland Ministries, 1978), 48.

given us the *gift* of salvation. We should *give* God our *gifts*. As we cannot *give* them directly to God, we should *give* [emphasis mine] them to the televangelist [or preacher]. When items are offered, they are always worth considerably less than the asked-for donation, gift, or "love offering."[95]

More importantly, because Jesus gave sacrificially, faithful believers should not only give but they should give their very best. The best gifts are those that reach the level of sacrifice and are above and beyond what is reasonably expected.

Because of its success in fundraising, seed-faith giving has flourished and evolved into more creative forms.[96] A good example of a seed-faith appeal is Juanita Bynum at the 1998 WTAL Conference. Bynum declared to conference participants, "The Lord just told me that every woman in this building is supposed to give a $98 seed offering! . . . God told me that there are twenty people in here that are to give $1000 offerings."[97] Cindy Trimm, one of the preachers that I witnessed at the 2009 WTAL Conference, went as far as telling congregants that she has a spiritual money tree growing in her backyard. She stated, "You can't see it because it is spiritual, only I can see it. Plant seeds, you get a tree! Whenever I need money, I don't pray for it—I create it! Seed! Seed! Seed! Get the revelation of the seed."[98] She also told congregants that she plants her seeds in $1,000 increments. The larger dollar amount of her seeds was used as evidence to show that she had advanced to a higher level of spirituality in her giving. These kinds of requests and testimonies are not unusual for many prosperity preachers. Another example of how seed-faith giving has evolved is that during the worship service congregants no longer wait until the offering to give their money. They are encouraged to walk

---

95. Steve Bruce, *Pray TV: Televangelism in America* (New York: Routledge, 1990), 145.

96. Bowler, *Blessed*, 128.

97. Frederick, *Between Sundays*, 163.

98. Cindy Trim, CD of 2009 Woman Thou Art Loosed Conference (Dallas, TX: T.D. Jakes Ministries, 2009).

in the middle of the sermon and throw money on the altar or pulpit.[99] In some churches, they not only place money on the altar, but their gifts include "jewelry, car titles, and other valuables."[100]

Prosperity preachers make quite a few appeals, and congregants are often encouraged to give money before they have actually earned it. As a result, Harrison asserts that believers can find themselves "in a very precarious position, threatening their ability to actually realize the promise of financial abundance."[101] Whether the actual finances manifest or not, many of the practitioners see themselves as having improved their life choices. As a result, they are rarely critical of the theology, nor of the prosperity rituals and practices. Seed-faith giving along with the religious practices of proof-texting and positive confession are prominent in theologies of prosperity, and are in many ways the litmus test for identifying a prosperity preacher and church.

A New Definition for Prosperity Preachers and Prosperity Theology

Bishop Jakes and other prosperity preachers tap into a very familiar refrain of American history and culture because these are popular folk theologies. The current definitions are inconsistent. The definition usually depends on how the scholar defines "culture," "religion," and "theology," as well as where that scholar places the border or division between the secular and the sacred. At other times, these definitions are described as a form of civil religion.[102] America's socio-religious beginnings in Puritanism and Calvinism complicate the definitions and often conflate or confuse prosperity theology

---

99. Lawrence Mamiya, *River of Struggle, River of Freedom: Trends among Black Churches and Black Pastoral Leadership: Pulpit and Pew Research on Pastoral Leadership Reports* (Durham, NC: Duke Divinity School, 2006), 11.

100. Tim Grant, "Collections Take New Form after Plates Are Passed." *St. Petersburg Times,* February 13, 2000, late Tampa edition.

101. Harrison, *Righteous Riches,* 71.

102. Simon Coleman, "America Loves Sweden: Prosperity Theology and the Cultures of Capitalism," in *Religion and the Transformations of Capitalism: Comparative Approaches,* ed. Richard H. Roberts (New York: Routledge, 1995), 171.

with the gospel of wealth. The American secular ideology is often referred to as "the gospel of wealth," "the gospel of success," and "the gospel of prosperity." David Bromley and Ansom Shupe expound on the definition. The gospel of prosperity

> is based on the belief that Americans have a special covenant with God—that in return for obeying [God's] mandates and creating a Christian nation that will eventually carry [God's] message and the American Way of Life to the entire world, God will raise up Americans, individually and collectively, as [God's] most favored people.[103]

Their definition encompasses religio-economic corporations like Amway and Mary Kay because these organizations incorporate themes like transcendent purpose, service, and achievement, and culturally integrate work, family, and religion.[104] Another definition includes religio-economic corporations, and "think-tanks affiliated with the new Religious Right, and a growing abundance of self-help guides in print, video, and television media" as examples of "prosperity theology."[105] These writers demonstrate the difficulty of presenting an adequate definition that is not only consistent, but can also be applied across the disciplines. For discourse purposes and with the hope of having scholars from a variety of fields participate, I propose a better definition for prosperity preachers and their contextual theologies. This definition is especially useful for black churches.

Prosperity preachers are pastors who use *Scripture and rituals such as seed-faith giving and positive confession to justify their personal economic empires. They affirm that it is God's will and a believer's right to*

---

103. David G. Bromley and Anson Shupe, "Rebottling the Elixir: The Gospel of Prosperity in America's Religioeconomic Corporations," in *In Gods We Trust: New Patterns of Religious Pluralism in America*, ed. Thomas Robbins and Dick Anthony, 2nd ed. rev. (New Brunswick, NJ: Transaction Publishers, 1996), 233.

104. Ibid., 234.

105. David W. Machacek, "Prosperity Theology," *Contemporary American Religion*, vol. 2, ed. Wade Clarke Roof (New York: Macmillan Reference USA, 1999), 561.

obtain prosperity or health and wealth. The simple definition is useful to classify the hundreds of prosperity preachers around the world. A clear definition is required for black churches, because black preachers are overwhelmingly represented as prosperity preachers with large black congregations.[106] Most of the successful prosperity preachers live in the United States and in Nigeria.[107] Bishop Jakes makes the list of richest preachers with a personal income of 18 million dollars.

The United States is the birthplace of the prosperity gospel, and other very American philosophies and mythologies contribute to the prosperity worldview. New Black Church theologies resonate with an American ideology that undergirds the economic empires of the preachers. They may claim to be prophetic and countercultural to secular interests, since the secular realm is often considered to be demonic or under the control of Satan. However, upon closer investigation, these pastors promote and represent a secular ideology—the gospel of wealth—that throughout American history continues to reemerge, especially in popular culture.

Theologies of Prosperity and the Ideology of the Gospel of Wealth

The gospel of wealth as an ideology is usually defined as secular, because its most prominent advocate was Andrew Carnegie, a professed atheist.[108] Carnegie was a millionaire industrialist who wrote a famous essay, entitled "The Gospel of Wealth," [109] that equated the accumulation of personal wealth with virtue, and the absence of wealth with sin.[110] Some scholars consider theologies of prosperity to simply be an improvement on the American gospel of wealth.[111]

According to church historian Vinson Synan, "After the Civil

---

106. Bowler, *Blessed*, 239.

107. Nkern Ikeke, "Ten Riches Pastors in the World," https://www.naij. com.

108. Brouwer, Gifford, Rose, *Exporting the American Gospel*, 22.

109. Andrew Carnegie, "The Gospel of Wealth," *The North American Review* 183, no. 599 (September 21, 1903): 526.

110. Bowler, *Blessed*, 30.

111. Brouwer, Gifford, and Rose, *Exporting the American Gospel*, 20.

War, a time of great prosperity blossomed in the Northern states because of the rising age of big industry, big railroads and big banks. Historians call this period from the Civil War to 1900 the 'Gilded Age' of rich 'robber barons' such as Cornelius Vanderbilt (railroads), John D. Rockefeller (oil), Andrew Carnegie (steel), James Duke (tobacco) and J. P. Morgan (banking)." This earlier generation of "enormously rich Protestant capitalists built monumental churches and hired preachers who would give a biblical rationale for their gigantic wealth." In popular culture at the same time, "a new genre of get-rich books became wildly popular, such as the books of Horatio Alger telling stories of poor, young people who became rich through hard work and smart business deals."[112]

The contemporary form of the gospel of wealth, according to Norton Garfinkle, is based on "laissez-faire economic philosophy," and "a celebration of the successful entrepreneur and investor as the source of prosperity and wealth."[113] This is what we see in T.D. Jakes, with his constant emphasis on his entrepreneurial pursuits. The gospel of wealth promotes the idea "that people get what they deserve out of the economy and that government has no business stepping in to even the odds."[114] No matter which era of history, Americans have negotiated, as well as justified, the vast economic inequalities between the rich and the poor—not only locally, but globally. In the words of Andrew Carnegie at the turn of the nineteenth century, "The problem of our age is the proper administration of wealth, so that the ties of brotherhood may still bind together the rich and the poor in harmonious relationship."[115] Americans need to "believe that America operates on the principle of fairness . . . [for] all citizens, and [is] not hopelessly skewed to those who, by dint of their wealth, can command greatest

---

112. Vinson Synan, "Word of Faith Movement Has Deep Roots in American History," http://www.believersstandunited.com.

113. Norton Garfinkle, *The American Dream vs. the Gospel of Wealth: The Fight for a Productive Middle Class Economy* (New Haven, CT: Yale University Press, 2006), 17.

114. Ibid.

115. Carnegie, "The Gospel of Wealth," 526.

control."[116] This is what Americans want to believe when they buy products from Wal-Mart or when they purchase the branded spiritual products from a WTAL Conference or a New Black Church ministry.

American history boasts of many public figures and clerics who have promoted the gospel of wealth in order to promote the illusion of American capitalist fairness. One of the most famous of these clerics was Russell H. Conwell from the First Gilded Age.[117] He was a Baptist preacher in Philadelphia who built the largest church in the United States. He traveled the country preaching his famous "Acres of Diamonds" sermon over six thousand times.[118] "Conwell's gospel of wealth focused on the Christian's duty to become rich."[119] Just like the clerics from earlier generations of the First Gilded Age, the prosperity New Black Church preachers of the Second Gilded Age emerged during 1980s and 1990s—a period of similar dramatic cultural change.

Black preachers in the New Black Church responded to this change by transforming deeply rooted symbols from both American secular culture and African American religious culture. As a secular ideology, the gospel of wealth promotes "the worship of the exceptional individual, the millionaire, the industrial magnate as prosperity's engine."[120] These exceptional individuals are supposed to be philanthropic. If they are, then their wealth is sanctioned or sacralized. Historically, this has meant that even "robber barons" such as Carnegie and John D. Rockefeller can be celebrated. Similar to their gospel of wealth counterparts, theologies of prosperity encourage giving as a sign of God's favor. Prosperity preachers instead are supposed to give tithes and offerings for the purpose of Christian evangelism. Just as Conwell was famous in the First Gilded Age, Bishop Jakes is a prominent example of the Second Gilded Age, with a large church and millions of books sold.

---

116. Garfinkle, *The American Dream*, 193-94.

117. Bowler, *Blessed,* 31-34.

118. Brouwer, Gifford, and Rose, *Exporting the American Gospel*, 22.

119. Sean McCloud, *Divine Hierarchies: Class in American Religion and Religious Studies* (Chapel Hill, NC: University of North Carolina Press, 2007), 114.

120. Garfinkle, *The American Dream*, 15.

The Gospel of Wealth of the Second Gilded Age
(1980s–1990s)

The majority of black prosperity theologians and their super-mega-churches were founded in the 1980s and 1990s and echo the cultural changes of the period. This is a very unique historical period for African Americans. The 1980s, in particular, represented "the triumph of upper America, an ostentatious celebration of wealth, the political ascendancy of the richest third of the population and the glorification of capitalism, free markets and finance,"[121] writes Kevin Phillips. It was also the beginning of unprecedented black middle-class ascendancy. The black middle class was no longer DuBois's "talented tenth." Instead, they became the "talented third."[122] Additionally, in the 1980s and 1990s the media helped to create the changes in the cultural landscape of African Americans by presenting a variety of appropriations of blackness and black affluence.

For example, one of the most popular television shows at the time was *The Cosby Show*. The successful show "presented a picture of a middle-class lifestyle and made it appear attainable to all, even African Americans."[123] As the post–civil rights era offered increasing access to financial and political resources, many African Americans began no longer to see themselves as occupying the margins of American society. One example is theologian Archie Smith's lament in 1982: "Some middle class blacks may no longer see themselves as members of an oppressed group and accept uncritically an exploitative, profit-centered economic and political system which, nevertheless, continues to deny them full humanity."[124] During this period, prominent African American religious figures such as T.D. Jakes, Creflo Dollar, and Fred Price became key spokespersons.

---

121. Kevin Phillips, *The Politics of Rich and Poor: Wealth and the American Electorate in the Reagan Aftermath* (New York: Harper Perennial, 1990), xvii.

122. Mamiya, *River of Struggle*, 10.

123. Harrison, *Righteous Riches*, 151. For an exhaustive treatment of blackness on television, see Herman Gray, *Watching Race: Television and the Struggle for Blackness* (Minneapolis: University of Minnesota Press, 1995).

124. Archie Smith, Jr., *The Relational Self: Ethics & Therapy from a Black Church Perspective* (Nashville, TN: Abingdon Press, 1982).

These African American men rose to fame during a time of great economic and cultural change and unrest. Both the First and the Second Gilded Age represent a time in history when economic disparity is tangibly visible. In sum, the periods are emblematic of a time when "the rich got richer and the poor got poorer."[125]

Far removed from the traditional stories of suffering and the U.S.'s segregated past, many African Americans in the Second Gilded Age became very comfortable in their middle-class American identity. In generations prior to this period, theologies of prosperity would have been considered on the fringe, illogical, and unorthodox.[126] However, post-1980, black congregants could confidently consider these theologies as not only credible but as a more rational faith alternative to the faith practiced in traditional churches. Prosperity preachers are able to capture the attention of many African Americans with worship services that resemble the worship and cultural traditions of the Black Church.[127] Yet, according to Lee, the preachers cleverly position themselves as "outsiders to the religious establishment, as enemies of religion and tradition, and as iconoclasts offering a new and vibrant religious experience"[128] They convince their congregants that their theologies are not only new, but different and better.[129]

These theologies provide existential explanations of economic conditions for both the rich and the poor, which is one reason why they continue to be successful and expand. Prosperity theologies provide the ideological backdrop to justify economic inequalities and are malleable and adaptable to new social and political contexts. Traditional and academic theologies are at a great disadvantage when compared to theologies of prosperity. The constant marketing and branding allow prosperity theologians to change their positions very quickly and immediately present them to parishioners and consumers. The brands are often renewed and repackaged like

---

125. Harrison, *Righteous Riches*, 150.

126. Brouwer, Gifford, and Rose, *Exporting the American Gospel*, 27. Lee, *T.D. Jakes*, 110. Frederick, *Between Sundays*, 145-46.

127. Lee and Sinitiere, *Holy Mavericks*, 75.

128. Lee, *T.D. Jakes*, 163.

129. Harrison, *Righteous Riches*, 83-84.

secular products and consumer firms. Because they provide existential explanations for suffering and economic hardship, prosperity preachers and their contextual theologies, as I have argued, should also be considered under the category of "theodicy."

Theologies of Prosperity as Theodicy

Theodicy, in theological and philosophical circles, is often defined as a concern for "the problem of evil." The problem of evil is shaped by theological propositions or questions: "If God is omnipotent, omniscient, and omnipresent, then God would prevent evil if God wanted to. And if God is a perfectly good God, then of course God would want to prevent evil if God could."[130] Several African American scholars have addressed the question of theodicy and its intimate relationship to black religion. Cornel West has argued that "Christianity is first and foremost a *theodicy*, a triumphant account of good over evil." He believes that Christianity is a religion particularly "fitted to the oppressed," and that the intellectual lives of oppressed peoples consist "primarily of reckoning with the dominant form of evil in their lives."[131]

In her sociological study of black churches after the civil rights era, Cheryl Townsend Gilkes mentions theodicy. She suggests that African Americans have "traditionally felt a deep anxiety over social class divisions," which is one of the "negative interpersonal consequences of social mobility." Because of the quick ascendancy of many African Americans to the middle class "a culturally relevant religious explanation of one's good fortune in the face of so many who had been left behind became necessary." Her conclusion is that "the nature of black social mobility is so precarious ('one paycheck away from poverty') that prosperity is both a blessing and a problem and *theodicy*."[132] Prosperity preaching "was a departure from

---

130. Katie Geneva Cannon, "'The Wound of Jesus': Justification of Goodness in the Face of Manifest Evil,'" in *Troubling in My Soul: Womanist Perspectives on Evil and Suffering*, ed. Emilie M. Townes (Maryknoll, NY: Orbis Books, 1993), 220.

131. Cornel West, *Prophecy Deliverance! An Afro-American Revolutionary Christianity* (Philadelphia: Westminster Press, 1982), 35 [emphasis mine].

132. Cheryl Townsend Gilkes, "Plenty Good Room: Adaptation in a

more traditional liberationist and perseverance themes." However, it had a purpose for the new black middle class in that the preaching "facilitated psychological relocation and integration in the world of affluence."[133] Providing individuals with remedies to oppression and suffering from both physical and financial suffering is very powerful, especially to those who have been disenfranchised.[134] Harrison concludes that prosperity theologies appeal "to those who have been left out of the mainstream of economic and social life, thus making it attractive to the poor who don't want to stay poor in America and elsewhere."[135]

Sociologist Peter Berger in *The Sacred Canopy* writes, "If a theodicy answers, in whatever manner, this question of meaning, it serves an important purpose."[136] He also says that "one of the very important social functions of theodicies is, indeed, their explanation of the socially prevailing inequalities of power and privilege."[137] Theologies of prosperity are attractive to both the rich and the poor. "Put simply, theodicies provide the poor with a meaning for their poverty, but may also provide the rich with a meaning for their wealth."[138]

The contextual theologies represented in the brands of T.D. Jakes and the New Black Church fit the religious definitions of theodicy. With their thousands of sermons and products, T.D. Jakes and other prosperity preachers are able to provide concrete explanations to congregants for economic and physical suffering. Moreover, the theodical question might be framed as, "How can a just God, who is all-powerful and all-seeing, allow some to be wealthy and healthy, while others (especially righteous, Bible-believing, church-going, tithing Christians) are not?"

Changing Black Church," *Annals of the American Academy of Political and Social Sciences* 558 (July 1998): 108 [emphasis mine].

133. Ibid.

134. Harrison, *Righteous Riches*, 152.

135. Ibid., 159.

136. Peter Berger, *The Sacred Canopy: Elements of a Sociological Theory of Religion* (New York: Anchor Books, 1967), 58.

137. Ibid.

138. Ibid.

The religiosity and ritual practices (tithing, seed-faith giving, prayer, and thinking positive thoughts) become a simplistic remedy and the answer to the complex theodical questions of why congregants are experiencing economic and physical suffering. Prosperity preachers are able to explain "why so many faithful Christians who tithe, give offerings, and financially support ministries in other forms do not prosper financially."[139] The answer given is that "they [congregants] just have to be taught *what the Bible really says* about wealth and who should possess it."[140] The blame oftentimes is placed on the believer and his or her lack of faith, as well as on the teachings of traditional churches. Word churches, especially, often admonish that too many "Christians have been taught in traditional denominational churches that Jesus was poor and that they should also be poor in order to identify with him. These people will never be able to receive prosperity from God until their subconscious minds have been relieved of their misconceptions about who Jesus was financially."[141]

Theologies of prosperity fulfill a need for certainty in response to the anxiety and fear that advanced capitalism generates for marginalized communities around the globe. Equally important, these churches and pastors offer what Cornel West suggests is lacking in the black liberation theology project—"a sketch of what liberation would actually mean in the everyday lives of Black people, what power they would possess, and what resources they would have access to."[142] Theologies of prosperity offer a picture of liberation that is not other worldly but rather is a liberation that resonates with the economic realities of African Americans who are comfortable with seeking what they consider to be their rightful place within the American dream.

The New Black Church's vision of liberation looks and feels attainable. It is reinforced in each broadcast and worship service.

---

139. Harrison, *Righteous Riches*, 11.

140. Ibid. [emphasis mine].

141. Ibid., 12.

142. Cornel West, "Black Theology and Marxist Thought," in *African American Religious Thought: An Anthology*, ed. Cornel West and Eddie S. Glaude, Jr. (Louisville, KY: Westminster John Knox, 2003), 878.

State of the art facilities, thousands of congregants in seats, expensive cars, tailored suits worn by preachers, and mansions become the tangible and visible examples of American success. Moreover, it communicates to African American congregants that success and liberation are available and attainable for people who look just like them. Prosperity preachers know the value in letting people know that they, too, used to be poor. This may serve their purposes of fundraising, but it also reinforces for congregants that success and liberation is possible for people just like them. Needless to say, the liberation that these theologies offer differs greatly from the liberation theology promoted in the academy.

Theologies of Prosperity as Pseudo Theologies of Liberation

The theologies of people of color and women defined as liberation theologies remain in the margins of the academy. Miguel A. De La Torre explains that "Eurocentric theologies have historically positioned themselves as the 'center' of worldwide theological thought, as though they were somehow more objective and thus more legitimate."[143] Understandably, academic liberation theologians have fought very hard to carve out a place for their discourses.

Latin American theologian Gustavo Gutiérrez coined the term "liberation theology." He describes it "as theological reflection based on the gospel and the experiences of men and women committed to the process of liberation."[144] Liberation theology is basically an "application to any group which might consider itself to be socially, economically, or politically oppressed or exploited or otherwise disadvantaged."[145] You cannot fully appreciate any liberation theology without understanding its specific historical, geographical, and religious context.

---

143. Miguel A. De La Torre, ed., *Handbook of U.S. Liberation Theologies* (St. Louis: Chalice, 2004), 2.

144. Gustavo Gutiérrez, *A Theology of Liberation* (Maryknoll, NY: Orbis Books, 1973), 209, quoted in Geoffrey Grogan, "Liberation and Prosperity Theologies," *Scottish Bulletin of Evangelical Theology* 9 (September 1991): 119.

145. Grogan, "Liberation and Prosperity Theologies," 118.

The Brazilian theologians Leonardo and Clodovis Boff, in *Introducing Liberation Theology*, express a commitment to the "collective" poor. They write:

> Every true theology springs from a spirituality—that is, from a true meeting with God in history. Liberation theology was born when faith confronted the injustice done to the poor. By "poor" we do not really mean the poor individual who knocks on the door asking for alms. We mean a collective poor, the "popular classes," which is a much wider category than the "proletariat" singled out by Karl Marx (it is a mistake to identify the poor of liberation theology with the proletariat, though many critics do): the poor are also the workers exploited by the capitalist system; the underemployed, those pushed aside by the production process—a reserve army always at hand to take the place of the employed; they are the laborers of the countryside, and migrant workers with only seasonal work.
>
> All this mass of the socially and historically oppressed makes up the poor as a social phenomenon.[146]

Liberation theologians provide a critique of capitalist systems and see the *poor* as a collective group fighting for social justice. Gutiérrez and the Boff brothers, as Catholic theologians, wrote in the context of the struggle for liberation in Latin America during the 1970s and 1980s. Their work was rooted in the reflection and praxis of "base communities," where the poor learned to read the Bible in light of their concrete circumstances. For each of these scholar-activists it was clear that liberation theology was never intended to be solely an academic discipline.[147]

Theologians of prosperity in the 1980s and 1990s do not provide a critique of capitalism. Preachers like Jakes are not interested in undertaking the momentous uphill struggle to dismantle and restructure capitalism. Instead, they offer the poor an economic

---

146. Clodovis and Leonardo Boff, *Introducing Liberation Theology*, 3.
147. Ibid., 18.

"liberation" *within* the existing system. For academic black liberation theologians the challenge is to evaluate whether the liberation
that these preachers present in their many brands is indeed liberating for black churches and black people.

Each liberation theologian, whether black, womanist, feminist,
or queer is privileged to speak *for* and *on the behalf of* a particular
ethnic or cultural community. These theologies, like most liberation
theologies, are usually based on oppositions. "Difference and conflict . . . are unavoidable and central to the theological enterprise,"[148]
writes Wesley Kort. All theological discourses, including those tied
to institutions such as black churches, are "oppositionally related to
one another but also . . . their meaning and power are generated by
such oppositions."[149] Kort explains:

> Discursive situations, including those that are recogniz-
> ably theological, include force as well as significance, and
> power reproduces and legitimates inequalities, repressions,
> and exclusions. Any theological situation, therefore, favors
> some participants over others; discourse is always going on
> in some way already, and some discourses are likely to be
> dominating the field at the expense of others.[150]

North American liberation theologians, like theologians of prosperity, speak on behalf of a particular community and are usually in
opposition or conflict with a group that they identify as dominant
or oppressive.

For instance, James Cone challenged classical theologians to see
the ontological blackness of God. He argued that God was on the side
of the oppressed. Most important is that black theology also presented
a new methodology that "gave preference to the lived experience of
African Americans instead of the experiences of whites. In other
words, it did not allow white Americans to view their experiences as

---

148. Wesley A. Kort, *Bound to Differ: The Dynamics of Theological Discourses* (University Park, PA: Pennsylvania State University Press, 1992), 2.
149. Ibid, 23.
150. Kort, *Bound to Differ*, 4.

the measuring stick for all people."[151] Rosemary Ruether with her feminist liberation theology critiqued the sexism of classical theology, and Jaqueline Grant has framed womanist theology in conversation with black and feminist theology. Speaking for black women, her theological discourse critiques racism, sexism, and classism.[152]

No matter how revelatory or liberating, all theologies are ideological constructions of the theologian. Many African Americans are supporting the prosperity hermeneutics of these preachers. Like academic black liberation theologians, Jakes and other preachers in the New Black Church interpret the most significant rites, symbols, and myths of black Christianity: God, Jesus, Exodus, and the Promised Land. [153] The theology of T.D. Jakes and other popular preachers is just one more location where the ultimate concern of black religion presents itself. Moreover, the liberation promoted in these brands represents a definitive cultural shift in the lives of African Americans and other marginalized communities.

The acceptance of these popular theologies speaks to the fact that more and more black Christians are concerned with "a new kind of liberationist agenda that can address the challenges people face in the twenty-first century."[154] This agenda differs from the expectations of those who participated in the social-justice movements of the past, and who clearly understood the need for a communal response. This new agenda focuses on the financial freedom of the individual as the path to liberation. As a result, theologies of prosperity differ greatly from the core ethic of liberation theologies—in particular, what is called "a preferential option for the poor."

---

151. Anthony B. Pinn, "Jesus and Justice: An Outline of Liberation Theology within Black Churches," *CrossCurrents* 47, no. 2 (Summer 2007): 224.

152. Rosemary Ruether, *Sexism and God-Talk: Toward a Feminist Theology,* 2nd ed. (Boston: Beacon Press, 1993); Jacqueline Grant, *White Women's Christ and Black Women's Jesus: Feminist Christology and Womanist Response* (Atlanta, GA: Scholars Press, 1989).

153. To say "rationally" also implies a certain epistemological and ideological worldview. Jakes's *rational* interpretations for academic theologians are not coherent. An academic might see his theology as irrational. However, this is not the case for the majority of his followers.

154. Lee, *T.D. Jakes*, 118.

Peter Berger, in an article in the *Wall Street Journal,* makes an important observation about theologies of prosperity: "There is no sentimentality about poverty in the prosperity gospel. There is an appeal to people not as victims but as responsible actors. There is also the confidence that generally people know what is best for themselves, better than any well-meaning outsiders."[155] Berger points out the syntax, that "the option is *for* the poor. That is, it is an option to be taken by those who are *not* poor." The preferential option for the poor is well intentioned by liberation theologians. However, Berger states that he understands why the poor, and I would include the congregants of the New Black Church, "are opting for a less patronizing message."[156] Many poor people are drawn to the messages of prosperity preachers and not to the messages and discourses of liberal or progressive Christians and academic theologians.

Popular theologies are more accessible to the average Christian. Moreover, if nothing else, theologies of prosperity offer *hope.* Philosopher and public theologian Cornel West argues that "the major enemy of black survival in America has been and is neither oppression nor exploitation but rather the nihilistic threat—that is, loss of hope and absence of meaning. For as long as hope remains and meaning is preserved, the possibility of overcoming oppression stays alive."[157] Jakes and other theologians of prosperity offer hope and what congregants consider to be rational prescriptions for economic liberation. As Jonathan Walton contends, prosperity preachers and "televangelists are ingeniously able to create a liminal space where the unjust realities of race, class, and gender are suspended long enough for viewers to imagine themselves living and thriving in such a world."[158]

Theology is always defined by the community. From the perspective of the congregants and the people participating in brands like WTAL, these theologies *are* theologies of liberation. To identify

---

155. Peter Berger, "Pennies from Heaven," *Wall Street Journal,* October 28, 2008, http://online.wsj.com.

156. Ibid.

157. Cornel West, *Race Matters* (New York: Vantage Books, 1994), 23.

158. Walton, *Watch This!,* 198.

them as such does not require any degree of acceptance or commitment on the part of academic theologians. As liberationists, we are called to challenge the interpretations and practices of any theologian (folk, lay, or otherwise) that speaks on behalf of black people.[159] The professional theologian, however, offers a scholarly critique—not just a rhetorical or popular response. This is what separates the academic theologian from the folk or popular theologian.

In the prosperity worldview, God is now miraculously working on behalf of congregants. The miraculous power of the faith message "can be utilized for any positive purpose whatsoever, so that it might overcome any and all material obstacles that the Christian encounters." There is nothing wrong with the poor "calling upon God's power through prayer in order to meet material needs."[160] Harrison shows that many of the congregants actually consider these theologies to be a kind of "poor people's movement."[161] The faith message in its own way calls for a redistribution of wealth when congregants quote the passages in Deuteronomy about the wealth of the wicked that is laid up for the righteous. Wealth is being transferred "out of the hands of 'sinners' into the hands of born-again *Christians*."[162] When congregants identify themselves as "chosen," "anointed," and when they are taking authority over Satan and their circumstances, they are essentially no longer being treated as hopeless victims. Instead, they are the protagonists in their own spiritual narratives. The faith brands of Bishop Jakes and others provide a way for those who have been marginalized and neglected in larger discourses to tell their story.[163] No different from secular brands, the faith brands tell others—including the dominant culture—who the consumers are, thereby establishing a religious and spiritual identity.

Prosperity preachers are extremely effective in presenting their congregants with a voice in the choices that they make in their own

---

159. Paul Tillich, *Systematic Theology*, vol. 1 (Chicago: University of Chicago Press, 1971), 4.

160. Brouwer, Gifford, and Rose, *Exporting the American Gospel*, 197.

161. Harrison, *Righteous Riches,* 148.

162. Ibid., 150.

163. Lee and Sinitiere, *Holy Mavericks*, 73.

lives. Theologies of prosperity offer a greater sense of personal agency along with "bottom-up" solutions for the poor.[164] T.D. Jakes, more than anyone, appears to give voice to the sufferings and concerns of African American women. He may not necessarily be empowering women in a mode that most feminists and womanists would identify as liberating. Many women, however, feel empowered and at times liberated when they assemble together at a WTAL Conference. *Feeling empowered,* however, is not the same as *being empowered.*

The hope that Bishop Jakes and other prosperity preachers offer is only for change in the individual, and is not for systemic or communal change. There is no critique of the overall oppressive system. Theologies of prosperity "dissuade congregants from evaluating the present economic order, merely persuading them to try to be amongst those who benefit from it."[165] When prosperity preachers convince congregants that financial wealth is not only attainable but a right, they essentially are removing any possibility that congregants will ever critique advanced capitalism and its many levels of exploitation.[166]

What is important for both academic and folk theologians to acknowledge is that Bishop T.D. Jakes and other pastors in the New Black Church do offer their followers a contemporary form of liberation. Unfortunately, the liberation that they offer is—at its best—only a pseudo liberation. The stories in the brands are uplifting and entertaining, but until individuals are inspired to change the broader system, the liberation of preachers like Bishop Jakes will never actually change the real lives and oppressive conditions of *all* God's people. The reality, for most people that buy the branded products, is that they will never have access to or be able to really enjoy the lifestyles of these preachers. Liberation has to reach in a systemic way all people—and not just those very few people who profit from the economic system.

---

164. Bradley A. Koch, "The Prosperity Gospel and Economic Prosperity: Race, Giving, and Voting" (Ph.D. diss., Indiana University, 2009), 4.

165. Paul Gifford, *The New Crusaders: Christianity and the New Right in Southern Africa* (London: Pluto Press, 1991), 65-66.

166. Frederick, *Between Sundays*, 152.

3

T.D. Jakes as Pastor/CEO and Theologian

There are always two people competing in my head: Bill Gates and Mother Teresa.   —T.D. Jakes

I was entrepreneurial before I was ministerial. It has always been a part of my destiny.   T.D. Jakes

In the biographies of T.D. Jakes and the majority of theologians of prosperity,[1] *pastor* and *entrepreneur* are the dominant images or

---

1. The theological method that I utilize in this chapter to study Jakes is based on James McClendon's book *Biography as Theology*. For the details of how I apply his method to study prosperity preachers, please refer to the original dissertation (Paula L. McGee, "The Wal-Martization of African American Religion: T.D. Jakes and Woman Thou Art Loosed" [Ph.D. diss., Claremont Graduate University, 2012], 147-49). McClendon's method calls for the professional theologian to seek out the central image, or a cluster of images, that is representative of how the person studied understands him or herself. The professional theologian observes how the chosen biographical subject has applied these images to their life. For McClendon, the application of these images answers "a (preliminary) theological question, *What is religion?*" (96). He defines religion as a "life lived out under the governance of a central vision" (152). For that reason, my application of his method is for the professional theologian to determine the images that best represent the central vision of the preacher he or she is studying. The images chosen should be those that characterize the preacher's theological contribution to the faith community.

metaphors.[2] Additionally, both images are critical to understanding the Wal-Martization of African American religion. Both pastor and entrepreneur (CEO) are cultural signifiers that define both the sacred and secular vocational identities of these preachers. Furthermore, both terms represent leadership roles that help define and justify success in American culture—especially economic success within advanced capitalism. The CEO has become the desired trope of empire—and the trope that has been far from the reach of African Americans.

T.D. Jakes's interpretation of himself as a CEO and how he shares his life story as a businessman and minister are foundational to his worldview and theological system. As Stacy Floyd Thomas chronicles in her research, T.D. Jakes "is keenly aware of his role as a CEO of a *new* type of business—the megachurch, which, he says, it is his job continually to define."[3] As a super-megachurch CEO, the power to define the new role of pastor/CEO is part of the reason that black megachurch pastors have so much epistemic, social, and cultural power. Jakes admits that pastors like him are responsible for "what is the equivalent of a small city."[4] Furthermore, T.D. Jakes, as America's preacher, is the exemplar of our "free enterprise system [that] is driven by acquisition. Consumers must consume, capitalists must accumulate capital, and labor must sell its labor."[5] He embod-

---

McClendon considers these archetypical images to be the very substance of religion. See James William McClendon, Jr., *Biography as Theology: How Life Stories Can Remake Today's Theology* (Nashville, TN: Abingdon, 1974).

2. In this chapter, when I use the term "pastor" as an image, I am including terms like "preacher," "evangelist," "televangelist," and "minister." Commentators and scholars use each of these terms to refer to Jakes's vocational identity as a pastor. The same applies for the image "entrepreneur." Whenever I use "entrepreneur," I am also including terms like "businessman," "CEO," "producer," "writer," and "record label owner"—in other words, any vocational identity that represents Jakes as a business owner or someone who is selling commercialized products.

3. Stacy C. Boyd, *Black Men Worshipping: Intersecting Anxieties of Race, Gender, and Christian Embodiment* (New York: Palgrave Macmillan, 2011), 76.

4. Ibid.

5. Bernard Brandon Scott, *Hollywood Dreams and Biblical Stories* (Minneapolis: Fortress Press, 1994), 143.

ies his celebrity or branded identity in his vocational performances as a pastor and CEO of his super-megachurch and several for-profit companies.

Bishop Jakes is consistently acquiring more companies and producing more products and events for African American church-women and others to buy and consume.[6] He also sells and profits from his access and relationship with parishioners.[7] Shayne Lee summarizes that Jakes "often defends his extraordinary wealth by reminding critics that he is both a businessman and a minister and that God has bountifully blessed both missions, but his followers are often naïve about how the nexus of businessman and minister forms a strategic multimillion-dollar machine."[8]

Jakes's personal life story as a pastor of a New Black Church is a lens into these new branded identities. The details of Jakes's life and his success in ministry illustrate the ideology and process of Wal-Martization and further solidify the ideological critique of the New Black Church. By voluntarily participating in the brand, the congregants and consumers are constructing their own branded spiritual and religious identities. The focus on Jakes does not in any way negate the importance of the women who follow Jakes and the formation of their own religious identity and sense of agency.

Bishop T.D. Jakes as Pastor

Jakes's ministry has both Baptist and Pentecostal roots. The ministry has always had some aspect of healing and addressing the hurts and pains of others. Jakes often points to the painful journey with his father's illness as the reason he has such compassion for others. "As a teenager, he watched his father slowly die of kidney disease. He

---

6. Carolyn M. Brown, "Sowing Seeds of Prosperity," *Black Enterprise* 44, no. 8 (April 2014): 58.

7. Jakes not only sells his own labor, which includes the selling of his image, story, and sermons, but he also sells the labor (writing, music, and preaching) of others.

8. Shayne Lee, *T.D. Jakes: America's New Preacher* (New York: New York University Press, 2005), 182.

had to shave, feed and clean his father every day for six years."[9] Jakes watched his father dwindle "from a tall strapping man of 280 pounds to a shadowy 130."[10] When Jakes's father died in 1972, "Jakes found refuge in the Bible. He carried one to high school and preached to imaginary congregations, so much so that neighbors dubbed him 'Bible Boy.'"[11] The early years of his faith were spent at First Baptist Church of Vandalia, West Virginia. In his late teens he would become the church's music director.[12] However, he would eventually leave the Baptist Church to join a Pentecostal church. Jakes sarcastically says that he was "looking for a deeper, more passionate understanding of God that didn't include discussions about whether the choir should sway during a song or march in before or after the congregation was seated."[13] Lee writes that Jakes liked the "Pentecostal experience where Christians thrive in power and holiness."[14]

The call to ministry came when Jakes was just a teenager. An "inner illumination" is how Jakes describes it. He says the calling meant knowing that "nothing would be as fulfilling or satisfying or meaningful than to do it."[15] Similar to the call narratives of many preachers, Jakes says that at first he was terrified. He had dropped out of high school to help his mother, and he did not think that anyone would believe he was called to preach.[16] Jakes later finished a GED and ran from his calling by going to West Virginia State College. While there, he was at a nightclub and a miraculous event gave him the motivation to return and accept his calling. Jakes tells the

---

9. John Blake, "Therapy and Theology: Atlanta's Megafest Shows Many Sides of T.D. Jakes Ministry," *Atlanta Journal-Constitution*, June 23, 2004, home edition.

10. Kaylois Henry, "Bishop Jakes Is Ready. Are You? The Nation's Hottest Preacher Brings His Message to Dallas," *Dallas Observer*, June 20, 1996.

11. Ibid.

12. Lee, *T.D Jakes*, 17, 23.

13. Henry, "Bishop Jakes Is Ready."

14. Shayne Lee and Phillip Luke Sinitiere, *Holy Mavericks: Evangelical Innovators and the Spiritual Marketplace* (New York: New York University Press, 2009), 63.

15. Henry, "Bishop Jakes Is Ready."

16. Ibid.

story of a stranger sitting on the bar stool next him who said, "You know, I had a dream that I saw you preaching."[17] After completing one year with a few classes in psychology,[18] Jakes returned to preach his first official sermon at Greater Emmanuel Gospel Tabernacle—an Apostolic church.[19] Apostolic churches are different from most Pentecostal churches in that they believe in the gifts of the Spirit and speaking in tongues, but they do not believe in the traditional Trinitarian doctrine. Often called Oneness Pentecostals, they argue that the believer has to be baptized in the name of Jesus alone to be saved, and that the Godhead is only in Jesus. Because of this connection, Jakes still receives inquiries about his theology.[20]

Jakes's bivocational and sometimes trivocational identity has been present from the beginning. He worked at the Union Carbide Chemical Plant in Charleston and took on a few other odd jobs as an "assistant manager for a store and a delivery truck driver."[21] The early preaching rarely generated enough income to pay the bills. Jakes was mainly preaching in "garages, storefronts, and small churches" in the "small coal-mining towns" and the "backwoods" of West Virginia.[22] In 1979 he organized his first church with just ten people.[23] The chemical plant eventually closed, as did many manufacturing plants across the country in the 1980s. The plant closure was the impetus that thrust Jakes into full-time ministry. During these early years Jakes and his new wife, Serita, often struggled with bouts of poverty. Jakes peppers his sermons and books with these stories of struggle. "I know also what it is to have my car repossessed, my children drinking milk provided by WIC,[24]

---

17. Henry, "Bishop Jakes Is Ready."

18. Lee, *T.D. Jakes*, 23.

19. Henry, "Bishop Jakes Is Ready"; Walton, *Watch This!*, 104.

20. Lauren Winner, "T.D. Jakes Feels Your Pain," *Christianity Today* 44, no. 2 (February 7, 2000): 55.

21. Lee, *T.D. Jakes*, 23.

22. Ibid., 24.

23. Ibid.

24. WIC stands for Women, Infants, Children. It is a government program that provides supplemental nutrition for low-income families and mothers.

to make a game with my boys out of feeling our way through the house when the electricity had been cut off for nonpayment."[25] At other times, he talks about poverty by referencing "the black and white T.V. set with the hanger hanging on top of it and the foil around the top." Stacey Floyd agrees that this is a "rhetorical strategy" to influence the audience to believe he is someone who understands the struggle of poor people.[26] Moreover, these personal stories improve his brand by making his life appear as a true Horatio Alger, rags-to-riches, American story.

The poor boy preacher from the Pentecostal storefront church with ten members in West Virginia makes good to become the CEO of a 30,000-member super-megachurch in the big city of Dallas, Texas. God has given the country boy divine favor and has elevated him to be a man featured on the cover of magazines, with a million-dollar mansion, a Bentley, and a private plane. Such a bootstrap story of rugged individualism strikes a powerful "American chord of self-determination."[27] If a poor black boy from West Virginia can do it—so can everyone else.

Bishop Jakes redefines his personal brand often. He has never been afraid to relocate and remake himself and his ministry. After starting Greater Temple of Faith in a storefront in Montgomery, West Virginia, in 1980, he moved his membership to Smithers in 1986. In Smithers he converted a dilapidated movie theater into a church and sanctuary.[28] After just five years he moved again to South Charleston, with a final move in 1992 to Cross Lanes, where his membership grew to about 1,000 members.[29] The most adventurous of his moves was when he moved to Dallas, Texas, in 1996. Jakes moved his staff and fifty families to start The Potter's House. Although many have suggested that Jakes made the move because

25. T.D. Jakes, *Reposition Yourself: Living Life Without Limits* (New York: Atria Books, 2007), 6.

26. Boyd, *Black Men Worshipping,* 74.

27. Ibid.

28. Lee, *T.D. Jakes,* 28.

29. Martha Jackson, "Jakes Hiked Long Road to Success," *Charleston Daily Mail,* November 18, 1995; Lee, *T.D. Jakes,* 29.

of pressure from local newspapers about his affluent lifestyle,[30] Jakes says the move was about growth: "He had outgrown the Charleston facility, which lacked a studio, and he needed to be in a city with better access to air travel and larger hotel facilities to accommodate conferences."[31] Dallas offered Jakes a larger local market and other resources, such as an international airport.

Jakes chose a new name for the new church in Dallas. The church's name, The Potter's House, is taken from a passage in Jeremiah: "Like clay in the hand of the potter, so are you in my hand, O house of Israel."[32] The brand and name of his super-megachurch match the way Jakes defines himself and his ministry. The words of the popular gospel song of the same name, tell the story: "the Potter wants to put you back together again!"[33] Jakes is someone that God as the potter is molding and leading to a divine destiny. The Potter's House is a church where people are invited to come and be healed from their hurts and pains, where they too can be molded by the Potter. They can, like Bishop Jakes, come and discover their individual divinely led destinies.

Jakes did his market research and conducted worship services for several months before he actually moved the entire congregation. The move was also a good financial move. He purchased the first property in Dallas from a discredited televangelist, W. V. Grant (convicted of tax evasion).[34] The campus had a 5,000-seat sanctuary, television studio, and 28 acres of land. The entire purchase cost about $3.2 million.[35] The $1.9 million mortgage was paid off in just six months.[36] Having already prepared for the move by conducting services while he was still living in Virginia, he doubled his member-

---

30. Lee, *T.D. Jakes*, 108.

31. Bill Broadway, "From His Pulpit, Messages on Prosperity, Pain," *Washington Post*, July 26, 1997, B7.

32. Sridhar Pappu, "The Preacher," *Atlantic Monthly* 297, no. 2 (March 2006): 100.

33. Walton, *Watch This!*, 111.

34. Broadway, "From His Pulpit," B7.

35. Lee, *T.D. Jakes,* 71.

36. Broadway, "From His Pulpit," B7.

ship to 2,000 at the first service.[37] After one year, the membership was up to 7,000.[38] Jakes eventually built another facility to accommodate the continuous growth.

The current facility for The Potter's House is a state-of-the-art facility that cost $45 million and has 191,000 square feet, seating about 8,200 people.[39] In just five years, The Potter's House was 30,000 members strong, and able to retire the entire debt.[40] Jakes does much of his entrepreneurial teaching and nonprofit work through the Metroplex Economic Development Corporation (MEDC), which he founded in 1998. The mission of the 501c3 not-for-profit corporation is "to remedy social and economic disparities, . . . [and] to bridge socio-economic voids existing in urban America."[41] Jakes has also expanded the campus to include the $11 million Clay Academy—a private Christian school, and the $150 million dollar Capella Park—a 1,500-unit single family residential development.[42]

Jakes considers The Potter's House to be the "prototype church for the twenty-first century."[43] "For Jakes, the positive fruits of faith and initiative embodied in such a facility are a testimony, pointing to God's presence and favor."[44] Although The Potter's House has outdistanced most churches in church growth, Jakes continues to be entrepreneurial. He is still remaking and expanding himself and his ministries. In 2010 and 2011 Jakes expanded to three more Potter's House locations: North Dallas and Fort Worth, Texas, and Denver, Colorado. Many prosperity preachers have taken on the franchise

---

37. William Martin, "American Idol," *Texas Monthly* 34, no. 8 (August 2006): 208.

38. Broadway, "From His Pulpit," B7.

39. "T.D. Jakes Biography," http://www.thepottershouse.org.

40. Hubert Morken, "Bishop T.D. Jakes: A Ministry of Empowerment," in *Religious Leaders and Faith-Based Politics: Ten Profiles*, ed. Jo Renee Formicola and Hubert Morken (Lanham, MD: Rowman & Littlefield, 2001), 29.

41. "T.D. Jakes Biography," http://www.thepottershouse.org.

42. Ibid.

43. Morken, "Bishop T.D. Jakes," 37.

44. Ibid.

or multisite model of one church in many locations.[45] They have one organization with several smaller church locations, but the main church functions as the corporate headquarters. This is not like traditional churches that often support new church plants. In the traditional Black Church, a local preacher would support a mentee or young preacher to start a new ministry. However, once the new preacher established him- or herself, the new preacher would have complete autonomy. In other words, they would be a separate church—a *sister church* that would remain in fellowship—but not with leadership from the mother church. However, in the franchise model, Jakes acts as a senior pastor and maintains much of the leadership control.

Alongside his vocation as a local pastor, Jakes has also spent time on the road as a traveling evangelist, revivalist, and conference presenter. He keynotes at the conferences of other preachers, as well as presents his own local and international conferences. For many Protestant traditions, an evangelist or revivalist is a minister who does not pastor a local church. Although national preachers like Billy Graham and Martin Luther King gave up their pastorates when they started their national and evangelistic ministries, T.D. Jakes has always retained clerical positions as both an evangelist and a local pastor. His first conference was a 1983 Back to Basics Bible Conference with about eighty attendees.[46] The first conference was the groundwork for many more.

Many of Jakes's conferences are tied to a book or a sermon. But the most prominent and profitable conference is WTAL (Woman Thou Art Loosed). As a local pastor in West Virginia, Jakes was counseling women and decided to start a Sunday School class with forty women. Each week the class kept growing. After discussing the success of the class with a friend, his friend invited him to present his first conference in Pittsburgh, Pennsylvania.[47] At first, Jakes was not

45. Lee, *T.D. Jakes*, 41.

46. Scott Billingsley, *It's A New Day: Race and Gender in the Modern Charismatic Movement* (Tuscaloosa, AL: University of Alabama Press, 2008), 117.

47. Jakes, in an interview, identifies the friend as the late Reverend Archie Dennis, who is also responsible for giving Jakes the idea of naming the confer-

sure what to call the conference, so his friend suggested taking the name from the Lukan biblical text. Jakes was surprised that 1,300 women registered for the conference. He moved it to a local hotel, and the conference in Pittsburgh became the first WTAL Conference.[48] Jakes then took the conference on the road. However, one invitation stands out in the history of his preaching at conferences. This invitation changed his life and the WTAL brand forever.

Jakes was asked to be a keynote speaker at Azusa in 1993. Carlton Pearson had created the annual conference as a renewal or celebration of the 1906 Azusa fellowship that birthed Pentecostalism.[49] According to Shayne Lee, the Azusa Conference was so popular in the 1990s that the keynote preacher could expect to "garner an extra $200,000 in annual income" from new preaching engagements.[50] Jakes had attended the conference in 1992 as a member in the audience.[51] The following year he preached two sermons—one on the main night and one session only for women. At the Azusa women's session Jakes preached the famous WTAL sermon from Luke 13:11-13. According to Lee, the products sold at Azusa from Jakes's appearance resulted in about $20,000 in revenue.[52] Consequently, Jakes quickly figured out how much income conferences like Azusa could generate. He returned to West Virginia and took $15,000 of his savings and self-published the first nonfiction version of the WTAL book.[53] Each book sold for about $10. After just a couple of weeks, Jakes had sold over 5,000 copies,[54] which meant that he netted close to $35,000. The content of the book was chiefly the material from the Sunday School lessons and the sermon.

---

ence Woman Thou Art Loosed. Michael Duduit, "Preaching to Mend Broken Lives: An Interview with T.D. Jakes," http:www.crosswalk.com.

48. Sam Wellman, "T.D. Jakes," http://www.heroesofhistory.com, p. 32.

49. Ibid., 40.

50. Lee, *T.D. Jakes,* 43.

51. Ibid., 46.

52. Ibid., 68.

53. Lisa Miller, "Prophet Motives: Grammy Nomination, Book Deal, TV Spots—A Holy Empire Is Born," *Wall Street Journal,* August 21, 1998, eastern edition, A1.

54. Billingsley, *It's a New Day,* 118; Miller, "Prophet Motives," A1.

The WTAL success was the impetus for other brands and more books. The counterpart for men of the WTAL book was *Loose That Man and Let Him Go.*[55] In 1993 Jakes added the national ManPower conferences for men only.[56] In 2003 he expanded his products for women by creating a second brand entitled God's Leading Ladies. The new brand and conference were geared to attract more business-minded women, who had advanced beyond the WTAL brand. In other words, they had already been *loosed* and were ready to be God's leading ladies. The God's Leading Ladies conferences are now held at The Potter's House under the leadership of his wife, Serita Jakes. In 2004 he took all of the conferences—WTAL, ManPower, and God's Leading Ladies—and branded them into a four-day festival called MegaFest.[57] He added the Mega Youth Experience in 2005 with events presented in several sites: the Georgia Dome, World Congress Center, Phillips Arena, and International Plaza. MegaFest had an attendance of over 560,000 people.[58]

Just as Jakes remakes himself, he also remakes his brands. He cancelled MegaFest in 2007 after it was in Atlanta for several years. He then rebranded the festival as MegaFest International and moved the conference to Johannesburg, South Africa.[59] Jakes promoted the move "as the next logical step in the evolution of the event." Jakes is quoted as saying, "As I looked out, the feel was much more aligned to an international event, than a U.S. specific event. . . . I believe the true purpose of the ministry is to go beyond the traditional walls and minister to the world."[60] MegaFest had several corporate sponsors and also required registration fees for many of the individual events. In an interview with *Jet* magazine Jakes said that the festival was too expensive. "Our overhead was unbelievable and when you add up the cost of the dome and all the various things it was just

55. T.D. Jakes, *Loose That Man and Let Him Go* (Tulsa, OK: Albury Publishing, 1995).

56. Billingsley, *It's a New Day*, 122.

57. Walton, *Watch This!*, 114.

58. Billingsley, *It's a New Day*, 123.

59. Lee and Sinitiere, *Holy Mavericks*, 68.

60. "Megafest Press Release," http://www.mega-fest.com.

very costly."[61] For Jakes, the criteria for ministry is not how many people are helped or how many souls have been evangelized. Morken states that Jakes believes that all of life has to have "profitability."[62] He writes, "Jakes asserts that profitability means adding something of value to the Kingdom of God, to oneself, to one's family, and to all humanity."[63]

Another explanation for moving MegaFest and changing the brand is that as a capitalist and entrepreneur, Jakes understands the nature of markets. When the U.S. market was oversaturated, he needed a new market with new customers. One of the challenges of these larger conferences and super-megachurches is that they require a lot of resources just to sustain the infrastructure. Much of the work is done by volunteers, but in order for a brand and conference to be successful the preacher has to always be satisfying the appetite of consumers and the market. One of the largest and most successful Megafest festivals was in 2013. Oprah Winfrey was the special guest. She filmed "a two-part series for her *Lifeclass* in which they discussed family issues related to fatherlessness and reconciliation."[64]

Along with his many vocational roles as preacher, conference presenter, evangelist, and speaker, Jakes has maintained a lucrative media ministry with radio, television, Internet, and social media. His first radio show in 1982 was called "The Master's Plan."[65] The Azusa Conference appearance with Carlton Pearson was also T.D. Jakes's first major television exposure. "Pearson arranged for TBN's Paul Crouch to hear a seven-minute clip, after which the TV mogul helped Jakes land his own show."[66] His weekly television show, *Get Ready with T.D. Jakes*, was broadcast nationally on TBN and BET

61. Dana Slagle, "The Personal Side of T.D. Jakes," *Jet* (July 2007): 60.

62. Morken, "Bishop T.D. Jakes," 35.

63. Ibid.

64. Marla F. Frederick, *Colored Television: American Religion Gone Global* (Stanford, CA: Stanford University Press, 2016), 165.

65. Billingsley, *It's a New Day*, 117.

66. Sarah Posner, *God's Profits: Faith, Fraud, and the Republican Crusade for Values Voters* (Sausalito, CA: PoliPoint Press, 2008), 54.

in 1993.[67] Similar to most televangelists that pastor churches, Jakes established T.D. Jakes Ministries as his personal ministry, set apart from the church's ministry.[68] The leadership structure in such cases usually entails the church having one team of leadership and the personal ministry having another. According to Ministrywatch. com, after moving to The Potter's House, Jakes made T.D. Jakes Ministries one of the ancillary ministries of The Potter's House.[69] Churches are not required to file the 990 income tax form that the Internal Revenue Service requires for nonprofits. As a result, T.D. Jakes does not file taxes for T.D. Jakes Ministries. Therefore, there is no way to measure how much income he has generated with his personal ministry. In 1995 Jakes also established TDJ Enterprises, LLP, the for-profit arm. This is the "umbrella" organization for "his books, movies, television programs, music CDs, digital properties, leadership training, and live events designed to entertain, educate, and empower not just Christian but mainstream audiences."[70]

Almost all of his sermons from his own conferences, as well as when he keynotes for others, are edited and reproduced as commercial products. The sermons are broadcast through his multilayered media ministry on television, radio, and Internet. Each of his half-hour television spots usually includes time for the core of the sermon as well as time to promote the next conference or book. More important, each media presentation always includes an appeal for members of the television audience to attend a conference, buy a CD, or become a monthly ministry partner.[71] Bishop Jakes has thousands of sermons and books in the marketplace. Some of the earlier books such as *Woman Thou Art Loosed* have been released so many times that the books can be purchased on Amazon.com for a penny. Hundreds of his sermons and speeches are uploaded on YouTube.

---

67. Jadell Forman, "Taking Religion to the Masses," *Texas Monthly* (September 1998): 121.

68. Brown, "Sowing Seeds of Prosperity," 55.

69. "T.D. Ministries," www.ministrywatch.com.

70. Brown, *Sowing Seeds of Prosperity*, 54.

71. Marla Frederick, *Between Sundays: Black Women and Everyday Struggles of Faith* (Berkeley: University of California Press, 2003), 145.

Because of the predominance of the media ministry, the actual physical space of The Potter's House serves as both a sanctuary for worship and a television studio for media production. The church bookstore is the storefront for all of the Bishop Jakes's merchandise, as well as the brands and products of his family members. Serita Jakes has several books. His daughter Sarah Jakes has started her writing and speaking career. Jacqueline Jakes, his sister, is also a part of the family branding. Jakes usually writes the foreword for the books.[72] Just as Jakes has expanded his brand with a variety of products, everyone that has any market appeal within the family also has a brand.

Any theme that can be branded, or any sermon that preaches well, will often become the next brand. Like most New Black Church pastors, the sermon remains the most likely medium for theology and the message of prosperity. After his exposure and relationship with Oprah Winfrey, Jakes began to produce new books and brands at a much faster rate. After publishing a book of a certain title, he would promote the new brand with a life class or television appearance.

Jakes has always been very careful to create two separate structures for not-for-profit organizations and the for-profit entity of T.D. Jakes Enterprises.[73] He is vigilant to make sure that he maintains his not-for-profit status. According to *Black Enterprise* magazine, Jakes has a "carefully constructed firewall which separates his church responsibilities from his business enterprises," with "two staffs" and two "different accounting systems and financial institutions."[74] However, no matter how much effort is put into the separation, it is extremely difficult to distinguish the ministry from the business. No matter

---

72. For books by family members the following are good examples, see Serita Jakes, *The Princess Within: Restoring the Soul of a Woman* (Bloomington, MN: Bethany House Publishing, 2011); Sarah Jakes, *Colliding with Destiny: Finding Hope in the Legacy of Ruth* (Bloomington, MN: Bethany House Publishers, 2014); Jacqueline Yvonne Jakes, *God's Trophy Women: You Are Blessed and Highly Favored* (New York: Hachette Book Group, 2006).

73. Nicole Marie Richardson, Krissah Williams, and Hamil Harris, "The Business of Faith," *Black Enterprise* (May 2006): 103.

74. Ibid.

what legal structures are in place, it is almost impossible to separate his vocational identity as a preacher from his identity as an entrepreneur and CEO.

T.D. Jakes as Pastor/CEO

Many biographers, interviewers, and scholars acknowledge the centrality of entrepreneur and preacher in Jakes's life story. Don Nori, the CEO of Destiny Image Publishers Inc., the company that published the WTAL nonfiction book, asserts that Jakes "is as good a businessman as he is a preacher. . . . In fact, some might say he's a better businessman than he is preacher."[75] *Forbes* magazine describes Jakes as "fervent preacher, ferocious capitalist."[76] Scott Billingsley asserts, "The confluence of business and ministry [is] so seamless that it [is] difficult to determine where one end[s] and the other beg[ins]."[77] Walton writes that Jakes conflates "the ecclesial and the economic realms. In fact, he embraces equally his roles as a Christian minister, business entrepreneur, author, recording artist, playwright, and movie producer. The bishop is multivocational when it comes to the respective spheres of the church and corporate America."[78] Without apology, Jakes defines himself as both a businessman and a preacher. In many interviews, Jakes reminds his admirers that he "could have been happy to be a businessman and not a preacher," but that the "harmonizing [of] those two things has been an exciting part of [his] life."[79] Jakes often reminds his followers that he is a fourth-generation entrepreneur: "I was entrepreneurial before I was ministerial. It has always been a part of my history, my destiny."[80]

Because of his Pentecostal roots, Jakes's role as a bivocational Black Church pastor is not that unusual. Pentecostals have often

---

75. Miller, "Prophet Motives," A1.

76. Jason Storbakken, "God Is in the T-Bills," *Forbes* 179, no. 12 (June 2007): 58.

77. Billingsley, *It's a New Day*, 109.

78. Walton, *Watch This!*, 116.

79. David Whitford, "So Shall Ye Reap," *FSB: Fortune Small Business* 15, no. 8 (October 2005): 32.

80. Brown, "Sowing Seeds of Prosperity," 56.

been characterized by their small storefront churches.[81] Many Pentecostal and black pastors are bivocational simply because their congregations are unable to financially support a full-time pastor.[82] However, Jakes's commitment to his bivocational identity has a more meaningful purpose. Jakes wants to be a role model for both African Americans and Pentecostals. Subsequently, his bivocation is for the purpose of embodying economic achievement. According to Jakes, our contemporary context demands a different understanding of the black preacher. Jakes says that we need preachers to be "believable heroes" for working-class black people. "We don't need preachers who have taken vows of poverty or who, on the other extreme, are living out of the collection plate. We need a preacher who, through writing, or some other honest means, has made the American dream work for him."[83] As a role model, like other prosperity preachers, Bishop Jakes embodies a kind of sacralized American exceptionalism.

This exceptionalism of prosperity preachers is simply a new version of the Puritan idea of America's calling to be "the city on a hill," or an "elect nation."[84] According to Lawrence Mamiya, black prosperity preachers like Jakes use "the old Puritan rationalization that poverty is a sign of God's curse and wealth a sign of God's blessing."[85] Whereas the Puritans were not supposed to enjoy their accumulation of wealth and material possessions, for prosperity preachers these things are the evidence of God's blessings. Jakes's position is that African Americans need to see successful people. He says, "Particularly in my culture we need to see some positive role models, who

---

81. Posner, *God's Profits*, 58.

82. Carter G. Woodson, *The History of the Negro* Church (Washington, DC: Associated Publishers, 1945), 146.

83. Winner, "T.D. Jakes Feels Your Pain," 59.

84. Mark Hellstern, "The 'ME GOSPEL': An Examination of the Historical Roots of the Prosperity Emphasis within Current Charismatic Theology," *Fides et Historia* 21, no. 3 (October 1989): 78-90.

85. Lawrence Mamiya, *River of Struggle, River of Freedom: Trends among Black Churches and Black Pastoral Leadership: Pulpit and Pew Research on Pastoral Leadership Reports* (Durham, NC: Duke Divinity School, 2006), 11.

are not selling drugs, who are not pimping women, who honorably pursued some gifting or talent—and become successful."[86] Bishop Jakes is able to profit from his celebrity status by branding himself as someone who has achieved the American dream.

The exceptionalism is communicated by the argument that if "worldly" people can have the finer things in life, then surely God wants God's people and servants to have that much more.[87] Jakes's lifestyle and secular success become the evidence of his exceptionalism and giftedness: "Once they see a black man who is successful, . . . and he's not selling drugs, but he's driving the same kind of car the pimp or drug dealer is, and he's not illegal and he's not immoral, it encourages young men. . . . They say, 'Hey, if God can do it for him.'"[88]

Jakes does not say that poverty is a curse, nor does he promote wealth as God's blessing to the same degree as most prosperity preachers. He does, however, promote the same cultural mythologies of success. Jakes spends a great deal of energy and time justifying his success as both a preacher and an entrepreneur. An excerpt from a speech at a two-day leadership conference at Southeastern University provides a vivid example of how Jakes interprets his identity as a pastor and entrepreneur. The theme of the conference was Ignite the Flame of Servant Leadership. Jakes's speech was entitled, "Reposition Yourself for Service." Reposition Yourself is one of his many brands. The forum included several well-known speakers such as Jack Welch of General Electric and Dave Ramsey, a national speaker who specializes in helping Christians get out of debt. Jakes began his speech by inviting the audience to get to know him a little better:

> It may help you to understand at least my thinking or to minister to my mentality and understanding. My brain probably breaks down in two parts. There are two people

86. "Gold and the Gospel: The Healer's Due," economist.com (May 31, 1997): 56.

87. Milmon F. Harrison, *Righteous Riches: The Word of Faith Movement in Contemporary African American Religion* (New York: Oxford Press, 2005), 63.

88. Broadway, "From His Pulpit," B7.

living in my head . . . [who] have a strong proclivity and interest in business. And I think that good business is in itself a ministry. . . . I have a passion for ministry. So I tell people sometimes half of my head is Bill Gates and the other half is Mother Teresa. The Mother Teresa in me wants to clothe the naked and feed the hungry, and do all sorts of good works around the world. And Bill and Mother argue all the time, because Bill says "Mother, you going to need some money for all that."[89]

Jakes's comparing himself to Bill Gates and Mother Teresa illustrates how pastor and CEO are always blending, and, at times, competing in his life story. The merger of the two images is also why his life story, his theology, and his worldview are so controversial.

Critics argue "that with his exorbitant speaking fees and excessive entrepreneurialism, Jakes turns religion into his most valuable commodity."[90] His life represents what they consider to be the uniting of two worlds that have contradictory worldviews and values. As a result, sometimes he is viewed as "a marketing genius who exploits people's pain, [and] a con artist who tells people what they want to hear—the 'Velcro Bishop' with a watered down gospel."[91] Others may not see him as negatively, but they still question his integrity. In an article in *Texas Monthly*, William Martin writes, "[Jakes] preaches and practices liberation of the poor and criticizes business and government for ignoring their plight, but he has gained great wealth by embracing and fully exploiting the free-market capitalism that exacerbates their plight. He encourages generosity, yet he cuts shrewd business deals and brooks little resistance from those who challenge him."[92] Many Christians are simply unable to reconcile

89. T.D. Jakes, "Reposition Yourself for Service," speech from The Forum When God Calls You to Lead, "Part 1 Reposition Yourself for Service," http://www.youtube.com.

90. Lee, *T.D. Jakes*, 3.

91. Ibid.

92. William Martin, "American Idol," *Texas Monthly* 34, no. 8 (August 2006): 124.

Jakes as a spiritual or moral leader who flaunts an affluent capitalist lifestyle. In their view, Jakes's "flashy affluence and relentless selling betray Christianity's core values of poverty and humility."[93] Jakes contends that these Christians and critics are the very people that need his ministry. His mission is to help Christians by providing balance to the extreme teachings of the church.[94]

Bishop Jakes argues that the extremists of prosperity preachers are not presenting a balanced gospel. "They believe that God's blessing can be counted in dollars and cents, and one's financial status is an indication of one's status in the eyes of the Lord."[95] The other extreme is the one that teaches a "monastic philosophy of frugalness."[96] So Jakes intends to preach to both extremes. He writes,

> Certain extremists in the faith based community teach that faith is only a matter of dollars and cents. They quote scriptures that promise great wealth. They don't emphasize the importance of a practical pragmatic plan of a faith-with-works ethic, education, and economic empowerment. . . . Others teach piety and asceticism and promote the idea that poverty should be worn as a badge of superiority, that it is somehow more godly to barely be able to feed your children than to be wealthy.[97]

Jakes's mission is to teach others by giving them the tools to become successful and prosperous like him. Morken states that what distinguishes Jakes's ministry is that Jakes offers a "prescription of rich and varied remedies."[98] Paraphrasing the words of Jesus, Jakes's life can be summed up as, "If you do not believe what I say, believe what I do."[99]

---

93. Miller, "Prophet Motives," A1.

94. T.D. Jakes, *The Great Investment: Faith, Family, and Finance* (New York: G. P. Putnam's Sons, 2000), 4.

95. Ibid., 4.

96. Ibid.

97. Jakes, "Reposition Yourself," 7.

98. Morken, "Bishop T.D. Jakes," 36.

99. Ibid., 37.

The Bishop says he is called to preach a much-needed message of liberation and economic empowerment—especially to minority communities. "Economically empowering minorities is a critical part of my mission,"[100] says Jakes. He sees his ministry as providing "African Americans with the life skills, emotional health, and psychological well-being to be successful."[101] Jakes's liberation is about "the renewing of the mind to conquer the victim mentality that precludes them from reaching their potential."[102] African American Christians and others must be liberated from the supposed faulty teachings on poverty and wealth. Although Jakes has worked hard to distance himself from Word of Faith, in his book *The Lady, Her Lover, Her Lord,* he writes,

> There seems to be a myth of poverty attached to Christianity. Many people, Christians and non-Christians alike, view accumulating wealth as un-Christian behavior. There's a tendency to think that a Christian must dress like a monk and live in a monastery, or he or she is not sincere. Well I bring a message of liberation. The Lord does not mean for you to forsake all ambitions in order to serve him. He just wants to be your priority.[103]

No different from the strategy that is often practiced by prosperity preachers, Jakes discredits any theology or Pentecostal piety that suggests Christians should be poor. Furthermore, Jakes disagrees with any doctrine that suggests that ministers have to live austere lives and take vows of poverty.

The bishop defends his God-given right to accumulate wealth as a pastor. He often accuses his critics of "occupational discrimination."[104] Wealthy doctors and lawyers don't receive the same

---

100. Richardson, Williams, and Harris, "The Business of Faith," 103.

101. Lee and Sinitiere, *Holy Mavericks*, 59.

102. Ibid.

103. T.D. Jakes, *Her Lady, Her Lover, Her Lord* (New York: Berkley Books, 1998), 201.

104. Miller, "Prophet Motives," A1.

criticism as wealthy pastors.[105] At other times, he has hinted that criticism of his wealth is also a form of racial discrimination. In West Virginia Jakes received his first major public criticism from the local newspaper. The *Charleston Gazette* wrote an article about the extravagant purchase of a $630,000, sixteen-room mansion that had seven bedrooms, a bowling alley, and an indoor swimming pool.[106] Jakes also purchased the house next door, which meant the total purchase for both houses was close to a million dollars.[107] Both homes were previously owned by white businessmen (a banker and motel owner).[108]

Jakes hinted that underneath the occupational discrimination was also a bit of racial discrimination because the newspapers never wrote any articles about the white businessmen who owned the houses: "In a state that is only 3 to 4 percent black, it is more polite for critics to deal with the occupational aspect, but there is a degree of racial overtones."[109] To describe and convince others of this occupational discrimination, Jakes also talks about how society treats athletes and entertainers: "This society pays thousands upon millions of dollars to watch men get out on the field and run into each other with helmets on, and that is completely acceptable. You can put on a silver glove and moonwalk across the stage for millions, and that is acceptable. But to reach into the gutters and help hurting people and strengthen them, and then be blessed by that, is not acceptable."[110] In other words, his identity as a preacher who helps people, combined with his identity as an entrepreneur, justifies his affluent lifestyle, his ambition, and his personal wealth.

---

105. Lib Copeland, "With Gifts from God: Bishop T.D. Jakes Has Made Millions by Reaching Millions. Not That There's Anything Wrong With That," *Washington Post*, March 25, 2001.

106. Ken Ward, Jr., "Successful Books, TV Exposure Allow Kanawha Minister to Live in Style," *Charleston Gazette*, April 5, 1995; Billingsley, *It's a New Day*, 121.

107. Billingsley, *It's a New Day*, 120.

108. Ward, "Successful Books."

109. Miller, "Prophet Motives," A1.

110. Miller, "Prophet Motives," A1.

Jakes often asserts, in a way that seems contradictory, that his wealth should not be a problem because he makes the majority of his income from his entrepreneurial ventures and not from his preaching. "The reality is [that] the majority of my income comes from my for-profit ventures. If I retired from preaching, I make enough to take care of my personal needs."[111] In his mind, the expectation that he should live differently because he is a preacher is the equivalent of asking him to live in the world as a second-class citizen. He says, "Then, you lock me in coach, but you want me to preach to first-class. Not only do I personally believe that it is not biblical, I don't think it is appropriate for these times."[112] *Ebony* magazine posed a direct question about his first-class lifestyle: "How do you respond to some commentators who have criticized you for living well and traveling first-class?"

> As you know, T.D. Jakes Enterprises co-owns *Woman, Thou Art Loosed* the movie; no other movie producer or record label owner would be called upon to defend the quality of his clothes or the stature of his home or how much income he makes. Additionally, the vast majority of the well-informed realized that any author who has sold 7 million books to his credit need not justify his enjoyment of some level of success as a reflection of his life's work.[113]

Again, Jakes's strategy is to remind his critics that he is not just a preacher, but an entrepreneur—a CEO. In this particular case, he emphasizes his entrepreneurial activities as a writer, movie producer, and record-label owner. By far, the history and success of WTAL are most representative of the blending of his preaching and his entrepreneurialism.

---

111. Kelly Starling, "Why People, Especially Women, Are Talking about Bishop T.D. Jakes," *Ebony* 56, no. 3 (January 2001): 114.

112. "Gold and the Gospel: The Healer's Due," economist.com (May 31, 1997).

113. "Five Questions for Bishop T.D. Jakes," *Ebony* 60, no. 2 (December 2004): 24.

Personal testimonies and stories are as prominent in prosperity preaching as their biblical exposition.[114] The preachers often share their life stories in order to impress upon congregants that the prosperity gospel works and that they are the living proof. Jakes is no exception. As a preacher and teacher of the gospel, Jakes convinces his followers that the God who inspires his "preaching of the Word" is the same God who inspires his "business ideas."[115]

In his book *The Great Investment,* Jakes testifies to how WTAL is an example of God's inspiring him both as a minister and as a businessman. He claims that through WTAL God taught him how to maximize all of his gifts:

> Years ago, God dropped an idea for a women's Bible class in my heart. The idea grew and became a book, a conference, a play, and a music CD. God gave the ability to take the idea and package it to reach a much larger audience than it would have reached if it had remained just a Bible class. As a businessman, I am successful because I see and understand the capacity God has given me and [I] am maximizing my moment. I am very blessed. I have my ministry, which is my passion, and I have business success, which is a result of my creativity and the source of my financial success.[116]

WTAL as a brand is the first of many other brands that Jakes packaged to reach larger audiences and bigger markets.

Although Jakes is very open about his entrepreneurial success and the maximizing of his gifts, he is not as open about how much he has profited from this success. In other words, he does not provide financial information or details about how much money he makes.[117] Writers and scholars can only estimate that he is worth about 150

---

114. Paul Gifford, "Prosperity: A New and Foreign Element in African Christianity," *Religion* 20 (1990): 376.

115. Jakes, *The Great Investment,* 43.

116. Ibid., 43-44.

117. Jakes rarely gives any information on how much income he actually makes. He no longer takes a salary from The Potter's House. In 1998 he told *Jet* that 35 percent came from the church.

million dollars.[118] Popular magazines list his empire to be worth 400 million.[119] Also, he rarely reveals to his followers how the profits from his entrepreneurial successes are directly tied to his preaching and the relationships that he has garnered as a preacher and spiritual leader. Unlike popular secular motivational speakers and writers, Jakes's many brands and branded products almost always start with a sermon, ministry, or worship experience. Jakes's fame and wealth are not the result of his entrepreneurial ventures alone. Furthermore, what fuels his entrepreneurial activities is Jakes's position as a pastor and preacher—not the other way around.

John Blake, a writer for the *Atlanta Journal-Constitution*, highlights that although Jakes wants to be "known as more than a preacher . . . Jakes built his reputation, though, in the pulpit. . . . He built his fortune by translating his preaching prowess into a multimillion-dollar industry built on the marketing of his sermons, books, gospel plays, music and video tapes."[120] Martin, in his article on Jakes, describes the relationship as symbiotic:

> T.D. Jakes Enterprises unquestionably benefits hugely from its symbiotic relationship with The Potter's House and T.D. Jakes Ministries. The church and the viewers who contribute to his ministry pay the tab for Jakes's telecasts, which in addition to carrying the message of the day and drawing people to The Potter's House, serve as infomercials for his books, CDs, DVDs, and other products. They also advertise at conferences in which these same products, including videos and tapes of conferences, are sold.[121]

---

118. Jonathan Walton, "Empowered: The Entrepreneurial Ministry of T.D. Jakes," *Christian Century* 124 no. 14, (July 10, 2007): 28.

119. Brown, "Sowing Seeds of Prosperity," 56; Matthew Faraci, "The Bishop's Life," *Variety* 330, no. 7 (December 2015): 119.

120. John Blake, "Theology and Therapy: Atlanta's Mega Fest Shows Many Sides of T.D. Jakes' Ministry," *Atlanta Journal-Constitution*, June 23, 2004, home edition.

121. William Martin, "American Idol," *Texas Monthly* 34, no. 8 (August 2006): 208.

Jakes takes full financial advantage of his role as a local pastor and international evangelist. He is well versed about the significance and history that the black pastor has played in churches and in the larger African American community.

Jakes describes the pastor's role in black churches as more important than that of the president of the United States. In an interview before Barack Obama became president, Jakes stated that "ministry is completely different in the African-American community . . . the church is everything. We've never had a president, we've only had preachers. So when we look to the preacher, he's the president. Many of us have not had fathers, so he's the daddy we didn't have. We take pride in him in a way white people don't understand."[122] Jakes has been able to take his social capital as a pastor and convert it into financial capital. His secular and non-Christian business partners are also aware of his appeal and his stature in the African American community. Jakes lists several secular partners on the website of T.D. Jakes Enterprises. They include Sony Pictures, Thomas Nelson, Bethany House Books, Radio One, CodeBlack Entertainment, Universal Christian Music Group (Dexterity Sounds), Atria Books—to name a few.[123] This list does not include other corporate sponsors like Coca Cola and American Airlines, and the smaller vendors that sponsor the larger conferences such as MegaFest, God's Leading Ladies, or WTAL.[124]

Jakes would argue that his entrepreneurial and secular vocations are the impetus for these financial partnerships. However, it is his vocation as a pastor more than as a writer, movie producer, or any other secular vocation that is the source for their involvement. Billingsley poses an excellent question: "without the institutional structure" that the ministries provide, would the "for-profit ventures" be as successful?[125]

Jakes's relationship with Putnam is a perfect example. Putnam is a division of Penguin Putnam, the second largest secular publisher

122. Winner, "T.D. Jakes Feels Your Pain," 59.
123. TDJ Enterprises, "Our Partners," http://enterprise.tdjakes.com.
124. Richardson, Williams, and Harris, "The Business of Faith," 106.
125. Billingsley, *It's a New Day*, 109.

in the country.[126] Jakes's first arrangement with Putnam was a two-book deal for $1.8 million.[127] An article in *Publisher's Weekly* describes Putnam's relationship with religious authors like Jakes: "Successful authors like T.D. Jakes have national and international ministries that reach millions of potential book-buyers through sold-out conferences, direct mailings, on-site and on-line bookstores, and various personal appearances. Jakes's publisher Putnam considers a writer's platform an important factor in the company's decision to sign them"[128] Destiny Image, a small charismatic press, sold two million copies of the WTAL nonfiction book. Destiny is committed to evangelism and Christian mission. As Morken writes, "Jakes transitioned from self-publishing, to small Christian publishers, to large Christian publishers, to a large secular publisher."[129] WTAL has now sold over 15 million copies worldwide and grossed over $75 million.[130] The success of WTAL, which is a religious text, led to the Putnam deal. The religious or spiritual success is what has fueled the secular success. Not the other way around.

Joel Fotinos, the religious director of Putnam, explains that "publishers *buy* authors as much as they buy their projects."[131] These companies are essentially buying Jakes and his relationship with his parishioners. In other words, it is not Jakes's role as an entrepreneur but his role as a pastor and evangelist that these corporate partners are buying. Like other prosperity preachers, Jakes unapologetically sells himself to the highest bidder in the global marketplace. He also sells his platform, which means that he profits from his relationship with his parishioners, ministry partners, and the thousands of congregants who attend the many conferences. Bishop Jakes is able to accomplish this by capitalizing on both vocational identities as a pastor and an entrepreneur. As a pastor preaching to millions and an

---

126. Forman, "Taking Religion to the Masses," 123.

127. Miller, "Prophet Motives," A1.

128. Marcia Ford, "Beyond Handselling," *Publisher's Weekly* (September 23 2002): S2.

129. Morken, "Bishop T.D. Jakes," 40.

130. Brown, "Sowing Seeds of Prosperity," 55.

131. Ford, "Beyond Handselling," S2 [emphasis mine].

author writing about God, Jakes is theologizing. He convinces his followers that they can be liberated. But what liberation is he offering, and what theology is he presenting in his brands?

T.D. Jakes as a Theologian of Prosperity

Theologies of prosperity are now mainstream and no longer sequestered along the margins of Protestant Christianity. Because of televangelism, media exposure, and how these popular preachers articulate for the masses their role as pastor and entrepreneur, the worldview and theological perspective can be seen all over the world. Television, more than any other medium, has provided mass exposure for these preachers and has contributed greatly to neo-Pentecostalism's emergence into the religious mainstream.[132] T.D. Jakes and these preachers tap into a long history in America of celebrity pastors and entrepreneurs as leaders who embody the American vision of success. But it is the theology that has such a great impact on everyday people. The preachers speak on behalf of God. They provide prescriptions and remedies for almost every aspect of life. With their brands they answer the question about the ultimate concern of many Christians.

The first generation of liberation theologians produced new Christologies, and their theologies were a counterdiscourse to what they considered to be the oppressive "Western articulated theologies and Christologies" that promoted "Western supremacist ideology."[133] The first liberation theologians argued for doing theology from the context of the oppressed. More important, they argued that the suffering of the oppressed had to be the starting point for any viable liberation theology. Consequently, they presented new theological reflections on Jesus, Exodus, and the Promised Land.

According to the testimonies of congregants, Bishop Jakes is not only a theologian; he presents himself as a kind of theologian of

---

132. Lee, *T.D. Jakes*, 37.

133. Jacqueline Grant, *White Women's Christ and Black Women's Jesus: Feminist Christology and Womanist Response* (Atlanta, GA: Scholars Press, 1989), 1.

liberation. It is important to keep in mind that lay people rarely use the academic term "theologian." More specifically, they do not usually articulate anything about systematic, constructive, or liberation theology. However, because liberation is critical to black churches and black identity, we need to place Jakes and other prosperity preachers in conversation with academic liberation theologians.

Bishop Jakes's interpretations of the Exodus narrative and how they differ from the theologies of Black Church preachers and academic liberation theologians are an important area for analysis and critique. The first generation of academic liberation theologians created counterdiscourses. In similar fashion, the theological appropriations of prosperity preachers are also counterdiscourses. However, their discourses are in opposition to those of the traditional Black Church and the theologies of academic theologians.

T.D. Jakes and other prosperity preachers argue that the theological discourses and interpretations by Black Church pastors and academics are oppressive and hegemonic.[134] In order to liberate African Americans and the members of their congregations, they feel compelled to present new and more liberating interpretations. In other words, they must create new (prosperity) Christologies. Consequently, in their interpretations, Jesus is no longer poor. He is not the co-sufferer of the Black Church tradition. Jesus is interpreted as a CEO with a national ministry. His disciples have also been transformed into antiquity's version of twelve members of his executive staff. Prosperity preachers use their interpretations of Jesus and the traditional stories of Exodus and the Promised Land to construct theological systems that are ideologically more compatible with the values of advanced capitalism and a global culture of empire. The life of T.D. Jakes as a pastor and entrepreneur tells the story.

In much of Jakes's teaching, Jesus is God—and not only because of his background as a Oneness Pentecostal. Many black Christians see Jesus as synonymous with God.[135] Therefore, most theological

---

134. Harrison, *Righteous Riches*, 149; Billingsley, *It's a New Day*, 107-8.
135. Grant, *White Women's Christ*, 213.

reflections are also christological. The statements about Jesus are often identical to the statements about God. Jakes's images of Christ are important because, first and foremost, Jakes is a preacher. In much of black preaching and black theology Jesus Christ is presented as God, and Jesus of Nazareth is one who is poor and on the side of the oppressed. Because Jesus is presented as poor, womanist theologian Jackie Grant asserts that African Americans and black women especially believed that Jesus associated with the lowly of his day and *the least of these*.[136] Women are able to believe that a poor Jesus understands that black women often suffer from the triple oppression of race, gender, and class. Dwight Hopkins, as a representative of black theology, offers a reading of how most black and womanist liberation theologians interpret Jesus the Christ:

> That is, Jesus Christ shows clear, conscious intent that God chose to manifest among specific oppressed groups in the real world. In Jesus, God publicly proclaims a heavenly mission on earth geared to freeing the poor and those victimized by discrimination. . . . And God, through Jesus, opted to die as a persecuted outlaw, a perceived threat to ruling powers and dominating church and theological authorities. Jesus Christ's funeral takes place with two thieves; lacking any resources, the Anointed One had to be buried in someone else's tomb.[137]

Liberation theologians argue that God chose to manifest in Jesus as one who is oppressed. This is why most liberation theologians argue for the *preferential option for the poor*.

Prosperity preachers tell a different story and have a different interpretation of the Christ narrative and event. The identity of Jesus has been changed into one that fits well within the tropes of global capitalism and empire. Jesus is not only wealthy, but is

---

136. Ibid., 217.
137. Dwight N. Hopkins, *Shoes That Fit Our Feet: Sources for a Constructive Theology* (Maryknoll, NY: Orbis Press, 1993), 213-14.

also a business mogul or CEO, and prosperity preachers usually cite examples from Scripture to justify their position. Oral Roberts, for example, gives seven reasons for believing Jesus was wealthy, from the kind of clothes Jesus wore, to the kind of house he had, to the fact that Jesus had a treasurer.[138] Similarly, Fred Price in an interview with *Religion and Ethics* argues:

> Jesus had plenty, and then he was always giving to people, always giving to the poor, and so he had plenty from a material point of view. He was responsible for twelve grown men—their housing, their transportation, their food, their clothing—for a three-and-a-half-year period of time. He had to have something. This concept of Jesus being poor is not biblically true; it's traditionally true.[139]

These arguments and interpretations of Scripture are intended to counter other traditional interpretations—especially those familiar cultural expressions of the Black Church and black theologians that present Jesus of Nazareth as poor. T.D. Jakes uses many of the same arguments as other prosperity preachers. More important, Jakes interprets both Jesus and God as businessmen with the characteristics of cosmic Wall Street investment bankers and venture capitalists—images of empire. In Jakes's worldview, God acts just like a CEO at the helm of a multinational corporation.

---

138. Oral Roberts writes in his chapter entitled "Seven Ways We Know Jesus was Not Poor": "1) Jesus has a house large enough for guests; 2) Jesus had money, enough to have a treasurer; 3) Jesus had a team, a large one that he had to support financially from city to city; 4) Jesus had a donor base, a faithful group of financial partners who 'ministered' to Him of their money. 5) Jesus wore good clothes, clothes that many people today might call designer clothes, clothes that were costly and unique to His needs. 6) Jesus was put in a rich man's trust to insure He had a proper burial place—actually, so that He might be buried with the rich. 7) It is Jesus' riches by which God said [God] would supply all your needs (see Philippians 4:19)." Oral Roberts, *How I Learned Jesus Was Not Poor* (Altamonte Springs, FL: Creation House, 1989), 11.

139. "Prosperity Gospel," episode no. 1051, *Religion and Ethics Newsweekly*, August 17, 2007, http://www.pbs.org.

Bishop Jakes's Christology

Jesus Is Not Poor

Jakes argues that the atonement of Christ provides the believer with access to the blessings of God. The believer must first accept a covenant relationship with God and be a good steward of the gifts that God has given him or her. Only then can believers expect God to invest in them and to bless their giftedness. It is God that gives gifts to believers, so that he or she can obtain wealth. Jakes's Christ image and his interpretation of the life of Jesus of Nazareth substantiate his contextual theology of empire and his prosperity worldview.

Jesus is not poor. Jakes says that "Christ's poverty is a religious myth."[140] Jakes provides several interpretations of Scripture as evidence that Jesus was rich and not poor. One interpretation is about the soldiers gambling for Jesus's cloak at the crucifixion. For Jakes, the gambling means that the coat must have been valuable. Therefore, Jesus could not have been poor.[141] He also argues that Jesus was able to comfortably fund a three-year ministry with his disciples.[142] Since Jesus was able to fund a ministry and take care of his disciples, Jesus is not only wealthy but he must be like a business mogul and CEO.[143] More important, Jakes frames the biblical image of ministry to resemble the international ministries of preachers like Jakes.

Jakes's interpretation of Matthew 19:23-24 is exactly like that of prosperity preachers. The text says that "it is easier for a camel to go through the eye of a needle than for a rich man to enter into the kingdom of God." Jakes contends that the "eye of the needle" in the verse refers to "an opening in the wall of Jerusalem sufficiently small that to pass through it, a camel had to get down on its knees."[144]

---

140. Martha Jackson, "Jakes Hiked Long Road to Success," *Charleston Daily Mail*, November 18, 1995.

141. Lee, *T.D. Jakes*, 109.

142. Henry, "Bishop Jakes Is Ready. Are You?"

143. Ibid.

144. Martin, "American Idol," 211.

Jakes sees the story as a lesson on humility: "We have a responsibility, like the camel, to humble ourselves, by giving back to people, by helping people who are less fortunate. I think God doesn't mind you having things; [God] minds things having you."[145] These are just a few examples. Jakes's reframing of Christ as rich is consistent with his reframing of God.

His teachings that present God as the cosmic investment banker and businessman can be found in his book *The Great Investment*. The book is an example of how Jakes takes scriptures and uses them to ideologically manipulate Black Church traditions to fit within the prosperity worldview and the gospel-of-wealth ideology. As a self-help guide on life, business, and family, the book is supposed to teach the believer how to be successful in life. In the preface, Jakes says that he is writing the book as an offering to God. So, he includes a prayer. In the prayer he identifies God as his financial advisor: "I am certain that whatever I have accomplished was simply a matter of Your divine favor. You are the best financial advisor, . . . thanks for giving me tips on stocks, bonds, annuities, people, places, and things. I have profited in every area through knowing You as my Lord."[146] Later in the book, Jakes uses the prosperity scripture of Deuteronomy 8:18 to make his claim that God wants the believer to be prosperous. Jakes says, "God will give you the power to get wealth, but you will have to take the power and get a plan and work the plan to make it happen."[147] Each believer is given "the capacity or means to get wealth. That power is in your will. It is in your talents. It is in your creativity."[148] Moreover, Jakes says that believers are to utilize this power to its fullest. They are encouraged to live beyond their limits. They should not limit themselves; they should aspire to live an affluent and opulent lifestyle. Jakes argues that God "is not offended by opulence or [God] would never have created Heaven with gold streets."[149]

145. Ibid.
146. Jakes, *The Great Investment*, xi.
147. Ibid., 42.
148. Ibid.
149. Ibid., 47.

Committed to proving "that God is not against us being affluent,"[150] Jakes is very much in line with the prosperity worldview that expects a hundredfold blessing from seed-faith giving. It is "through our sacrifice and giving, [that God] honors with a hundredfold return,"[151] writes Jakes. Moreover, he asserts that this hundredfold blessing is not for some day later in heaven. The return from God is for material blessings in the here and now. He says, "This return is not in Heaven; as Jesus plainly promised, a hundredfold return will be gained in this life! Why would I need a hundredfold return in Heaven? I need a return on my investment in this life while recognizing that the greater wealth is still, as [Jesus] so aptly puts it, eternal life. [Jesus] has promised that to those who sacrifice for [Jesus'] divine purpose."[152]

In Jakes's worldview, Christians are encouraged to use seed-faith giving and positive confession to access the divine power that is guaranteed through their covenant relationship. The more wealth that Christians possess, the more they will be able to further the kingdom of God for evangelism. The ultimate goal of wealth is evangelism; therefore, Jakes is careful to stress that the focus should not be just about money or just wealth. Money is simply a tool and a currency that God uses.[153] He often reminds believers, however, that wealth is always supposed to come back to the ministry for evangelism. Moreover, in the prosperity worldview you give *to God* by giving *to ministries*. Jakes elaborates that God wants "godly people" to have money "so that it might flow back to the ministry."[154]

In contrast to some prosperity preachers, Jakes not only encourages Christians to sow into the ministry; he also includes advice on how to invest and save with his prosperity prescriptions:

[God's] covenant is established when we use [God's] provision to bring glory to [God's] name and establish [God's]

---

150. Ibid., 28.
151. Ibid.
152. Ibid., 28.
153. Ibid., 47.
154. Ibid., 48.

Kingdom among the nations. Supporting God's work is why [God] gives us the power to get wealth. But we must also understand that sowing into ministry is only part of the plan. *Investing, saving,* thinking thoughts that are prosperous and progressive—these are the prerequisite for the next move of God.[155]

The God of Jakes's worldview is a businessman who thinks and makes investments like an American CEO on Wall Street.

More important, Jakes's God blesses *only* those individuals who are able to provide a profitable return on an investment. Like any good venture capitalist, God is not going to bless those individuals who are not going to guarantee a financial return. Jakes argues,

> It is your wisdom and ability to handle success that causes God *to invest* in you even more. You have to attain the ability to be a good steward over every opportunity in order to have the good success that God has promised his people. *God is a businessman.* [God] *is not* going to do business with someone who shows no sign of potential return. [God] invests in people who demonstrate an ability to handle what [God] has given them.[156]

The implication is that God rewards those who are able to accumulate more, and the more one accumulates, the more God will bless and give to that person. The converse is implied as well, however. For those who do not accumulate more wealth—those who have not been financially successful—God will not reward them with wealth. In other words, individuals who are not wealthy have not received God's reward because they show no sign for a potential return, or because they have not demonstrated to God that they can handle the wealth.

The believer must give tithes and offerings to ensure their access to divine power. Jakes says that the tithe is the "key to releasing the

---

155. Ibid. [emphasis mine].
156. Ibid., 60 [emphasis mine].

blessings of God in our life."[157] The tithe is defined as "ten percent of our gross income given to support the work of the local church." Jakes's position is no different from that of many prosperity preachers; he argues that "the tithe is seed planted into the kingdom of God, and just like investments in the stock market, it will produce a harvest. The harvest may come soon or it may come later, but God will release blessing to those who faithfully, obediently, and generously give."[158] For the poor, or anyone for whom giving 10 percent of their gross income might be difficult or a sacrifice, Jakes says not to worry. They may not see their reward right away: "You may not see a check in the mail on Monday to compensate for the money you placed in the offering plate on Sunday, but in time you will see [God's] blessing."[159] Nonetheless, Jakes expects them to keep tithing and to keep looking for their return. Ultimately, tithing and sacrificial giving is so fundamental to the prosperity worldview and to Jakes's theological system that it is also the ideological backdrop for how Jakes interprets the Exodus narrative.

Bishop Jakes as Theologian of Liberation

Exodus and the Promised Land

Images of Exodus and the Promised Land have been vital to Black Church identity and the theme of liberation. In his earlier writings, James Cone used the Exodus story to argue that God is on the side of the oppressed. Martin Luther King also interprets the Exodus story as God leading the people of Israel out of their bondage, but leading them as a community, not just as individuals. Pharaoh and Egypt, in Cone's and King's interpretations, represent systems of oppression. Jakes's interpretation of the Exodus narrative is quite different.

Bishop Jakes's version of the story is about individual and personal salvation. The main focus is on financial freedom and liberation. More important, the entire narrative is interpreted in the

---

157. Ibid., 73.
158. Ibid., 74.
159. Ibid.

language of *economic dependency*, which is a familiar ideological trope used to justify the gospel-of-wealth ideology. Bishop Jakes writes, "I believe that one of the most damaging traits that subverts and impedes the progress of many people is dependency on others."[160] In his interpretation of the Exodus story, God had "to wean [the people of Israel] from the breast milk of dependency to the strong nutrition of self-reliance, and greater God reliance."[161] Furthermore, he contends,

> Israel had a right to the wealth of Egypt. . . . There is no other way to interpret this Exodus passage than to see that God was paying Israel back for her years of uncompensated labor and for the faithfulness of her father Joseph as a tithe of blessing to the Egyptian people. Joseph faithfully served God's purpose, as did the Israelites for four hundred years, and the spoils of Egypt were the interest accrued from years of dedicated living.[162]

Jakes's interpretation is ideologically consistent with the supposed redistribution of wealth promoted by prosperity preachers who claim that the wealth of the wicked is laid up for the righteous.[163] Whereas liberation theologians argue for liberation that eliminates communal and systemic oppression (gender, race, and class), Jakes, in contrast, argues for liberation that focuses only on financial and material oppression.

Additionally, in Jakes's interpretation, Joseph symbolically represents the sacrificial tithe. Joseph, as a character in the Exodus story, is sold into slavery by his brothers, falsely accused by Potiphar's wife, and then imprisoned.[164] The systemic oppression of the Israelites by the Egyptians is also interpreted as a *voluntary* sacrificial gift. The God in Jakes's theological worldview is a cosmic venture capitalist

---

160. Ibid., 33-34.
161. Ibid., 34.
162. Ibid., 75.
163. Ibid., 11-12.
164. Ibid.

and investment banker; this God must now return to Israel a financial return with accrued interest.

Jakes correlates the Exodus story with three levels of economic striving: *not enough, just enough,* and *more than enough.* He says, "There are stages of success. No one achieves success without going through these stages."[165] Jakes adds, "When the people of Israel were living in Egypt, they were depending on Pharaoh. [Pharaoh] gave them not enough. . . . God delivered them from scarcity. [God] led them out of Egypt, through the Red Sea, and through the wilderness, and for forty years they depended on God. . . . [God] delivered them to the wilderness and delivered them from *not enough.*"[166] The second level is when "[God] delivered them through the wilderness and delivered them to *just enough.*"[167] There is a divine purpose, according to Jakes, for the just-enough stage. He says that we have to experience this stage so that God may "determine if we have the will and tenacity to go on to the final stage of success and rest comfortably in the stage of *'more than enough.'"*[168]

According to Jakes, Christians, who are supposed to be on their individual journeys, will be led by God in the same way that God led Israel to its final destination: "[God] delivered them [Israel] from the wilderness and delivered them to more than enough." Therefore, the conclusion is that Christians should expect that their final destination will be like that of Israel: "[God] gives us the power to have 'more than enough.' . . . God wants you to have more than enough. [God] wants you to be financially independent. [God] wants you to use your faith to unlock your finances."[169]

Bishop Jakes's interpretation of the Exodus passage is a perfect example of how stories, Scripture, and rituals are revamped by prosperity preachers to resonate with the economic realities of advanced capitalism. Thus, God is not the same liberator as the God of black liberation theology. Jakes takes the historic Exodus narrative, the

---

165. Ibid., 35.
166. Ibid., 35-36.
167. Ibid.
168. Ibid., 36 [emphasis mine].
169. Ibid., 37.

key characters and places (the people of Israel, Exodus, Egypt, Pharaoh, and Joseph), and transforms the entire story from one of black liberation into one of *economic investment* and *return*. More important, his use of the story affirms the prosperity religious practices of tithing, seed-faith giving, and an endorsement of the constant pursuit of wealth.

In the prosperity worldview, Christians have a God-given right to the wealth of the wicked. Therefore, in Jakes's interpretation, the people of Israel have a right to the wealth of the Egyptians. Israel, like the individual believer, receives a promise (the Abrahamic covenant), makes a financial investment or tithe, and is rewarded with the wealth of Egypt. Israel (and the individual believer) receives a return on its investment. Jakes echoes the same ideological position of Word of Faith: "When God makes a promise, [God] keeps [God's] word. However, it is often required that we lay hold on the promise by acting on it in an aggressive way. . . . The miracle begins when we remove the training wheels of dependency on others."[170] The story is shared with the ideology of a very familiar trope in American neoliberal political discourse—the rhetoric of *dependency*.

Dependency is a familiar trope in American discourse about the deserving poor and welfare reform. The term "carries strong emotive and visual associations and a powerful pejorative charge. In current debates, the expression 'welfare dependency' evokes the image of the welfare mother, often figured as a young, unmarried black woman (perhaps even a teenager) of uncontrolled sexuality."[171] The gospel-of-wealth rhetoric about dependency often makes the welfare queen the main perpetrator in its neo-liberal discourse. Jakes's version of the Exodus story is ideologically consistent with the neo-liberal gospel-of-wealth rhetoric, which says that we should *not* provide safety nets for the poor, because doing so will only create a culture of dependency.[172] Jakes's interpretation, like much of his contextual

---

170. Ibid., 37.

171. Nancy Fraser and Linda Gordon, "A Genealogy of Dependency: Tracing a Keyword of the U.S. Welfare State," *Signs* 19, no. 2 (Winter 1994): 311.

172. Norton Garfinkle, *The American Dream vs. The Gospel of Wealth: The*

theology, indirectly blames the poor for needing help and celebrates individuals who are financially independent.

The most disappointing aspect of Jakes's interpretation of the Exodus narrative is not only that it has been reframed into a story of individual economic salvation. The real tragedy is that by suggesting that Joseph and the four hundred years of oppression was a tithe and a sacrifice, Jakes places God *not* on the side of the oppressed but on the side of the oppressors and empire. "God is weaning them from the breast milk of dependency to the strong nutrition of self-reliance, and greater God reliance."[173] God, as the cosmic investment banker, requires the oppression of Israel as a gift in the heavenly gift economy. Then this God rewards the people of Israel by essentially making them into oppressors, who now must claim the wealth of their oppressors. This is a normal refrain for the extremists of prosperity preachers; God intends for God's people to take the wealth from those who are not Christian. Only Christians have God's favor as the "chosen" and "anointed."

Although Jakes works hard *not* to align himself with the extremists of Word of Faith preachers, ideologically he privileges the same tropes of empire, with the CEO/rich entrepreneur as the model of economic and spiritual success. His worldview and interpretation encourage congregants to believe that anyone who is still in an economically oppressive situation—the not enough or the just enough—is not where Jakes's capitalist God expects them to be. "Financial success will come only to those who take what they have been given and invest it, plant it in good soil in hopes of a good harvest."[174] In Jakes's theology of empire and the prosperity worldview, there is no room for the losers or victims of capitalism. Only winners are welcomed—only those who are financially independent and are financial winners in the global marketplace. These believers have arrived; they have made it to their final destination—the Promised Land. God has blessed them because they are worthy of

173. Jakes, *The Great Investment*, 34.
174. Ibid., 46.

an investment. Only these Christians are blessed to manifest their personal economic destinies and empires.

In sum, Jakes's Christ image and his interpretation of the Exodus story are similar to those of other prosperity preachers. In addition, how he shares his life story as a pastor and entrepreneur is also similar to that of many of the popular preachers on the continuum. Both images are central to the life story and brand of Bishop T.D. Jakes. Jakes may have the businessman Bill Gates and the pastor/humanitarian Mother Teresa competing in his head. However, his theological system, his contextual theology, the prosperity worldview, and his religious practices all suggest that it is Bill Gates and not Mother Teresa who is definitely winning.

4

T.D. Jakes and
the Brands for Women

Woman Thou Art Loosed

Bishop T.D. Jakes, the Sam Walton of the New Black Church, is the case study for this book. Just one brand, WTAL—his most popular brand and the impetus for his success—is the center of our investigation. The success with the WTAL brand is a reflection of the process of Wal-Martization and a mirror into Jakes's relationship with African American women.

As a contemporary academic theologian I combine the roles of researcher and cultural critic to seek answers to my critical questions about the New Black Church, its branding, and theology. How do this theology and branding affect its audience of African American women? How are biblical texts appropriated throughout the brand and its products? What exactly is the "liberation" that Bishop T.D. Jakes is offering to black women?

Preachers like Jakes draw their brands from many aspects of popular culture. However, in order to make the secular acceptable for evangelical and fundamentalist faith, the brand messages are sacralized or Christianized.[1] Through strategic marketing and other rhetorical devices, the preachers often reinterpret traditional texts and

---

1. For an example of how themes are sacralized and Christianized, see Rosalind I. J. Hackett, "Charismatic/Pentecostal Appropriation of Media Technologies in Nigeria and Ghana," *Journal of Religion in Africa* 28, no. 3 (August 1998): 258.

symbols to strengthen and boost the content and messages of their brands. Pastors usually start a brand by focusing on a particular biblical story or theme. Then, through testimony or a series of sermons, they connect the brand's story to their own personal story. In doing so, they brand themselves with the message of the brand. Once the preacher is successfully branded to the story of the brand, the next step is to make the brand's story resonate with the life story of the individual consumer. The brand is marketed in such a way as to meet the spiritual, social, emotional, and psychological needs of the consumer.

Participant observation is an important way for me to examine the phenomenon of the New Black Church. Most academic theologians are unfamiliar with the language and nature of prosperity churches and their brand communities, and the women in these churches are typically unfamiliar with academic black, womanist, and feminist theologies. In fact, they are often suspicious of most academic researchers, especially those attempting to examine something as important as their worship and their faith.[2] Participant observation also ensures that the impact of Jakes as a preacher and theologian are not discussed only from a top-down, minister-only perspective.[3] The perspective of the parishioner/consumer is as important as that of the pastor/CEO to comprehend how black women and parishioners are experiencing the theology of the New Black Church and the many brands.[4] In addition, participation in the brand means using

---

2. Marla Frederick, *Between Sundays: Black Women and Everyday Struggles of Faith* (Berkeley, CA: University of California Press, 2003), 18-23.

3. For a discussion about the limitations of earlier research on black churches, see Daphne Wiggins, *Righteous Content: Black Women's Perspectives of Church and Faith* (New York: New York University Press, 2005), 6.

4. I recognize that certain limitations exist with my method. Conducting interviews with women of the faith community would have also been a valuable methodology. However, because of my insider status in these prosperity faith communities as a preacher and congregant, I see myself as an insider. Furthermore, because of the space limitations of this project and the limited research on theologies of prosperity, I decided not to conduct interviews with individual women. I did attempt to interview T.D. Jakes. Wanting to interview Jakes was not simply a result of my decision to use the biography-as-

the products and sharing in the worship services in order to witness the social construction of religious identity, and to experience the ideological impact of the branding.

African American women are Jakes's target audience for the WTAL brand. As a group, African American women face an *intersectionality* of oppressions (race, gender, and class) within the matrix of domination.[5] As a result, they have also been marginalized and historically silenced within most academic discourses.[6] And yet African American women are not only Jakes's parishioners, customers, and ministry partners;[7] several women have been critical to his success. For instance, Sarah Jordan Powell, an African American woman, strategically introduced Jakes to the then-power broker for black Pentecostalism, Carlton Pearson.[8] Pearson's 1993 Azusa Conference is where Jakes received his first national exposure,[9] and Pearson shared Jakes's sermon with Paul Crouch of the Trinity Broadcasting Network (TBN).[10]

---

theology methodology. I wanted an interview with the preacher so that the voice of the preacher/pastor/CEO would be included. More important, as a scholar, I would be more likely to present a fair critique. However, even with several attempts, Bishop Jakes declined. I am not the only scholar to have been refused an interview by Jakes. Whereas T.D. Jakes is always doing interviews with the popular press and media, he does not provide the same access to scholars. I can only assume that the critical questions of the scholar do not help with the promotion of his many brands and products.

5. Kimberlé Williams Crenshaw, "Mapping the Margins: Intersectionality, Identity Politics, and Violence Against Women of Color," *Stanford Law Review* 43, no. 6 (July 1991): 1241-99.

6. Wiggins, *Righteous Content*, 6.

7. Johnnetta Cole and Beverly Guy-Sheftall, *Gender Talk: The Struggle for Women's Equality in African American Communities* (New York: One World/ Ballantine Books, 2003), 125.

8. Jonathan L. Walton, *Watch This! The Ethics and Aesthetics of Black Televangelism* (New York: New York University, 2009), 105; Sarah Posner, *God's Profits: Faith, Fraud, and the Republican Crusade for Values Voters* (Sausalito, CA: PoliPoint Press, 2008), 54.

9. Shayne Lee, *T.D. Jakes: America's New Preacher* (New York: New York University Press, 2005), 67; Walton, *Watch This!*, 106.

10. Shayne Lee and Phillip Luke Sinitiere, *Holy Mavericks: Evangelical*

For the women who attend the conferences and send monthly gifts to T.D. Jakes Ministries, their time, talents, and gifts (spiritual and financial) are exchanged ultimately in what they consider to be a spiritual or faith realm—a kind of divine-gift economy. Their religious practices such as prayer and tithing are gifts given in an exchange between themselves, their God, and their pastors.[11] As with other faithful Christians, "their gifts of money, like their gifts of words or habits, do not go to any man or ministry, but instead go directly to God and represent obedience to [God]."[12] The New Black Church is where they exercise their individual agency,[13] and where they feel they have access to a divine power that empowers them. What is often overlooked with theologies of prosperity is the underlying requirement that believers "bless others." Being in the position to be the donor, as opposed to just the recipient of charity, Frederick posits, transforms "would-be victims into victors, the needy into benefactors.[14] "It is through their gifts (offering, prayer, and praise) that they claim a power not only to liberate themselves but also to liberate others. As Loosed Women their gifts provide them the opportunity to evangelize and exercise power over Satan, "the wicked," and others.[15] In many cases, the financial exchange of a tithe or sacrificial offering as a special gift is expected to unleash a power that even obligates God to act on their behalf.

Innovators and the Spiritual Marketplace (New York: New York University Press, 2009), 64.

11. Susan Friend Harding, *The Book of Jerry Falwell: Fundamentalist Language and Politics* (Princeton, NJ: Princeton University, 2000), 122.

12. Ibid.

13. For an example of how women exercise personal power and agency, see Milmon F. Harrison's discussion of a woman named Cassandra in *Righteous Riches: The Word of Faith Movement in Contemporary African American Religion* (New York: Oxford Press, 2005), 27.

14. Marla Frederick, *Colored Television: American Religion Gone Global* (Stanford, CA: Stanford University Press, 2016), 84.

15. "The wealth of the wicked is laid up for the righteous." Proverbs 13:22b KJV is one of the many scriptures often cited by New Black Church pastors as an example of how women exercise their power to gain wealth.

Woman Thou Art Loosed (WTAL)—the Brand

Bishop Jakes with his sermons, books, films, and music has thousands of items available to use for research to evaluate the brand and its underlying theology. As much as possible, I chose the products and the religious experiences of the average congregant or consumer. The products and events of the WTAL brand for this investigation include the 1993 sermon at the Azusa Conference, the 1993 nonfiction book, the 2004 WTAL movie with screenplay, and the 2009 WTAL Conference at The Potter's House.[16]

The 1993 Azusa sermon marks the beginning of the brand, and the sermon is an example of the products and events that were sold during the early years of Jakes's ministry. The 1993 nonfiction book is the first major revenue-generating product,[17] as well as the first of many books that Jakes would later author. Jakes often references the nonfiction book as an example of when God gave him the power to get wealth.[18] The 2004 WTAL film is an example of the rhetorical and story-telling power of film. The film has given T.D. Jakes his greatest exposure as a celebrity preacher and CEO. The success of the film was leveraged for the deal with Sony Pictures. Finally, the 2009 WTAL Conference is critical because one cannot really experience or comprehend the WTAL brand without attending a live conference. At the peak performances of the brand, the annual conferences had over 50,000 women. The success of WTAL also helped launch other brands and national conferences such as ManPower,[19]

---

16. While Jakes produces music at each conference, and music is important to the brand, I did not include any music in my investigation because I did not feel qualified to do so. I had quite a few WTAL products with sermons, books, articles, and the movie.

17. Lee, *T.D. Jakes*, 67-68.

18. T.D. Jakes, *The Great Investment: Faith, Family, and Finance* (New York: G. P. Putnam's Sons, 2000), 43-44.

19. Deborah Kovach Caldwell, "The Power at The Potter's House," *Dallas Morning News*, July 5, 1997, home final edition.

God's Leading Lady,[20] and MegaFest.[21] Later WTAL conferences were featured along with Megafest. The conferences and the women who participate are now identified as the WTAL movement.[22]

The conferences also act as an international platform to launch the ministries of other prosperity preachers and new brands.[23] Many scholars do not think that the women who buy the brand are making agentive decisions about their own lives. From my research and also from the statements from black women who follow Jakes, interviewed by Marla Frederick, one can conclude that the women consider the teaching of T.D. Jakes and preachers like him to be "liberating them from destructive and abusive relationships, low self-esteem, and financial instability."[24] Frederick actually describes what the women experience as a "subversive, even feminist discourse that confronts the conundrums of their personal lives."[25] She writes that the women "come to respect themselves more deeply and to demand respect from men."[26]

To ignore the voices of the women who follow T.D. Jakes and other preachers in the New Black Church, and to assume that the women are not making decisions about their lives, gives T.D. Jakes and these preachers too much power. In other words, it too easily reinscribes the preachers and T.D. Jakes as *powerful*, and the women

---

20. T.D. Jakes, *God's Leading Lady: Out of the Shadows and into the Light* (New York: G. P. Putnam's Sons, 2002).

21. Megafest is an international conference/festival that included several of Jakes's conferences in one location at one time. The conference was first held in 2004 in Atlanta, GA. The festival met for several years. Jakes then cancelled the festival in 2007. He changed the brand to Megafest International, and in 2008 MegaFest International was held in South Africa. Oprah filmed her show from the 2013 Megafest in Dallas. Information is available at http://www.megafest.org.

22. See "Woman Thou Art Loosed," http://wtalmovement.org.

23. Lee, *T.D. Jakes*, 107.

24. Marla Frederick-McGlathery, "But It's Bible: African American Women and Television Preachers," in *Women and Religion in the African Diaspora: Knowledge, Power, and Performance,* ed. Ruth Marie Griffith and Barbara Dianne Savage (Baltimore, MD: Johns Hopkins University Press, 2006), 277.

25. Ibid.

26. Ibid.

as *powerless*.[27] Many layers exist in understanding the ideology and power of the brand. One aspect often missed is how the brand provides respectability to women. A closer examination of the many layers of the brand is needed to explain why most academic scholars and the congregants that follow Jakes have such diverse reactions to his ministry and theology.

WTAL and Respectability in the Second Gilded Age

Contemporary African American women who attend the WTAL conferences are also participating in discourses of respectability.[28] Higginbotham's book *Righteous Discontent* is one of the few scholarly projects that specifically explores the lives of women in the Black Church. She coined the concept of "the politics of respectability" to describe their "opposition to the social structures and symbolic representations of white supremacy."[29] In a parallel phenomenon, Darlene Hine has described what she calls "a culture of dissemblance." In order for African American women to seek justice and protect themselves from the oppression of rape and other intimate violations, they have often silenced themselves and "created the appearance of openness and disclosure but actually shielded the truth of their inner lives and selves from their oppressors."[30] Womanist ethicist Katie

---

27. For a discussion on reinscribing power to the powerful, see James C. Scott, *Domination and the Arts of Resistance: Hidden Transcripts* (New Haven, CT: Yale University Press, 1990), 4-5.

28. For a discussion on contemporary black women and the politics of respectability, see Frederick, *Colored Television*, 90-92; Ayana Weekley, "Why Can't We Flip the Script: The Politics of Respectability in Pearl Cleage's What Looks Like Crazy on an Ordinary Day," *Michigan Feminist Studies* 21, no. 1 (Fall 2008): 24-42. Also see Elsa Barkley Brown, "What has Happened Here: The Politics of Difference in Women's History and Feminist Politics," *Feminist Studies* 18, no. 2 (Summer 1992): 295-312.

29. Evelyn Brooks Higginbotham, *Righteous Discontent: The Women's Movement in the Black Baptist Church, 1880–1920* (Cambridge, MA: Harvard University Press, 1993), 186.

30. Darlene Clarke Hine, "Rape and the Inner Lives of Black Women in the Middle West," *Signs* 14, no. 4 (Summer 1989): 912.

Cannon highlights how similar practices also take place in black churches. African American churchwomen live "between the razor-blade tensions of heteronormativity and hypersexuality." Cannon asserts that as a defensive "survivalist strategy,"[31] with the hopes of combatting "negative stereotypes," women have used the politics of respectability and "socially conservative, circumscribed notions of super-morality." Simply put, "claiming respectability through manners and morality furnish[es] an avenue for African Americans to assert their will and agency to redefine themselves outside the prevailing racist [and sexist] discourses."[32]

According to Higginbotham, black women have appealed to the politics of respectability because they were always "ever-cognizant of the gaze of white America, which in panoptic fashion focus[es] perpetually upon each and every black person and record[s] his or her transgressions in an overall accounting of black inferiority."[33] She asserts, however, that "it was in the church, more than any other institution, where black women of all ages and classes found a site for 'signifying practice'—for coming into their own voice."[34] The church is where black women assert "agency in the construction and representation of themselves as new subjectivities—as Americans as well as blacks and women."[35]

The majority of New Black Churches emerged during the 1980s and 1990s. This period is described as "rich with struggles, debates, and transformations in race relations, electronic media, cultural

31. Katie G. Cannon, "Sexing Black Women: Liberation from the Prisonhouse of Anatomical Authority," in *Loving the Body: Black Religious Studies and the Erotic*, ed. Anthony Pinn and Dwight Hopkins (New York: Palgrave Macmillan, 2004), 12.

32. Kali N. Gross, "Examining the Politics of Respectability in African American Studies," in *Almanac* 43 no. 28, http:// www.upenn.edu.

33. Higginbotham, *Righteous Discontent*, 196.

34. I am not suggesting that black women and churches have not changed since the early nineteenth and twentieth centuries, but I am inferring that for black women the church more than any other institution of power is still considered a safe space for self-representation.

35. Higginbotham, *Righteous Discontent*, 186.

politics and economic life."[36] Black identity was politically inscribed through several tropes. The policy makers associated black identity with "welfare queens, drug dealers, criminals, school dropouts, teenage pregnancy, and single-mother households to justify as assault upon the liberal welfare establishment."[37] Many people did not see this discourse as "ostensibly racist" because television shows and other media often presented several images of black achievement.[38] The truth, however, is that "the harsh realities of the Reagan era economic policies for the nation's most vulnerable were very different from what was being portrayed of American life by the mass entertainment media."[39] In the First Gilded Age, the black Baptist women of 1880–1920 whom Higginbotham studied were responding to what French theorist Michel Foucault defines as the *technologies of power*.[40] In the Second Gilded Age (1980s and 1990s),[41] black women did not control the technologies of power, and like their foremothers they had to respond to the same kind of negative stereotypes and sexual images.

The brand of WTAL is an attempt to counter the many negative tropes and identities presented by the majority culture. The tropes of the 1980s that described black women as welfare queens, teenage mothers, and single mothers are gendered inscriptions that placed

---

36. Kevin Phillips, *The Politics of Rich and Poor: Wealth and the American Electorate in the Reagan Aftermath* (New York: Random House, 1990).

37. Herman Gray, *Watching Race: Television and the Struggle for Blackness* (Minneapolis: University of Minnesota Press, 1995), 2.

38. Michael Battle, *The Black Church in America: African American Spirituality* (Malden, MA: Blackwell Publishing, 2006), 25.

39. Harrison, *Righteous Riches*, 150.

40. Higginbotham uses Foucault's term "technologies of power." She describes "the technologies of power at the everyday level—films, newspapers, school textbooks." See *Righteous Discontent*, 189. Also see Michel Foucault, *Discipline and Punish: The Birth of the Prison*, trans. Alan Sheridan (New York: Vintage Books, 1977).

41. Gray, *Watching Race*, 28. Also see Janet R. Nelson, "Walter Rauschenbusch and the Social Gospel: A Hopeful Theology for the Twenty-First Century Economy," *Crosscurrents* 59, no. 4 (December 2009): 455n6.

the majority of the blame for America's ills on the backs and bodies of black women. Vivyan Adair explains that welfare queen or

> stories of the welfare mother intersect with, draw from, reify, and reproduce myriad mythic American narratives associated with a constellation of beliefs about capitalism, male authority, the "nature" of humans, and the sphere of human freedom, opportunity, and responsibility. These narratives purport to write the story of poor women in an arena in which only their bodies have been positioned to "speak."[42]

T.D. Jakes received his first national exposure and introduced the WTAL brand with these policies and images in place. Thousands of black women around the country began to attend his conferences and buy his products. Instead of being labeled as welfare queens, black women were now Loosed Women. The women-only gatherings of WTAL were for many women a reprieve from their more oppressive home churches.[43] The women who attend the conferences, purchase the products, and watch Jakes on television see these religious meetings as redemptive, and a place where they can safely heal their deepest hurts.[44] The social influence of black churches is not as widespread as it was in the segregated America of the late-nineteenth and early-twentieth century. Black churches, however, still influence normative values of respectable and nonrespectable behavior.[45] The church, for many women, is still the safest gathering place for black churchwomen to construct identity and to create new subjectivities that counter racist stereotypes and negative sexual images.

At the all-women conferences they are *not* presented as victims, nor are they positioned as the cause of all of society's ills. Instead, they are encouraged to reach for all the privileges supposedly afforded to them by the American Dream—a dream sanctioned by a God who answers prayers, if only they live right by giving their offerings, pray-

---

42. Vivyan C. Adair, "Branded with Infamy: Inscriptions of Poverty and Class in the United States," *Signs* 27, no. 2 (Winter 2002): 455.

43. Frederick-McGlathery, "But It's Bible," 280.

44. Frederick, *Colored Television*, 103-7.

45. Ibid., 112-14.

ing correctly, and believing. Furthermore, Jakes becomes the celebrity and prototype who confirms that success is possible.

Many black churches do not allow women to pastor or participate in leadership positions. Jakes, in contrast, strategically employs women preachers as keynote speakers. Thus, the WTAL brand, with its products and worship experiences, provides an opportunity for women to experience other women in positions of power. This is not to suggest that the messages preached or heard by the women in the pews transcend traditional patriarchal and submissive roles.[46] However, scholars who label these women only as victims and passive participants or reduce their participation to a form of false consciousness miss the power and the everyday forms of resistance experienced both by the women preachers and the conference participants.

1993 Live at Azusa WTAL Sermon

Bishop Jakes's power as a preacher, the effectiveness of the brand, and his relationship with African American women are evident from the very first sermon at Azusa. I was able to secure a VHS version of the 1993 Azusa sermon. Captured on the videotape are the women enthralled with the worship experience. The power of Bishop Jakes's sermon is apparent in the cathartic response of the thousands of women assembled at his appearance there. The Sunday School class that Jakes taught in West Virginia and the subsequent sermon that he preached at Carlton Pearson's 1993 Azusa conference mark the origin of the brand.

The Azusa Conference was held at the Mabee Center at Oral Roberts University in Tulsa, Oklahoma.[47] The videotape begins with an introduction (obviously added later) by T.D. Jakes and highlights the promises he makes to the women consumers who purchase the video. The introduction illustrates how Jakes informs viewers about

---

46. See Victor Anderson, *Creative Exchange: A Constructive Theology of African American Religious Experience* (Minneapolis: Fortress Press, 2008), 158; Marcia Riggs, *Plenty Good Room: Women versus Male Power in the Black Church* (Cleveland, OH: Pilgrim Press, 2003), 80.

47. T.D. Jakes, *Woman Thou Art Loosed: Live at Azusa,* VHS (1993; Dallas, TX: T.D. Jakes Ministries, 1998).

Figure 5. T.D. Jakes preaching the WTAL sermon at 1993 Azusa Conference at Mabee Center on the campus of Oral Roberts University and the cover for the VHS *Woman Thou Art Loosed: Live at Azusa.*

what they can expect, and how to participate in the religious experience. More important, the introduction shows how Jakes's early products and events were marketed:

> Jesus is speaking and healing women all over the country just as he did in the Bible. He saw a woman who was lost in the crowd who was wounded and twisted and fragmented, had been through eighteen years of adversity that had left her a mere shadow of what she could have been. He saw her and called her. He spoke to her and he said "Woman, thou art loosed!" He spoke to her femininity. He spoke to her self-esteem. He spoke to the rose in her, the silk in her—the lace in her. He spoke to all of her dreams and all of her hopes and all of her goals, and when he loosed her he loosed everything around her. Get ready for a word from God that's going to change everything in your life as he speaks to the silky issues in your life and touches you in your femininity. Jesus said "Woman, thou art loosed!" Get ready for a miracle![48]

48. *Woman Thou Art Loosed: Live at Azusa.*

Prosperity preachers often make promises to their congregants about the power or "anointing" present in their branded products. The Azusa sermon is the first of many in the overall brand. Every time Jakes preaches to women at WTAL he is adding to the overall brand. The gendered language is evident with calls to her femininity, the rose, the silk, the lace in her. Moreover, the product informs the consumer and worshiper that she will get a word from God that's going to change everything. She simply has to get ready for a miracle.

Following the introduction, the worship service begins. The video shows several thousand women participating in worship at the Azusa Conference. Those familiar with Jakes's later appearances cannot fail to observe the obvious differences in Jakes's early aesthetic. In the video Jakes is wearing an ill-fitting, purple, off-the-rack gabardine suit and purple loafers—a signal of his humble beginnings. He has an unstylish haircut, gold-plated watch, and inexpensive cuff links—all in strong contrast to the tailored suits he now wears. The majority of the women are dressed in white. An insider would immediately recognize that both the fashions of Jakes and the women are hints of a black Pentecostal holiness tradition. The white dresses are worn by the women as one aspect of the politics of respectability and as an outward symbol of holiness, while Jakes's off-the-rack purple suit is a marker of the bishop's poor country roots.

The holiness tradition and the ecstatic worship of Pentecostals have not always been celebrated by other denominations. Carlton Pearson asserts that Jakes "makes Pentecostalism pretty," [49] and that his ability to do so is part of the reason he has been so successful. The video is a reminder that Jakes changes his attire and his physical appearance as his brand changes, especially because he wants to reach broader audiences beyond his Pentecostal roots. New Black Church pastors, and Jakes included, now wear expensive suits in an attempt to look like and perform the trope of CEO. In 1993, Jakes had not yet retained consultants like Larry Ross of A. Larry Ross Communications. Ross also works with clients such as Rick Warren

---

49. Sarah Posner, *God's Profits*, 58.

and Billy Graham.[50] He was responsible for helping Jakes cross over to secular audiences by getting him a front-page article in the *Wall Street Journal.*[51]

Jakes seeks credibility beyond the poverty of West Virginia and the boundaries of traditional Pentecostalism. Higginbotham reminds us that respectability is always "a process, a dialogue with oneself and with one's fellows, never a fixed position."[52] The dialogue and process are determined by the group or people to whom one wishes to appear respectable. In general, Iris Marion Young adds that "the norms of respectability in our society are associated specifically with professional culture. Professional dress, speech, tastes, and demeanor all connote respectability."[53] What this means is that the women are not the only ones performing respectability. Jakes also participates in a politics of respectability. With attention to his branding, Jakes has remade himself to fit the culture of the larger cross-over audiences. He has intentionally removed as many of those class signifiers as possible. Walton affirms that "[Jakes's] personal aesthetic has become more conservative in recent years as he has traded in the purple and canary-yellow suits for navy blue, black, and gray."[54] It is obvious that like many prosperity preachers, Jakes has not only remade and repackaged his brands, he has also remade himself.

Not only is the aesthetic noticeable in the video of Azusa in 1993, before Jakes preaches the sermon, the video provides a glimpse of how Jakes prepares women for his preaching. With many of the women already in tears, Jakes, in a baritone voice and sympathetic tone, invites the women to openly share their hurts and struggles:

---

50. Strawberry Saroyan, "Christianity, the Brand," *The New York Times Magazine,* April 16, 2006, http://www.nytimes.com.

51. Ibid.

52. Brian Harrison, *Peaceable Kingdom: Stability and Change in Modern Britain* (New York: Oxford University Press, 1982), 161, quoted in Lee and Sinitiere, *Holy Mavericks,* 67; Walton, *Watch This!,* 195.

53. Iris Marion Young, *Justice and the Politics of Difference* (Princeton, NJ: Princeton University Press, 1990), 57.

54. Walton, *Watch This!,* 117.

Spirit of the living God, breath in this place. Release an anointing because somebody in this room is in trouble. Somebody's Mama is in trouble. Somebody's wife is in trouble. Some mother of the church, some first lady is in trouble; encumbered with duties and responsibilities. Functioning like a robot but bleeding like a wounded dog . . . that the Spirit of the Lord God would permeate this place and resurrect our evangelists and our missionaries and our ministers and raise up Mamas and raise up wives and raise up our sisters that have been slain by circumstances. I pray in the name of Jesus that the Holy Spirit would release a glory in this place.[55]

Jakes positions himself as the male preacher who understands the suffering of women. "Somebody's Mama is in trouble." He speaks as the one with power from God to change their lives so that they might be resurrected to their vocational destinies as missionaries and ministers. After the initial prayer, he then reads the famous WTAL biblical text in Luke. Jakes preaches for almost an hour. At the close of the sermon he speaks to the women now standing and fully invested in ecstatic worship and praise. Many are shouting and some are prostrate at the altar. Jakes closes with his declaration to the women at Oral Roberts University and perhaps those watching the video:

Many thousands of women are going to be loosed in this place today. You're going to be loosed today. Suicide is going to be loosed from you today. Spirits of depression are going to be loosed from you today. Homosexuality is going to be loosed from you today. Right women in wrong relationships is going to be loosed today.[56]

Through the power of God by the Holy Spirit, Jakes declares to

55. *Woman Thou Art Loosed, Live at Azusa*. See Lee, *T.D. Jakes*, 58.

56. *Woman Thou Art Loosed, Live at Azusa*. Also see Frederick, *Between Sundays*, 163, for her rendering of the same passage.

the women that they are *loosed*. He is able to loose them with his positive confession. Furthermore, like many Pentecostal, charismatic, and Word of Faith preachers, Jakes is also able to loose demonic spirits, homosexuality, and wrong relationships. Jakes affirms for the women that, "When you get loosed, everything in your house is going to get loosed."[57]

The *Woman Thou Art Loosed* Nonfiction Book

The product that Jakes says launched the brand and the start of his empire is the nonfiction book *Woman Thou Art Loosed,* published by Treasure House, an imprint of Destiny Image. As Jakes says, "Years ago, God dropped an idea for a women's Bible class in my heart. That idea grew and became a book, a conference, a play and a music CD."[58] Jakes cites God as the source of his success. God may have generated the idea; yet, Jakes also highlights his own expertise as an exceptional individual. "I am successful because I see and understand the capacity God has given me."[59] Additionally, Jakes credits the book as launching his career as a writer[60] and providing the revenue to purchase his mansion in Charleston.

One of the reasons that the brand has been so successful is because Jakes interprets the biblical story of the infirmed woman to suggest that Jesus is the great physician and healer. "The Holy Spirit periodically lets us catch a glimpse of the personal testimony of one of the patients of the Divine Physician Himself. . . . There are three major characters in this story. These characters are the person, the problem and the prescription."[61] The story is interpreted not only to be about physical healing but also healing from all emotional and spiritual issues. As a result, the WTAL brand is able to encompass a wide

---

57. *Woman Thou Art Loosed: Live at Azusa.*
58. T.D. Jakes, *The Great Investment,* 44.
59. Ibid.
60. Lee, *T.D. Jakes,* 106.
61. T.D. Jakes, *Woman Thou Art Loosed: Healing the Wounds of the Past* (Shippensburg, PA: Treasure House, 1993), 1.

Figure 6. The first edition of Bishop Jakes's self-published book *Woman Thou Art Loosed: Healing the Wounds of the Past*. The book was published by Destiny Image but has gone through several different versions with various publishers.

range of products and events that speak to the physical, psychological, and emotional healing of women.

Jakes presents himself as an expert who sympathizes with, and understands, the problems of women. Moreover, the women feel that he has *real* solutions to their *real* problems. Jakes writes that counseling may not be the ideal solution for women in need of healing: "What I want to make clear is that after you have analyzed the condition, after you have understood its origin, it will still take the authority of God's Word to put the past under your feet!"[62] Similar to other prosperity preachers, Jakes is not an advocate for women to seek professional counseling. Instead, he points them to the Bible; all of life's solutions are in God's Word. For Jakes, natural problems are ultimately spiritual problems: "I realize that these are natural problems [child abuse, rape, wife abuse, or divorce], but they are rooted in spiritual ailments."[63]

Excerpts from the book demonstrate that the WTAL brand is about spiritual healing and spiritual infirmities. However, Jakes also includes prescriptions for his version of liberation. These prescriptions support my argument that, for his congregants, Jakes speaks as

---

62. Jakes, *Woman Thou Art Loosed: Healing the Wounds*, 2.
63. Ibid., 5.

a contemporary theologian of liberation. In other words, T.D. Jakes perceives loosing women as an act of liberation. Surprisingly, especially for academic liberation theologians, Jakes writes about oppression in terms of race, gender, and class:

> Jesus simply shared grace and truth with that hurting woman. He said, "Woman thou art loosed." Believe the Word of God and be free. Jesus our Lord was a great *emancipator of the oppressed* [emphasis mine]. It does not matter whether someone has been oppressed socially, sexually, or racially; our Lord is eliminator of distinctions. . . .
>
> It is wonderful to teach prosperity as long as it is understood that the Church is not an elite organization for spiritual yuppies only, one that excludes other social classes.[64]

Although it is difficult to imagine or place preachers like Jakes in the same vein as other liberationists, the preachers in the New Black Church see themselves as bringing a much-needed message of liberation.

Jakes's type of liberation is modeled after the infirmed woman in Luke. Like the story tied to the brand, other scripture texts are mediated by this norm. For instance, chapter 10 in Jakes's book is entitled "Daughter of Abraham." Included in the chapter is the story of the daughters of Zelophehad (Numbers 27:1-3). Biblical characters from a different text are interpreted as women who are no different from the infirmed woman in Luke, and by extension, they are no different from the women of the WTAL brand community. Jakes's use of the story illustrates how the brand is what theologians identify as the theological norm. A theological norm is the concept or criterion that *judges* all biblical scriptures, books, and sermons for a particular theology. In other words, the biblical passage in the Gospel of Luke is interpreted to fit the brand, the prosperity worldview, and the related practices of seed-faith and positive confession. Jakes writes,

> Like the infirmed woman, you are a daughter of Abraham if you have faith. . . . Why should you sit there and be in

---

64. Ibid., 11-12.

need when your Father has left you everything? Your Father is rich, and He left everything to you. . . . There is no need to sit around waiting on someone else to get what is yours. Nobody else is coming. The One who needed to come has already come. Jesus said, "I am come that they might have life, and that they might have it more abundantly" (John 10:10b). That is all you need.[65]

The identification with Abraham is a reference to the Abrahamic covenant, which prosperity preachers say gives the believer access to God's promises. Furthermore, the suggestion that Jesus has provided everything through the atonement is also a familiar refrain. John 10:10 is a Word of Faith scripture that is often quoted by Word of Faith practitioners. Jakes even encourages women to use positive confession as a means to get wealth. He writes, "The power to get wealth is in your tongue. You shall have whatever you say."[66] He adds,

> When you start speaking correctly, God will give you what you say. You say you want it. Jesus said, "And all things, whatsoever you shall ask in prayer, believing, ye shall receive" (Matt. 21:22). . . . God will give you whatever you ask for (John 14:13). God will give you a business. God will give you a dream. He will make you the head and not the tail (Deut. 28:13).[67]

Through such words the women are encouraged to believe that they can have everything that they ask from God—including a business and a dream.

Jakes uses prosperity scriptures, offers prescriptions for liberation, and directs women to give seed-faith offerings and use positive confession. Ultimately, Jakes performs like the majority of New Black Church pastors, as a theologian of prosperity. In other words, the nonfiction book, along with other products within the brand, makes

---

65. Ibid., 129-30.
66. Ibid., 130-31.
67. Ibid.

women believe that they need to be loosed and that Bishop Jakes is the one that God has anointed to loose them.

The *Woman Thou Art Loosed* Movie

In terms of mass appeal, revenues, and the medium itself, the WTAL movie is the most important cultural text within the overall brand, not just because of its financial success but because as a medium, the film provides the greatest exposure. Jakes was able to leverage the success of the film into a nine-picture deal with Sony Pictures. Tatiana Siegel in 2006 describes the deal as a "three year production and distribution deal with Sony Pictures Entertainment for theatrical releases and DVD exclusives generated by his production company TDJ Enterprises."[68] The second installment of the WTAL movie, *Woman Thou Art Loosed: On the 7th Day*, was released in April 2012.[69] The second WTAL movie did not do very well in the box office. However, the other films did very well. Each of the films focus on African American life. However, the most successful movie, *Heaven Is for Real*, does not have an African American cast. Todd Burpo, who wrote the book that the film was based on, chose Jakes because he felt that he could trust Jakes to translate his story with integrity.[70]

The WTAL movie was advertised as being produced and written by Bishop T.D. Jakes. Like African American filmmakers Tyler Perry and Spike Lee, Jakes also stars in the movies that he produces. The difference is that Tyler Perry and Spike Lee play different characters in their movies; they do not usually play themselves. In WTAL, Jakes plays himself. In later movies such as *Ties Not Easily Broken* and *Jumping the Broom*, he still plays a minister, but he doesn't play himself. However, WTAL is the first introduction and branding of himself as a pastor who is also an actor and filmmaker. Some critics

---

68. Tatiana Siegel, "Author Jakes Lands Inspiring Deal with SPE," *The Hollywood Reporter,* April 18, 2006.

69. *Woman Thou Art Loosed: On the 7th Day*, http://www.tdjakeswtal movie.com.

70. Matthew Faraci, "The Bishop's Life," *Variety* 330, no. 7 (December 2015): 120.

noted, "the film has drawn criticism as a 'T.D. Jakes vanity project'—Jakes plays himself, and there are lingering scenes spotlighting his ability to stir up his congregation."[71]

Film (Distributor)	Release Date	Budget	Domestic Gross
Heaven Is for Real (Sony TriStar)	April 16, 2014	$1.2 m	$91.4 m
Black Nativity (Fox Searchlight)	Nov. 27, 2013	$17.5 m	$7 m
Winnie Mandela (Image Ent.)	Sept. 6, 2013	n/a	$80.6 k
Sparkle (TriStar)	Aug. 17, 2012	$14 m	$24.4 m
Woman Thou Art Loosed: On the 7th Day	April 3, 2012	n/a	$1.2 m
Jumping the Broom (Sony TriStar)	May 6, 2011	$6.6 m	$37.3 m
Not Easily Broken	Jan. 9, 2009	$5 m	$10.6 m
Woman Thou Art Loosed (Magnolia)	Oct. 1, 2004	$3 m	$6.9 m

Figure 6. Jakes was able to leverage the success of the *Woman Thou Art Loosed* film into an nine-picture deal with Sony Pictures. The figure shows the revenue for each film. Source: Matthew Faraci, "The Bishop's Life," *Variety* 330 no. 7 (December 8, 2015): 119.

Nevertheless, the WTAL film became "a cult hit" that grossed close to $6.9 million and sold over one million DVDs.[72] Jakes talks about his movie success and his work as a movie producer in the same way that he talks about his books and his vocation as an author. Both are evidence to his followers that he is both a spiritual and a secular success. My approach to the film was to treat it as an important source for theology and to view it as a just another

71. Jeffrey Overstreet, "Reconciliation on Screen: Recent Films Explore Conflict, Retaliation, and Peacemaking," *Seattle Pacific University Response* 27, no. 4 (Autumn 2004), https://spu.edu.

72. Faraci, "The Bishop's Life," 120.

product of the brand. As a consumer of black films, I had already seen the film when it was first released in 2004. I also watched it again on DVD. However, for research purposes, I purchased the WTAL Special Edition Gift Set,[73] and I then viewed the film from the perspective of a scholar, theologian, and critic of ideology.

The movie tells the story of Michelle Jordan, who is a victim of a childhood rape and molestation. She later has bouts with drug abuse and prostitution. As a result, she finds herself in prison. Her mother, Cassie, who has never admitted to the abuse, is a churchwoman with a chronically unemployed live-in boyfriend named Reggie. Reggie is the man who raped and molested Michelle when she was just a girl. At the end of the movie we discover that Reggie is also hooked on crack. Bishop Jakes is able to get Michelle out of prison on an early release from a three-year sentence. One of the requirements of her early release is that Michelle must attend three nights of revival. On the last night of the revival, Michelle walks to the altar and finds that Reggie, her perpetrator, is also seeking redemption. He too has been moved by Bishop Jakes's altar call. Out of her rage she pulls a gun out of her purse and kills him.

Bishop Jakes then visits Michelle in prison on death row, where she tells her painful story of rage and victimization. Eventually, Michelle is able to find forgiveness for herself and for her perpetrator. Bishop Jakes, through counseling and prayer, leads her to the path of forgiveness and reconciliation. In other words, Michelle is a woman who is loosed from her past. Moreover, she is loosed by Bishop T.D. Jakes.

Several scenes of Michelle's prison cell with T.D. Jakes as her counselor are strategically placed throughout the film and serve as defining moments. The first scene where T.D. Jakes is identified as Bishop T.D. Jakes is when he is walking into the prison to meet Michelle. Jakes's outfit and his dialogue both signal how Jakes brands himself as a liberator in the stories and lives of African American women. The WTAL brand's target audience is women like the character Michelle. The brand has always focused on reaching victims

---

73. *Woman Thou Art Loosed*, DVD, directed by Michael Schultz (2004; Beverly Hills, CA: Twentieth Century Fox Home Entertainment LLC, 2006).

of domestic violence and incest. The first scenes, especially those of Jakes walking into the prison, give the audience an opportunity to see T.D. Jakes's branded identity as a celebrity preacher, the pastor of a super-megachurch, and a healer of women. Kimberly Elise, as the character Michelle, and T.D. Jakes, as Bishop Jakes, are always visually positioned on the screen so that the audience quickly identifies Michelle as a woman who needs to be loosed, and Jakes as the one able to loose her.

When Jakes first walks down death row at the prison, he is wearing a dark suit with a clerical collar and he is carrying a big, black Bible. Michelle is in a cell in an orange two-piece prison outfit. Bishop Jakes says, "You did request to see me?" Michelle responds, "I didn't think you'd really come. I saw you on the cover of *Time* magazine. 'Is this man the next Billy Graham?' You don't expect somebody like that to take a stroll down death row to preach to me."[74] This detailed information introduces Jakes as more than just a black Pentecostal preacher. Bishop T.D. Jakes is a preacher on the cover of major magazines. He is a preacher as important as Billy Graham. More important, the scene suggests to filmgoers that Jakes is a pastor who actually visits women on death row. T.D. Jakes pastors thirty thousand people, but is still able to honor a member's request to visit her daughter in prison. The dialogue is revealing, but so is the way that Michelle and Jakes are positioned in each of the counseling scenes.

For most of the film Michelle is on the floor of the prison cell, preoccupied with the construction of a small toothpick house. The screenplay describes the first scene and the character Michelle Jordan: "She's in her early thirties, with her legs crossed and folded childlike, she trembles as she glues a matchstick onto the skeleton of a small matchstick house."[75] In the final scene the matchstick house is complete.

---

74. *Woman Thou Art Loosed*, special edition DVD. Interestingly, many people missed Jakes on the cover of *Time* magazine because his cover story was released on September 17, 2001, which was immediately following the events of 9/11.

75. Stan Foster, *Woman Thou Art Loosed*, screenplay.

Figure 7. Bishop Jakes stars has himself in the *Woman Thou Art Loosed* movie. Kimberly Elise stars as the young woman incarcerated for shooting her abuser in church.

The last scenes of the movie are perhaps the most troubling. Michelle kills her perpetrator in a violent rage while he is walking toward her at the altar to ask for forgiveness. Reggie, her perpetrator, has decided during the altar call to come not only to seek his reconciliation with Michelle but also to seek redemption. Reggie has admitted his mistake and is begging Michelle for forgiveness when she reaches into her purse and pulls out a gun, killing him in front of the entire congregation. After the audience witnesses the tragic shooting in the church, the final scene shows Jakes in his last counseling session with Michelle.

Michelle is now ready to release her anger and to seek forgiveness by taking full responsibility for what she has done. Visually, this is first time that Michelle stands up in these scenes. She then sits next to Bishop Jakes. Her dialogue and movement in the scene tell her story:

> You can never get even. What I did was wrong. No matter what he did to me it was wrong. [She then stands and moves to sit next to Jakes.] When you talk to God again, ask him to forgive me. I know that I can't bring life back. Tell my mother that I love her and that I forgive her. I have always loved her. I hope that we can get to know each other. No

matter what I felt I didn't have the right to take something from her. Just pray for me.[76]

In this scene Michelle does not pray for herself, nor is she capable of having a conversation on her own with her mother. Both women (Cassie and Michelle) need Bishop Jakes to be the mediator, not only between the women themselves but also between them and God. Responding to her request for prayer, Bishop Jakes tells her:

> I have been praying. I been praying for a little girl. I been praying that she wouldn't die. I been praying that she wouldn't give up and that somehow you would get through this. I been praying that you wouldn't allow these bars and this chaos and all this stuff to destroy your spirit. Now I know that she's alive and well and I know in my heart Michelle you're going to be O.K. I know it in my heart. Stay free! Stay free, Michelle! You hear me. I am going to be praying for you and you know what, you're going to make it.[77]

The fact that Jakes addresses Michelle, a grown woman, as if she were still a little girl, is only one small problem. Perhaps, one can assume that Jakes is speaking metaphorically to the little girl who remains a part of a grown woman's story of pain and suffering—the little girl who was never healed from the trauma. What is more troubling theologically, and from a gender perspective, is that Jakes is the male preacher who determines the meaning of liberation for Michelle, his female congregant. Instead of Michelle claiming her own subjectivity and defining her own liberation, Jakes declares what it means for her to be free: "Stay free! Stay free Michelle!"

Bishop Jakes boldly declares that Michelle is going to be okay. Unfortunately, what we see on the screen is that Jakes leaves the cell and the prison, while Michelle remains behind bars. She is free. She is loosed. But, she is still incarcerated and still in prison. She is still oppressed. She is still on death row. In other words, no matter what

---

76. *Woman Thou Art Loosed*, special edition DVD.
77. Ibid.

Bishop Jakes declares and confesses, Michelle is not really *liberated* and she is not really *free*.

We can celebrate the fact that Michelle is no longer bound by guilt and unforgiveness. However, for the viewing audience, the film suggests that Jakes responds to the needs of an individual parishioner (Cassie, the mother of Michelle). But in the real world, as is the case with other prosperity celebrity preachers, Jakes and the women of The Potter's House and the customers in the WTAL brand community rarely have face-to-face time with Jakes—unless, of course, the women are Bishop Circle V.I.P.'s and have already given their seed-faith offering or a financial gift.

The freedom and liberation that Jakes offers Michelle and other women is mainly a spiritual liberation that exists only in the individual. By ignoring the systemic inequities, it blames the victims. Furthermore, this liberation exonerates the systems that the movie identifies as having failed Michelle. More important, scenes of the movie with dialogue effectively serve to brand T.D. Jakes as the priest, healer, counselor, pastor, and liberator. Jakes brands himself as the one who *looses* these women, including Cassie, the mother of Michelle. Women are those in need of liberation, and Jakes is the one who provides the liberation. Furthermore, this liberation is usually located in the context of a product or experience that places him as the one in power and not the women themselves: his preaching, his counseling, and his contacting the warden. Ideologically, the WTAL brand repeatedly sends the message that it is T.D. Jakes who looses women, and not the women themselves.

The movie also demonstrates how Jakes is able to cloak his entrepreneurial ventures in theological language and convince his followers that his ventures have more to do with ministry than business. In this particular case, Jakes ties the film to the church's mission to evangelize. He argues that movies are no longer just entertainment but are a new medium for Christians to participate in the Great Commission. The film is not just about more revenue; Jakes insists that his work on the silver screen is about ministry. In one of the interviews in the WTAL limited edition, Jakes says that "Jesus said go into the world and preach the gospel to every living creature. Well, the world is going to the movies so the best place to reach the world is to go where the world is going."[78] Prosperity preachers often present a new product or medium as an opportunity to spread the gospel: "I think that WTAL is a great opportunity to define the fact that the pulpits of the twenty-first century are not hidden behind stained-glass windows all the time. They're over the Internet. They're on television and they are on the silver screen. Hence, *Woman Thou Art Loosed* the movie."[79] The film is also supposed to correct the previous images of the Black Church as presented by secular film-makers. His commentary about the WTAL movie can also be interpreted as a critique of what I have defined as the traditional Black Church. Jakes remarks, "I was excited to do it [WTAL] because most of the things that I have seen Hollywood do were done in small churches with MLK fans and fat women in white."[80]

Jakes may say that the film is about women, but a more accurate reading is that the movie is really about T.D. Jakes and his ministry *to* women. Jakes successfully brands himself as Bishop T.D. Jakes, the megachurch celebrity preacher, who counsels and preaches to women. In the movie, T.D. Jakes as a personality and as a character is so prevalent that almost every character in the movie has to hear or go see him. He is not just a celebrity preacher, however; he is also a preacher with the power to alter the decision of a white prison warden. Later in the movie he also gets the governor to consider giving Michelle a stay, and perhaps a new trial. Essentially, Jakes is presenting himself as what most black people have come to expect from the traditional Black Church preacher like Martin Luther King. Whereas King used his celebrity status and influence to join in the systemic struggles of African Americans, Jakes does not challenge systems like the prison in which Michelle is incarcerated. He often allows women in prison to participate in the conferences by viewing his sermons via technology but does not critique the overall system.

Another way that the movie brands T.D. Jakes as the looser of women is that no other character is able to bring healing and

78. "Making of the Featurette," Interview with T.D. Jakes, *Woman Thou Art Loosed*, DVD.

79. Ibid.

80. Ibid.

liberation to Michelle, who was sexually abused, raped, on drugs and working as a prostitute—not probation officers, not her supportive boyfriend, not a halfway house, not even her mother. Although Bishop Jakes recommends a three-day revival as a requirement of her early release, even the church fails Michelle because Michelle resorts to violence and shoots her perpetrator at the altar. Ultimately, the solution for her healing is facilitated by Bishop T.D. Jakes alone. This is powerful branding, and Jakes accomplishes this branding by using the characters, visual images, and the dialogue in the script.

The branding occurs throughout the film. The movie begins with "T.D. Jakes Enterprises LLP presents *Woman Thou Art Loosed.*" If that were not enough exposure, Jakes plays himself in the movie— Bishop T.D. Jakes. And, besides the sermons that are strategically placed throughout the film, as well as counseling sessions with the main character and voice-overs of sermons, the dialogue completely points to T.D. Jakes being the preacher who was on the cover of *Time* magazine and who might be the next Billy Graham.

Finally, the role of T.D. Jakes is in stark contrast to the cast of victims who make up the other characters in the film: a long list of black people, especially women, who need to be loosed. Cassie, the mother, never admits to the molestation of her daughter and is in a relationship with a man who is not only chronically unemployed but also addicted to crack. We also find out in Cassie's confessional that she too was sexually molested as a child. Michelle, the main character, has not only been raped by her mother's live-in boyfriend, but she is also a recovering addict who has a history of working in a strip club and finds herself on death row after shooting her assailant in church. Even Todd, the handsome childhood sweetheart of Michelle, is a victim. As we learn, he is a single father who was abandoned by his wife when she left him and their daughter for a gangbanger. The remaining cast of characters is also made up of victims: recovering addicts, pimps, and drug dealers. The mother's friend, who supports Michelle, is positive, but she too is unable to really help bring about reconciliation between the mother and the daughter. The only person who is able to provide any healing and to *loose women* is Bishop T.D. Jakes.

2009 WTAL Conference in Dallas, Texas

I attended the 2009 WTAL Conference in Dallas, Texas, at The Potter's House. The theme of the conference was "Thankful Women." While a seminary student in Atlanta, Georgia, I attended an earlier WTAL Conference at the Georgia Dome when the conferences had close to fifty thousand women in attendance. For the 2009 conference, approximately eight thousand women were in attendance. Registration was available on-line for $50. I received a badge at the onsite registration that identified for the ushers where I would be allowed to sit. The best seating was reserved for the ministry partners. Although thousands of women paid the registration fee, offerings were still raised at the general sessions—a perfect example of how Jakes blends worship and entertainment. Charging a registration fee makes the WTAL Conference like secular conferences or similar to entertainment; yet, the offerings are what one expects in worship.

The conference was scheduled for three days—Thursday night through Saturday afternoon. Before each session conference participants were lined up at least thirty to forty minutes outside the doors, waiting in long lines. Ushers would direct people to special seating and would give early entrance to ministry partners based on the amount of their giving; these women partners were put into categories such as Aaron's Army, Bishop Circle, and Bishop Circle V.I.P. The better seating—the seats closest to the stage—were reserved for women at the higher levels of giving. After the seating of the ministry partners and registered conference participants, the general public would be admitted. While we waited for the services to start, the large screens on the side of the pulpit played the trailers for Jakes's latest movie.[81] The Potter's House often markets Bishop Jakes's conferences and products. Jakes apparently takes advantage of every opportunity to promote his books and future events.

---

81. In 2009 the movie being advertised was *Ties Not Easily Broken,* starring Morris Chestnut.

 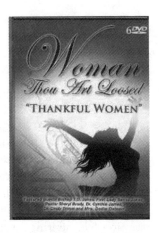

Figure 8. The theme for the 2009 WTAL Conference was "Thankful Women." Most events and conferences are advertised with photos of the speakers and a particular layout for the particular conference. The six-CD set was available for purchase after the conference. The theme and layout are the same as the other products.

While at the conference I purchased one CD from one session.[82] I later ordered the entire six-CD set of all of the sermons from the conference to evaluate the differences, if any, from the live worship services. I also needed to see the branding and marketing differences between the products that were available immediately after a worship service, and their packaged edited version. The six-CD set included edited versions of the longer live sermons of each speaker. Each of the sermons by the women speakers, however, was introduced on the CD with a short introductory message from T.D. Jakes. The CD that I purchased immediately after the conference did not include the introduction. Obviously, the same day of the conference, there is not enough time to add the extra edits including the introduction from Jakes.

All of the products have similar packaging—the same color, logo, and conference theme. From a marketing standpoint all products

---

82. *Woman Thou Art Loosed: Thankful Women*, CD (Dallas, TX: T.D. Jakes Ministries, 2009).

and events must be consistent with the brand. The packaging usually has a marketing hint or teaser that alerts the customer to what unique spiritual experience they can expect with the purchase. The back cover of 2009 WTAL Conference CD package reads:

> Have you ever felt broken or bound by your situations? If so, get ready to be loosed and restored as you hear the inspirational messages from eminent speakers including Bishop T.D. Jakes, First Lady Serita Jakes, Pastor Sheryl Brady, Dr. Cynthia James, Dr. Cindy Trimm and Mrs. Dodie Osteen. These explosive messages from the Woman Thou Art Loosed Conference will transform your life forever![83]

The caption is an example of how the WTAL brand works for T.D. Jakes, the women preachers, and the consumers. The consumer is first queried if she *feels broken or bound*. If yes, she is supposed to *get ready*, because the WTAL sermons will *loose* and *restore* her. The sermons are explosive and inspirational from eminent speakers. The woman who purchases the product and participates in the WTAL brand will live transformed forever.

The speakers for the conference included Bishop Jakes, his wife Serita Jakes, and Pastor Dodie Osteen. Her son is also a televangelist and the pastor of Lakewood, a super-megachurch located in Houston, Texas. Osteen is a prosperity preacher who is even more popular and famous than T.D. Jakes.[84] The 2011 WTAL Conference was actually held at Osteen's church. Prosperity preachers often promote the other's brands by being guest speakers at one another's conferences. Pastor Sheryl Brady not only speaks at WTAL but is the co-pastor of The Potters' House in North Dallas. One of the newer faces at the 2009 conference was Cindy Trimm, the speaker who most vividly represented the prosperity theology worldview and seed-faith giving. Trimm told congregants that she has a spiritual money tree in her backyard, and then asked everyone who wanted

---

83. *Woman Thou Art Loosed: Thankful Women*, CD.
84. Mara Einstein, *Brands of Faith: Marketing Religion in a Commercial Age* (New York: Routledge, 2008), 122.

Figure 9. Brochure advertising a new book and brand *The 40 Day Soul Fast,* by Cindy Trim. The foreword is written by Bishop T.D. Jakes. This is an example of how Jakes creates other brands for his women speakers.

to be a millionaire to stand for a prayer.[85] Trimm is a prime example of how the conferences allow women preachers to create their own brands. Since the 2009 conference Dr. Cindy Trimm has gained more prominence and has created her own brands, for example, her book, *The 40 Day Soul Fast: Your Journey to Authentic Living.* The foreword for the book is written by T.D. Jakes.[86] The women

---

85. See Chapter 2 on theologies of prosperity. I use Cindy Trimm as an example of how seed-giving has evolved in recent years.

86. Cindy Trimm, *The 40 Day Soul Fast: Journey to Authentic Living* (Shippensburg, PA: Destiny Image, 2011), 77.

whom Jakes promotes usually stay connected to his brand. Jakes's writing the foreword for Cindy Trimm's book is an illustration of the symbiotic financial relationships he maintains. However, the women preachers are rarely positioned or marketed as his equals or as peers, nor do they share equally in the profits. Jakes always controls his brands. On other occasions, he also controls the brands of the women. The women are not colleagues of equal status; rather, they remain his de facto daughters in ministry.

Shayne Lee records that Juanita Bynum was ostracized when she asked Jakes to let her share in the financial success of her own 1998 "No More Sheets" sermon. The sermon eventually became a book and one of her many brands.[87] Like a true capitalist, Jakes used his influence and power to make sure that the larger black churches would no longer invite Bynum. She was not reinstated as a member of the WTAL brand until she returned in 2003. At that conference in front of thousands of women, she gave a public apology to Jakes. The entire legal dilemma was couched in a testimony in which she repented and confessed that it was her pride that was the problem. According to Bynum it was God, not T.D. Jakes, who removed her from her national platform. She proclaimed, "God said get your behind out there in exile. So the invitations stopped coming, and for two years God said 'nope, nope.' And for two years God only let me preach in storefront churches."[88]

Presenting herself as a daughter who had betrayed her father in the ministry, Bynum told the audience, "The Holy Ghost said, 'Ain't nobody used you. He [Jakes] gave you a chance that nobody would give you. He platformed you when nobody else would touch you. Those were his tapes. That's his stuff!' "[89] This event confirms that Jakes controls his image and his brands, as well as the women who have a business or spiritual relationship with him; they must respond according to his terms.

---

87. Juanita Bynum, *No More Sheets: The Truth about Sex* (Lanham, MD: Pneuma Life Publishing, 1998).

88. "A Renewed Covenant 2–Juanita Bynum," http://www.youtube.com.

89. Ibid.

Aaron's Army Ministry Partner

After attending the live conference and in order to experience the brand as even more of an insider, I became an Aaron's Army monthly ministry partner. Prosperity preachers encourage not only seed-faith giving but covenant partnering. Financially, a monthly commitment from the partners provides more income for the ministry than one seed offering at a worship service. More important, the congregants are placed on the mailing list that allows the ministry to send more appeals and offers. T.D. Jakes Ministries has several levels of partnership. I signed up as a partner at the 2009 WTAL Conference. However, via the website, congregants can have their monthly gift deducted by automatic debit.

> Your convenient auto-debit gift of any amount is appreciated and establishes your growing covenant relationship with this ministry as a friend and regular supporter. Giving is an expression of love and commitment to advance the work of the Kingdom of God. Know that your monthly donations help us to continue and expand our reach and help proclaim the glorious Gospel of Jesus Christ.[90]

This appeal is a good example of the expectations of the relationship between the prosperity preacher and the congregant. Although the general appeal says "any amount," the website outlines three partnership levels (Aaron's Army, Bishop Circle, and Bishop Circle V.I.P.). The bigger the financial commitment that the congregant makes, the more "partner benefits" he or she receives. The Aaron's Army requires an auto-debit gift of $30/month. Bishop Circle requires $50/month or one gift of $500.[91] The highest level of membership is Bishop Circle V.I.P.; the very important person (V.I.P.) designation is assigned to those partners who contribute a $100 gift per month or a one-time advance gift of $1,000.[92]

---

90. "Ministry Partners," *T.D Jakes Ministries*, http://www.tdjpartners.org.
91. Ibid.
92. Ibid.

Figure 10. The welcome letter from T.D. Jakes Ministries after becoming an Aaron's Army ministry partner.

Figure 11. I also received a certificate with the Aaron's Army logo and an official-like gold stamp with T.D. Jakes's logo.

One of the brochures outlines that "Bishop Circle VIP Partners receive all of the Bishop Circle's benefits, plus a two-night stay at a scheduled partner's event, and exclusive access to Bishop Circle VIP partner gatherings with Bishop and Mrs. T.D. Jakes."[93] Thus, the Bishop Circle partners receive face-to-face meetings with Jakes, special seating, and other privileges at the conference.

As only an Aaron's Army member, I received a startup package in the mail. The packet included a certificate, several CDs, and an Aaron's Army CD holder. The one-time donation of $30 also placed me on the mailing list. I immediately began receiving monthly direct-mail letters from T.D. Jakes. Each letter always ended with an appeal to send more money or to purchase more products. I also signed up to be on the email list. Jakes often sends letters or e-blasts that encourage congregants to give money—as "unto God"—and to give sacrificially. The letters are part of the branding and become one more communication between the preacher and the congregant.

The language and the messages usually include some of the familiar prosperity language. For example, a direct mail letter sent February 2010 reads:

Dear Ms. McGee:

Your love, your prayers, and your steadfast support have turned the dreams of many into a reality. God has taken the financial seeds you've sown and He has multiplied it to touch the hearts and lives of thousands all around the world. . . . The heart of T.D. Jakes Ministries is to help the hurting people in all we do. Through the support of friends and partners like you, we have been able to bring hope to so many who otherwise might not have hope. We are so thankful for your partnership and for standing in covenant with this ministry.[94]

93. T.D. Jakes, brochure, donor letter from T.D. Jakes Ministries, February 2010.

94. Ibid.

Figure 12. Monthly letter after becoming an Aaron's Army ministry partner.

The letter reveals how congregants are encouraged to plant financial seeds, with the implied expectation that God produces a spiritual harvest by multiplying the seed or gift of the congregant. In this particular instance, the promise is not that the seed will produce a direct financial return for the congregant. Rather, the return for the congregant is evangelism; the congregant will be reaching thousands of people around the world.

In the prosperity worldview, the covenant relationship is not simply a contractual agreement. Instead, the financial gift is the catalyst for a spiritual relationship between the preacher and the ministry partner. Covenants have theological implications that bind in ways that contracts do not. With one contribution, the congregant expects special access to Bishop Jakes and his ministry. More important, the partner is connected to his anointing. In terms of branding and marketing, the ministry partners become a recognizable way to measure how many people are loyal to Jakes's brand. Moreover, for his secular partners, these individuals represent verifiable numbers of potential customers. The secular business partners may not be interested in Christian discipleship, but they are very interested in Jakes's brand loyalty.

In sum, studying the movie, book, and conference all show that that Jakes is able to successfully brand himself as a pastor and theologian. The women who attend these conferences and participate in the brand, although liberated spiritually, are not really loosed from more devastating effects of systemic oppression. We must not forget that ultimately brands, including faith brands, are about identity creation.[95] We communicate to those around us with the brands that we buy. Hence, when black women purchase a book, go to the movie, or attend a WTAL Conference, they are expressing to others who they are. Moreover, they are telling the world who they are in the eyes of God. During these conferences the women preachers and the congregants are constructing a counternarrative to the negative identities promulgated about black women by the dominant culture. Moreover, they are also responding to the negative portrayals of themselves in their home churches.

Black churches and worship experiences like WTAL remain central to identity formation for African American Protestants. Jakes continues to convince women that they need to be loosed, and that they need to be loosed by him. Their participation in the brand may in fact be spiritually liberating. But, for most of these women, they are really only loosed to buy more products and to send more money to Bishop T.D. Jakes.

---

95. Einstein, *Brands of Faith*, 13.

CONCLUSION

Wal-Martization: "Keeping It Real"

Theology, as a function of the Christian church, must serve the needs of the church. A theological system is supposed to satisfy two basic needs: the statement of the truth of the Christian message and the interpretation of this truth for every new generation. —Paul Tillich, *Systematic Theology*

In today's context the majority of theological and religious discourses about black churches are framed around two models: the Black Church and the New Black Church. T.D. Jakes's ministry is representative of the New Black Church. Furthermore, Bishop Jakes as a preacher and the WTAL brands are an example of the pastor/CEO and parishioner/consumer relationship characteristic of the New Black Church. The women who follow Jakes are socially constructing their collective and individual identities by participating in his church and the brand communities. Furthermore, Jakes's branded identity is successful because of his relationship with African American women.

As the Sam Walton of the New Black Church, Jakes represents a definite cultural paradigm shift in black religion and spirituality. The women who follow Jakes believe that Bishop Jakes tells their story and that he speaks to those intimate and painful issues that are often ignored or avoided in other churches. As one woman stated, "I love my pastor. Because he lets people know, '*I'm Bishop Jakes, but I go through things too.*' *He's just about keeping it real.*"[1] Many of the women who follow Jakes echo the same sentiments. Women, pastors, ministry partners, and brand consumers in the New Black Church believe his story, including the branded biblical stories that make up his brand.

When he tells his life story, he combines the cultural signifiers of pastor and entrepreneur/CEO. Additionally, as a practitioner of Christian capitalism, he strategically blurs the sacred and the secular. In other words, Jakes is as much a businessman as he is a pastor. As a result, it is almost impossible to discern where one vocation begins and the other ends. This provides him with epistemic privilege and status in both the church and the corporate world. The pastors of the New Black Church are described as creative religious entrepreneurs. Secular entrepreneurs may be accountable only to the market and are *not* expected to tell the truth in the stories and myths that they present in their brands. For preachers and pastors, however, we expect honesty and authenticity.[2] In other words, I think that pastors and preachers are expected to "keep it real." However, based on the research, it is difficult to believe that Bishop T.D. Jakes is keeping it real, not only because of his lack of transparency[3] but because much of what he brands is not always completely true.

For instance, although he has a GED and only one year of college at an accredited institution of higher learning, he claims that he has completed both a master's and a doctoral degree. Several prosperity preachers have degrees from the same institution—Friends

---

1. Shayne Lee and Phillip Luke Sinitiere, *Holy Mavericks: Evangelical Innovators and the Spiritual Marketplace* (New York: New York University Press, 2009), 71.

2. Marla Frederick, *Colored Television: American Religion Gone Global* (Stanford, CA: Stanford University Press, 2016), 88-89.

3. Ministrywatch.com, an organization that posts information for donors about nonprofits and Christian ministries, gives T.D. Jakes Ministries and The Potter's House of Dallas an "F" for its lack of transparency. "T.D. Jakes," http://www.ministrywatch.com.

Figure 13. Website of FICU explaining that they are not accredited by any accrediting agency recognized by the United States Secretary of Education. The photos are of the other preachers who have also received degrees. Friends International Christian University, "Accreditation," http://www.ficuflorida.com.

International Christian University (FICU) in Merced, California. Unfortunately, the majority of Jakes's followers do not know that his doctorate is not from an accredited institution. FICU is more of a correspondence school than an institution of higher learning. On the school's own website it admits that the school is not accredited by any agency that is recognized by the U.S. Department of Education.[4]

We have also seen that Jakes promotes himself as a role model—a self-made man and an expert on successful Christian living in the twenty-first century. His main justification for his wealth is that God has given him the power to achieve wealth. Jakes asserts that he can effectively pastor thirty thousand members and boasts of being financially successful, but not as a result of his ministry. His suc-

---

4. "Accreditation," Friends International Christian University, http://www.ficu.edu.

cess is actually from his entrepreneurial work as an author, speaker, playwright, and movie producer. Therefore, he claims he has a God-given right to his wealth and to his financial empire, which is estimated to be worth $400 million.[5]

Jakes feigns a pseudo-Protestant ethic that undergirds the idea of American meritocracy—with both the Horatio Alger and the exceptionalism myths. Bishop Jakes even argues that it is occupational discrimination to suggest that he not earn as much income as possible in the global marketplace. He often provides a long list of his accomplishments as evidence of just how hard he has worked, which is supposed to justify his conspicuous consumption.

Bishop Jakes brags that he is a successful author who has written several books. He implies that all of the work and labor are his own. Therefore, he should be rewarded for both his labor and his impeccable work ethic. However, Shayne Lee has documented that Jakes employs "talented researchers and ghostwriters to help produce his books," and that he requires these writers "to sign waivers prohibiting them from discussing their contributions to his books."[6] These co-authors do not receive any name recognition or acknowledgment for their work. Another example of Jakes responding as a capitalist is the WTAL novel. The novel is an expanded version of the screenplay, which was written by Stan Foster. Just one glance at the screenplay next to the novel is proof positive that the two are almost identical.[7] The WTAL movie was marketed and promoted as "based

---

5. Jim Haskins and Kathleen Benson, *African American Religious Leaders* (San Francisco: Jossey-Bass, 2008), 150.

6. Shayne Lee, *T.D. Jakes: America's New Preacher* (New York: New York University Press, 2005), 148.

7. The screenplay reads as follows: "Sounds of shoe heels klip-klopping in the distance. The sound grows louder and louder as the walker seems to be coming closer. FEMALE VOICE (O.S.) Black man walking. FEMALE VOICE #2 (O.S.) Is that him? The preacher on TV? Bishop T.D. Jakes. FEMALE VOICE (O.S.) *T.D. Jakes*, you ignorant." (Stan Foster, *Woman Thou Art Loosed*, screenplay, 1-2). The similarities are obvious. The novel reads as follows: "Klip klop . . . klip klop . . . klip klop . . ." "Is that him," an inmate asked. "You know, that preacher on TV? Bishop T.D. Jakes?" (Bishop T.D. Jakes, *Woman Thou Art Loosed* [New York, Berkley Publishing Group], 7).

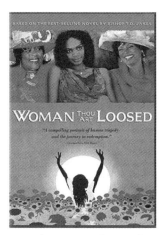

Figure 14. The *Woman Thou Art Loosed* movie is advertised as based on the novel, and the *Woman Thou Art Loosed* novel is advertised as based on the book. Both statements cannot be true.

on the best-selling novel" by Bishop T.D. Jakes.[8] Yet, the cover of the novel says, "based on the award-winning motion picture."[9] It cannot be both! Foster, the actual writer of the screenplay, on his website writes, "People actually think that the story came from T.D. Jakes's novel, or self- help book." His position is clear, "the novel was actually based on my script, in many places word for word."[10] As a capitalist, Jakes presents the work as his own and reaps the full profits. Without a doubt, he is an example of Wal-Martization.

Several scholars and academic theologians argue that advanced capitalism is functioning like a religion in our contemporary society. The word "Wal-Martization" expresses their concerns. The term also speaks to the branding, as well as to the ideological influence of the branding, on the individual and the collective identities of people and institutions. As a theoretical concept, Wal-Martization

---

8. *Woman Thou Art Loosed*, DVD special edition, front cover.

9. Jakes, *Woman Thou Art Loosed* (the novel), cover.

10. Stan Foster, "Woman Thou Art Loosed Movie," http://www.stan foster.com.

exemplifies both the *ideology* and the *process* that corroborates the cultural and generational differences between the New Black Church and the Black Church.

Brands are ultimately cultural stories, especially stories that are repeated with the appropriate marketing. Wal-Martization explains the branding and storytelling at every level of representation of the New Black Church. The 1980s and 1990s mark the expansion of black megachurches as well as the beginning of Wal-Mart's growth and expansion. Today, Wal-Mart is not only the largest corporation in America, but in the world—the "template industry," setting the bar for its competitors.[11] Bishop Jakes as a New Black Church pastor of The Potter's House has the same iconic and celebrity presence as Wal-Mart founder Sam Walton. In other words, with the same storytelling ability and notoriety, T.D. Jakes is the Sam Walton of the New Black Church.

The similarities between the black churches of the New Black Church and Wal-Mart are notable. Many of the poor women who shop and work at Wal-Mart are ideologically influenced by the leadership in the same way that churchwomen are influenced by their pastors. Both Wal-Mart and black churches are places to socialize and find community—where people assemble often, sometimes on a weekly basis. The size of the megachurches and their impact on communities also have a host of similarities. Stacey Floyd-Thomas shows that the size and popularity of super-megachurches have led to "the demise of many small-town traditional churches."[12] Wal-Mart because of its size and power has the same destructive effect on smaller community retail stores.[13]

Both Wal-Mart and black churches are successful because women

---

11. Wal-Mart Stores, Inc., not only grew in stature from a mere "276 stores to 1528, but also in sales from 1.2 to 26 billion dollars." Justin R. Watkins, "Always Low Prices, Always at a Cost: A Call to Arms Against the Wal-Martization of America," *J. Marshall Law Review* 40 (2006–2007): 274.

12. Stacey Boyd, *Black Men Worshipping: Intersecting Anxieties of Race, Gender, and Christian Embodiment* (New York: Palgrave Macmillan, 2011), 74.

13. Watkins, "Always Low Prices," 288.

are the main stakeholders as volunteers, workers, parishioners, and consumers, but they are not really represented in the formal leadership. Both black churches and Wal-Mart carry an ideological mythology of representing the concerns of the marginalized. However, in both instances, the economic disparities do not always match the storytelling and brand mythology. Sam Walton is known for his Horatio Alger story and for providing low prices and jobs for Middle America. However, the truth is that at Wal-Mart, women, who are 90 percent of the cashiers, are the lowest paid workers.[14] For the majority of these women, their annual salary places them near or below the poverty line.[15] These numbers should be placed in perspective with the socioeconomic status of the Wal-Mart leadership. If Sam Walton were living he would be the richest man in the world. According to a *Forbes* magazine list, Sam Walton's children, who inherited his wealth, are five of the ten richest individuals in the world.[16]

The disparity between CEO or pastor and the average customer or parishioner is also similar. The most glaring example of the changes and the cultural influences of empire can be summed up in a comparison of the compensation packages of the CEO of General Motors (GM) in 1950 and the CEO of Wal-Mart in 2003. In 1950, the CEO of GM earned *135 times* that of the average assembly worker. In 2003, the CEO of Wal-Mart, by contrast, earned *1,450 times* that of a full-time employee.[17] This same disparity of the preacher/CEO and the members of the congregation in these churches astoundingly resembles empire. The theology of T.D. Jakes and his many brands highlights that capitalism has overwhelmingly impacted black churches and their historical social-justice mission.

Without question, the theology of Bishop Jakes and other popular preachers is important for how we understand and do theology

---

14. Liza Featherstone, *Selling Women Short: The Landmark Battle for Worker's Rights at Wal-Mart* (New York: Basic Books, 2004), 97.

15. Ibid., 129.

16. Featherstone, *Selling Women Short, 57.*

17. Erin Johansson, "Checking Out: The Rise of Wal-Mart and the Fall of Middle Class Retailing Jobs," *Connecticut Law Review* 39, no. 4 (May 2007): 1464-65.

as black Christians. I have offered an interdisciplinary method of theological research. In disagreement with other scholars, I argue that Jakes and other New Black Churches should be treated as theologians. More specifically, Bishop Jakes is a theologian of prosperity, and he offers his own brand of liberation to his followers.

Prosperity preachers and their theologies vary based on geography, denominational background, and historical context. The theologies fall on a continuum, reflecting what Bowler describes as *hard* and *soft* prosperity.[18] I define a prosperity preacher or theologian of prosperity *as anybody who interprets Scripture and uses rituals such as seed-faith giving and positive confession to create theologies that justify their personal economic empires. They also believe and affirm that it is God's will and a believer's right to obtain prosperity or health and wealth.* Based on this definition, because of Jakes's theology, worldview, affluent lifestyle, and religious practices, without a doubt, Bishop Jakes and many of the pastors in the New Black Church are theologians of prosperity.

I am suggesting that ideologically all of Bishop Jakes's brands, as well as how he shares his life story as a pastor and entrepreneur, serve to encourage other pastors and churches to believe that the New Black Church is a credible model of ministry. The truth, however, is that apart from Bishop Jakes, most other televangelists and Black Church pastors do not have a team of marketers, publicists, co-authors, and others to create their brands and promote their branded identities. Nor do they have Bishop Jakes's multimillion dollar deals with corporate partners.

Jakes's lifestyle and practices promote the values that undergird the gospel of wealth, which blames the poor for their poverty and diverts attention from the systemic problems of capitalism. Neoliberalism has become the new orthodoxy. His model supports the ideology of advanced capitalism. Jakes and the preachers who follow him wish to perform the ultimate trope of empire—the celebrity corporate CEO. Moreover, Jakes wants others to believe that the

18. Kate Bowler, *Blessed: A History of the American Prosperity Gospel* (New York: Oxford University Press, 2013), 7-8.

New Black Church is actually a better model, and the best model, for contemporary black Christians to achieve liberation.

A prime example of his branding and promotion of this ideology is taken from his book *The Great Investment*. Jakes gives a prescription to his readers for how to obtain wealth, explaining just how easy it is for Christians to become millionaires:

> If you have a take-home pay of $20,000 per year and spend it all on eating out at the finest restaurants and purchasing the latest designer clothes you will have a full stomach and a packed closet, but your pockets will be empty. If instead you invested even 10 percent—$2000 per year—in, say, a mutual fund that averaged a 15 percent return per year, after ten years you would have over $49,000. After twenty years that amount grows to just about $267,000. And in thirty years you could retire a millionaire with more than $1,200,000. Are you willing to give up a few dinners out and a couple pair of new shoes to be a millionaire? The choice is yours.[19]

He implies that someone who is netting $20,000 a year can, with a little discipline and hard work, one day be a millionaire. However, he lays out a financial plan that does not adjust for inflation and the cost of living. Similarly, Jakes infers in this passage that someone living on less than $20,000 per year has the luxury to irresponsibly spend money on fancy dinners and designer clothes. In a later chapter, he encourages readers to tithe 10 percent not off the *net* but off their *gross* income.[20] As I have demonstrated, in the prosperity worldview, tithing is mandatory for adherents if they want God to give them the power to get wealth. Therefore, the take-home pay in his illustration is actually only about $18,000. Moreover, most mutual funds do not guarantee a consistent 15 percent return on an investment. If we are *keeping it real*, most working-class people, after

19. T.D. Jakes, *The Great Investment: Faith, Family, and Finance* (New York: G. P. Putnam's Sons, 2000), 50.

20. Ibid., 57.

living expenses, do not have money for expensive designer clothes, nor do they always have a $2,000 per year surplus to save consistently over a twenty- or thirty-year period. This is just one more example of how Jakes promotes this very familiar American gospel-of-wealth ideology, which says that everyone can be wealthy, if they just work hard.

The stories that Jakes presents in WTAL and other brands for African American women are not much better. In sum, whether Jakes is seductively painting a picture of the godly man who is waiting to sweep black women off of their feet, or he is inspiring them to have financial dreams that look more like the Emerald City than the black-and-white farmland of Kansas, the stories and the brands that Bishop Jakes lifts up for women are not their reality.

The brands and stories that Jakes presents through his books, movies, and conferences, including the story of the infirmed woman in Luke 11, may inspire and encourage women, but Jakes does not really empower or liberate women with these stories. He is an outstanding preacher. More important, he provides a voice for women who are often forgotten in their local churches and larger society. But, in terms of empowerment, these women are being empowered primarily to stay loyal to Bishop Jakes's brand and to remain women who need *to be loosed*. Essentially, Jakes has empowered them to attend more conferences, purchase more products, and become ministry partners. The stories promoted within the brand are mythological, and ideologically persuasive, but they are not the "truth" for most African American women. Jakes encourages women to seek individual success within an oppressive system.

These women are enticed or seduced by a very familiar politics of respectability and an uplift ideology—traditions from the traditional Black Church. Given the many demonizing negative tropes and stereotypes (such as welfare queen) of the dominant culture and the fact that many black churches do not even ordain women or have them in leadership, I acknowledge and understand why the stories that Jakes tells may be so inviting, even intoxicating. As bell hooks has argued, "marginalized groups, deemed Other, who have been ignored, rendered invisible, can be seduced by the emphasis on

Otherness, by its commodification, because it offers the promise of recognition and reconciliation."[21]

Jakes presents the trope of CEO as if it were easily accessible to everyone, even African American women. However, most women will rarely have the opportunity to be a CEO. In other words, they will never be able to achieve the ultimate trope of empire. Furthermore, the majority of women and men who attend Jakes's church and his conferences do not have, and never will have, the same celebrity status as Jakes.

No different from the Waltons at the helm of Wal-Mart, only a few of the leaders or pastors in the New Black Church will participate within the same economic ranks that Jakes enjoys. Just like Wal-Mart, the financial success of these CEO/preachers is usually supported by the labor and purchasing power of women. Sadly, both the women preachers and the thousands of Pentecostal and charismatic women attendees who are poor or newly middle class—no matter how hard they try, give offerings, and pray—will not have access to the top echelons of economic power. They will more than likely not live like Bishop T.D. Jakes, with a mansion, Bentley, and private plane.

Whether Jakes's theology and his brands communicate a message that meets the standards of academic systematic theology or not, many black Christians and women name Jakes as pastor, leader, and liberator. Bishop T.D. Jakes, Creflo Dollar, Fred Price, Juanita Bynum form a new generation of popular theologians who are successfully presenting their contextual theologies to millions. I am comfortable with naming Jakes as a theologian. But, I am just as convinced that the theology he offers and prescribes for black pastors, ministry partners, and his brand communities is only a *pseudo liberation.* Jakes gives his followers what Jonathan Walton defines as "a liminal space where the unjust realities of race, class, and gender are suspended long enough for viewers [and

---

21. bell hooks, "Eating the Other," in *Black Looks: Race and Representation* (Boston, MA: South End Press, 1992), 26.

brand participants] to imagine themselves living in the world and thriving in such a world."²²

Bishop Jakes's lifestyle and his *theology of empire* endorse a "preferential option for the rich," rather than a "preferential option for the poor." Jakes encourages black women to pursue success and wealth within a system that has proven to be racist, sexist, and classist. As Walton queries, "Is it really possible to 'be loosed' from poverty and attain means of economic wealth when one turns a blind eye to unjust systems of America's capitalist economy that is based on a patristic and exploitative relationship with the underclass?"²³ My answer is "No!"

Liberation has to be more than a liminal space, a moment in worship, or freedom from spiritual infirmities. This is true about all forms of liberation, whether it is the woman in the Gospel of Luke or the character Michelle Jordan from the WTAL movie. Jakes prays for her and says, "Stay free!" Yet, Bishop Jakes exits and Michelle remains incarcerated. Liberation must also be resistance to, and liberation from, economic and political systems that keep black people and women oppressed. The prophetic call is to speak truth to power and facilitate the liberation of women from all situations of oppression.

This book is a challenge and a call for academicians and liberation theologians to speak and to offer more than a caricature or homily about these popular preachers. My goal has been to judge *the model* more *than the man*. No scholar or theologian can determine the integrity of any preacher, nor whether that preacher actually believes his or her own brands and theological propositions. There is no way to know or discern when evangelism and ministry (not-for-profit) become only for-profit. Consequently, because of the "mega-ness," branding, consumerism, and the constant desire for pastors to accumulate wealth, I can only conclude that the New Black Church is a problematic model for African Americans and black churches. More

---

22. Jonathan Walton, *Watch This!: The Ethics and Aesthetics of Black Televangelism* (New York: New York University, 2009), 198.

23. Walton, *Watch This!*, 201.

research is needed by a community of scholars and theologians to understand this very complex model of ministry.

It may be that, like Sam Walton and Wal-Mart, good intentions and early theological or philosophical missions are no contest for the pervasive seductions and cultural influences of advanced capitalism. Perhaps it is like the emperor and his "new clothes": any individual, institution, and its representatives may be systematically co-opted and seduced into the larger hegemonic framework. It is the call of the prophet to proclaim that the emperor is naked, and the call of the scholar to show the nakedness and to challenge all those participating in the parade.

I have presented a clear picture and definition of prosperity theology or theologies of prosperity. I have also presented a theological research method for academicians to place these theologies in dialogue with other theologies and scholarly discourses. This is only the beginning of many more conversations about black churches. Finally, I hope that I have made a small contribution to pay back my personal debt to those many women who nurtured the little girl in the black church across the street from my grandmother's house. Hopefully, as Paul Tillich has urged, I have interpreted the truth of the Christian message for a new generation. Prayerfully, these words are truth for a new generation of black women who will continue to find healing in these places of worship that we continue to identify as black churches.

Bibliography

Adair, Vivyan C. "Branded with Infamy: Inscriptions of Poverty and Class in the United States." *Signs* 27, no. 2 (Winter 2002): 451-71.

Alcoff, Linda. "The Problem of Speaking for Others." *Cultural Critique* 20 (Winter 1991–92): 5-32.

Althusser, Louis. *Essays on Ideology.* London: Verso, 1984.

Anderson, Victor. *Beyond Ontological Blackness: An Essay on African American Religious and Cultural Criticism.* New York: Continuum, 1995.

———. *Creative Exchange: A Constructive Theology of African American Religious Experience.* Minneapolis, MN: Fortress Press, 2008.

Andrews, Dale P. *Practical Theology for Black Churches: Bridging Black Theology and African American Folk Religion.* Louisville, KY: Westminster Press, 2002.

Ayeboyin, Deji Isaac. "A Rethinking of Prosperity Teaching in the New Pentecostal Churches in Nigeria." *Black Theology* 4, no. 1 (2006): 70-86.

Baer, Hans A., and Merrill Singer. *African American Religion: Varieties of Protest and Accommodation.* Knoxville, TN: University of Tennessee Press, 1992.

Baldwin, Lewis V. "Revisiting the 'All-Comprehending Institution'; Historical Reflections on the Public Roles of Black Churches." In *New Day Begun: African American Churches and Civic Culture in Post-Civil Rights America*, edited by R. Drew Smith, 15-38. Durham, NC: Duke University Press, 2003.

————. *The Voice of Conscience: The Church in the Mind of Martin Luther King, Jr.* New York: Oxford University Press, 2010.

Balmer, Randall. *Mine Eyes Have Seen the Glory: A Journey into the Evangelical Subculture in America.* 3rd ed. New York: Oxford University Press, 2000.

Banet-Weiser, *Authentic™: The Politics of Ambivalence in a Brand Culture.* New York: New York University Press, 2012.

Bannon, Bruce. *The Health and Wealth Gospel.* Downers Grove, IL: InterVarsity Press, 1987.

Barnhart, Joe E. "Prosperity Gospel: A New Folk Theology." In *Religious Television*, edited by Robert Abelman and Stewart M. Hoover, 159-64. Norwood, NJ: Ablex Publishing, 1990.

Barr, James. "The Fundamentalist Understanding of Scripture." In *Conflicting Ways of Interpreting the Bible*, edited by Hans Küng and Jürgen Moltmann, 70-74. New York: T. & T. Clark, 1980.

————. "The Problem of Fundamentalism Today." In *Explorations of Theology* 7, edited by James Barr, 65-90. London: SCM Press, 1980.

Battle, Michael. *The Black Church in America: African American Spirituality.* Malden, MA: Blackwell Publishing, 2006.

Bellah, Robert. "Civil Religion in America." *Daedalus* 117, no. 3 (Summer 1988): 97-118.

Berg, Bruce L. *Qualitative Research Methods for the Social Sciences.* Boston, MA: Pearson Press, 2004.

Berger, Peter L. "Pennies from Heaven." *Wall Street Journal,* October 24, 2008.

————. *The Sacred Canopy: Elements of a Sociological Theory of Religion.* New York: Anchor Books, 1967.

Bevans, Stephen B. *Models of Contextual Theology.* Maryknoll, NY: Orbis Books, 1992.

Beverland, Michael. *Building Brand Authenticity: 7 Habits of Iconic Brands.* New York: Palgrave Macmillan, 2009.

Billingsley, Scott. *It's a New Day: Race and Gender in the Modern Charismatic Movement.* Tuscaloosa, AL: University of Alabama Press, 2008.

Blake, John. "Bishop's Charity Generous to Bishop: New Birth's Long Received 3 Million." *Atlanta Journal-Constitution,* August 28, 2005.

———. "Therapy and Theology: Atlanta's Megafest Shows Many Sides of T.D. Jakes Ministry." *Atlanta Journal-Constitution,* June 23, 2004, home edition.

Boff, Leonardo, and Clodovis Boff. *Introducing Liberation Theology.* Maryknoll, NY: Orbis Books, 1987.

Bosshart, David. *Cheap: The Real Cost of the Global Trend for Bargains, Discounts, and Consumer Choice.* Philadelphia: Kogan Page Business Books, 2006.

Bowler, Kate. *Blessed: A History of the American Prosperity Gospel.* New York: Oxford University Press, 2013.

Boyd, Stacy C. *Black Men Worshipping: Intersecting Anxieties of Race, Gender, and Christian Embodiment.* New York: Palgrave Macmillan, 2011.

Bridges, Flora Wilson. *Resurrection Song: African American Spirituality.* Maryknoll, NY: Orbis Books, 2001.

Broadway, Bill. "From His Pulpit, Messages on Prosperity, Pain." *Washington Post,* July 26, 1997.

Bromley, David G., and Anson Shupe. "Rebottling the Elixir: The Gospel of Prosperity in America's Religioeconomic Corporations." In *In Gods We Trust: New Patterns of Religious Pluralism in America,* 2nd rev. ed., edited by Thomas Robbins and Dick Anthony, 233-54. New Brunswick, NJ: Transaction Publishers, 1996.

Brouwer, Steve. *Conquest and Capitalism, 1492–1992.* Carlisle: Big Books, 1992.

Brouwer, Steve, Paul Gifford, and Susan D. Rose. *Exporting the American Gospel: Global Christian Fundamentalism.* New York: Routledge, 1996.

Brown, Carolyn. "Sowing Seeds of Prosperity." *Black Enterprise* 44, no. 8 (April 2014): 54-60.

Brown, Delvin, Sheila Greeve Davaney, and Kathryn Tanner, eds. *Converging on Culture: Theologians in Dialogue with Cultural Analysis and Criticism.* New York: Oxford University Press, 2001.

Bruce, Calvin E. "Black Spirituality, Language and Faith." *Religious Education* 71, no. 4 (July-August 1976): 363-76.

Bruce, Steve. *Pray TV: Televangelism in America*. New York: Routledge, 1990.

Bryman, Alan. *The Disneyization of Society*. Thousand Oaks, CA: Sage Publications, 2004.

Bucher, Glen R. "Toward a Liberation Theology of 'the Oppressor.'" *Journal of the American Academy of Religion* 44, no. 3 (September 1976): 517-34.

Butler, Anthea D. *Women in the Church of God in Christ: Making a Sanctified World*. Chapel Hill, NC: University of North Carolina Press, 2007.

Butler, Anthea D., Jonathan L. Walton, Ronald B. Neal, William D. Hart, Josef Sorett, Edward Blum, and Eddie S. Glaude, Jr. "The Black Church is Dead—Long Live the Black Church." *Religion Dispatches.org*, March 9, 2010. http://www.religiondispatches.org.

Butler, Lee. *Liberating Our Dignity, Saving Our Souls*. St. Louis, MO: Chalice Press, 2006.

Buttrick, David G. *Homiletic Moves and Structures*. Philadelphia: Fortress Press, 1987.

Bynum, Juanita. *No More Sheets: The Truth about Sex*. Lanham, MD: Pneuma Life Publishing, 1998.

Caldwell, Deborah Kovach. "The Power at The Potter's House." *Dallas Morning News*, July 5, 1997, home final edition.

Cannon, Katie G. *Katie's Canon: Womanism and the Soul of the Black Community*. New York: Continuum, 1995.

———. "Sexing Black Women: Liberation from the Prisonhouse of Anatomical Authority." In *Loving the Body: Black Religious Studies and the Erotic*, edited by Anthony Pinn and Dwight Hopkins. New York: Palgrave Macmillan, 2004, 12.

———. "Structured Academic Amnesia: As If the Womanist Story Never Happened." In *Deeper Shades of Purple: Womanism in Religion and Society*, edited by Stacey Floyd-Thomas, 19-28. New York: New York University Press, 2006, 19-28.

———. "'The Wound of Jesus': Justification of Goodness in the Face of Manifest Evil." In *Troubling in My Soul: Womanist Perspectives on Evil and Suffering*, edited by Emilie M. Townes, 219-31. Maryknoll, NY: Orbis Books, 1993.

Carrette, Jeremy, Richard King. *Selling Spirituality: The Silent Take-over of Religion.* New York: Routledge, 2005.

Carnegie, Andrew. "The Gospel of Wealth." In *The North American Review* 183, no. 599 (September 21, 1903): 526-37.

Castelli, Elizabeth A., Stephen D. Moore, Gary A. Phillips, and Regina M. Schwartz. "Ideological Criticism." In *The Postmodern Bible: The Bible and Culture Collective,* edited by Elizabeth A. Castelli, Stephen D. Moore, Gary A. Phillips, and Regina M. Schwartz, 272-307. New Haven, CT: Yale University Press, 1995: 272-301.

Chesnut, R. Andrew. "Pragmatic Consumers and Practical Products: The Success of Pneumacentric Religion among Women in Latin America's New Religious Economy." *Review of Religious Research* 45, no. 1 (September 2003): 20-31.

Cobb, John. "Economic Aspects of Social and Environmental Violence." *Buddhist and Christian Studies* 22 (2002): 3-16.

Cobb, Kelton. *The Blackwell Guide to Theology and Popular Culture.* Malden, MA: Blackwell Publishing, 2005.

Cohen, Cathy J. *The Boundaries of Blackness: AIDS and the Breakdown of Black Politics.* Chicago: University of Chicago Press, 1997.

Cole, Johnetta, and Beverly Guy-Shetfall. *Gender Talk: The Struggle for Women's Equality in African American Communities.* New York: Ballantine Books, 2003.

Coleman, Simon. "America Loves Sweden: Prosperity Theology and the Cultures of Capitalism." In *Religion and the Transformations of Capitalism: Comparative Approaches,* edited by Richard H. Roberts, 161-79. New York: Routledge, 1995.

———. "Charismatic Christianity and the Dilemmas of Globalization." *Religion* 28, no. 3 (1998): 245-56.

———. "Conservative Protestantism and the World Order: The Faith Movement in the United States and Sweden." *Sociology of Religion* 54, no. 4 (Winter 1993): 353-73.

———. *The Globalisation of Charismatic Christianity: Spreading the Gospel of Prosperity.* Cambridge, UK: Cambridge University Press, 2000.

Collier-Thomas, Betty, and James Turner. "Race, Class and Color:

The African American Discourse on Identity." *Journal of American Ethnic History* 14, no. 1 (Fall 1994): 5–31.

Cone, Cecil W. *The Identity Crisis in Black Theology*. Nashville, TN: AMEC, 1975.

Cone, James H. *A Black Theology of Liberation*. 2nd ed. Maryknoll, NY: Orbis Books, 1989.

———. *For My People: Black Theology and the Black Church. Where Have We Been and Where Are We Going?* Maryknoll, NY: Orbis Books, 1984.

———. *God of the Oppressed*. New York: Seabury Press, 1975.

———. "The Sources and Norm of Black Theology." In *The Black Experience in Religion: A Book of Readings*, edited by C. Eric Lincoln, 110-26. New York: Anchor Books, 1974.

Cooke, Phil. *Branding Faith: Why Some Churches and Non-profits Impact Culture and Others Don't*. Ventura, CA: Regal Publishing, 2008.

Copeland, Lib. "With Gifts from God: Bishop T.D. Jakes Has Made Millions by Reaching Millions. Not That There's Anything Wrong with That." *Washington Post*, March 25, 2001.

Cotterell, Peter. *Prosperity Theology*. Leicester, UK: Religious and Theological Studies Fellowship, 1993.

Cox, Harvey. *Fire from Heaven: The Rise of Pentecostal Spirituality and the Reshaping of Religion in the Twenty-First Century*. Reading, MA: Addison-Wesley, 1995.

———. "Mammon and the Culture of the Market: A Socio-Theological Critique." In *Meaning and Modernity: Religion, Polity, and Self*, edited by Richard Madsen, William M. Sullivan, and Steven M. Tipton, 124-35. Berkeley, CA: University of California Press, 2002.

Davis, Donald Mark. "Paul Tillich's Theological Method and the Globalization of Capitalism." Ph.D. diss., University of Iowa, 1999.

Dawson, Michael C. *Black Visions: The Roots of Contemporary African-American Political Ideologies*. Chicago: University of Chicago Press, 2001.

Dodson, Jualynne E. "The Lincoln Legacy: Challenges and Considerations." In *How Long This Road: Race, Religion and the Legacy of C. Eric Lincoln*, edited by Alton B. Pollard and Love Henry Whelchel, Jr., 77-90. New York: Palgrave Macmillan, 2003.

————. *Engendering Church: Women, Power, and the AME Church.* New York: Rowman & Littlefield, 2002.

Douglass, Kelly Brown. "Marginalized People, Liberating Perspectives: A Womanist Approach to Biblical Interpretation." In *I Found God in Me: A Womanist Biblical Hermeneutics Reader,* edited by Mitzi J. Smith. Eugene, OR: Cascade Books, 2015, 80-86.

Drucker, Peter F. "Management's New Paradigms." *Forbes* 162, no. 7 (October 5, 1998): 152-77.

Du Bois, W. E. B., ed. *The Negro Church.* Atlanta, GA: University Publications, 1903.

————. *The Souls of Black Folk.* New York: Signet Classic, 1969 [1903].

Ebony. "Five Questions for Bishop T.D. Jakes." *Ebony* 60, no. 2 (December 2004): 24.

Economist. "Gold and the Gospel: The Healer's Due." Economist. com (May 31, 1997): 28.

"8 Black Pastors Whose Net Worth is 200 Times Greater Than Folks in Their Local Communities." July 6, 2014, http:// atlantablackstar.com.

Einstein, Mara. *Brands of Faith: Marketing Religion in a Commercial Age.* New York: Routledge, 2008.

Evans, Curtis J. *The Burden of Black Religion.* New York: Oxford University Press, 2008.

Evans, James H., Jr. *We Have Been Believers: An African American Systematic Theology.* Minneapolis: Fortress Press, 1992.

Faraci, Matthew. "The Bishop's Life." *Variety* 330, no. 7 (December 2015): 119.

Featherstone, Liza. *Selling Women Short: The Landmark Battle for Worker's Rights at Wal-Mart.* New York: Basic Books, 2004.

Fee, Gordon D. *The Disease of the Health and Wealth Gospels.* Vancouver, BC: Regent College Publishing, 2006.

Fishman, Charles. *The Wal-Mart Effect: How the World's Most Powerful Company Really Works—and How It's Transforming the American Economy.* New York: Penguin Books, 2006.

Ford, Marcia. "Beyond Handselling." *Publisher's Weekly* (September 23, 2002): S2.

Forman, Jadell. "Taking Religion to the Masses." *Texas Monthly* 26, no. 9 (September 1998): 120.

Foster, Stan. *Woman Thou Art Loosed.* Screenplay.

Franklin, Robert M. *Another Day's Journey: Black Churches Confronting the American Crisis.* Minneapolis, MN: Fortress Press, 1997.

————. *Crisis in the Village: Restoring Hope in African American Communities.* Minneapolis, MN: Fortress Press, 2007.

————. "The Gospel of Bling." *Sojourners Magazine* 36, no. 1 (January 1, 2007): 19-23.

Fraser, Nancy, and Linda Gordon. "A Genealogy of Dependency: Tracing a Keyword of the U.S. Welfare State." *Signs* 19, no. 2 (Winter 1994).

Frazier, Edward Franklin. *The Negro Church in America.* New York: Schocken Books, 1963.

Frederick, Marla. *Between Sundays: Black Women and Everyday Struggles of Faith.* Berkeley, CA: University of California Press, 2003.

————. *Colored Television: American Religion Gone Global.* Stanford, CA: Stanford University Press, 2016.

Frederick-McGlathery, Marla. "'But, It's Bible': African American Women and Television Preachers." In *Women and Religion in the African Diaspora: Knowledge, Power, and Performance*, edited by Ruth Marie Griffith and Barbara Dianne Savage, 266-92. Baltimore, MD: Johns Hopkins University Press, 2006.

Gaines, Kevin K. *Uplifting the Race: Black Leadership, Politics, and Culture in the Twentieth Century.* Chapel Hill, NC: University of North Carolina Press, 1996.

Garfinkle, Norton. *The American Dream vs. The Gospel of Wealth: The Fight for a Productive Middle Class Economy.* New Haven, CT: Yale University Press, 2006.

Geertz, Clifford. *The Interpretation of Cultures: Essays by Clifford Geertz.* New York: Basic Books, 1973.

Gifford, Paul. *Christianity and Politics in Doe's Liberia.* Cambridge Studies in Ideology and Religion. New York: Cambridge University Press, 1993.

————. "Christian Fundamentalism and Development." *Review of African Political Economy* 52:9-20.

————. "Expecting Miracles: The Prosperity Gospel in Africa." *Christian Century* 124, no. 14 (July 10, 2007): 20-24.

————. *Ghana's New Christianity: Pentecostalism in a Globalizing African Economy.* Bloomington, IN: Indiana University Press, 2004.

————. *The New Crusaders: Christianity and the New Right in Southern Africa.* London: Pluto Press, 1991.

————. "Prosperity: A New and Foreign Element in African Christianity." *Religion* 20 (1990): 373-88.

Gilkes, Cheryl Townsend. *"If It Wasn't for the Women . . . :" Black Women's Experience and Womanist Culture in Church and Community.* Maryknoll, NY: Orbis Books, 2001.

————. "Plenty Good Room: Adaptation in a Changing Black Church." *Annals of the American Academy of Political and Social Sciences* 558 (July 1998): 101-21.

Glaude, Eddie, Jr. "The Black Church Is Dead." *The Huffington Post,* February 24, 2010. http://www.huffingtonpost.com.

————. "Myth and African American Self-Identity." In *Religion and the Creation of Race and Ethnicity: An Introduction,* edited by Craig Prentiss, 28-42. New York: New York University Press, 2003.

Grant, Jacqueline. *White Women's Christ and Black Women's Jesus: Feminist Christology and Womanist Response.* Atlanta, GA: Scholars Press, 1989.

Grant, Tim. "Collections Take New Form after Plates are Passed." *St. Petersburg Times,* February 13, 2000, late Tampa edition.

Gray, Herman. *Watching Race: Television and the Struggle for Blackness.* Minneapolis, MN: University of Minnesota Press, 1995.

Griffin, David Ray, John B. Cobb, Jr., Richard A. Falk, and Catherine Keller. *The American Empire and the Commonwealth of God: A Political, Economic, Religious Statement.* Louisville, KY: Westminster John Knox, 2006.

Grogan, Geoffrey. "Liberation and Prosperity Theologies." *The Scottish Bulletin of Evangelical Theology* 9 (September 1991): 118-32.

Gross, Kali N. "Examining the Politics of Respectability in African

American Studies." *Almanac* 43, no. 28 (1997). http://www. upenn.edu.

Grossberg, Lawrence, Cary Nelson, and Paula A. Treichler. *Cultural Studies*. New York: Routledge, 1992.

Gutiérrez, Gustavo. *A Theology of Liberation*. Maryknoll, NY: Orbis Press, 1973.

Hackett, Rosalind I. T. "Charismatic/Pentecostal Appropriation of Media Technologies in Nigeria and Ghana." *Journal of Religion in Africa* 28, no. 3 (August 1998): 258-77.

Hadden, Jeffrey K., and Anson Shupe. *Televangelism: Power and Politics on God's Frontier*. New York: Henry Holt and Company, 1988.

Hall, David D., ed. *Lived Religion in America: Toward a History of Practice*. Princeton, NJ: Princeton University Press, 1997.

Hall, Stuart. "Cultural Studies: Two Paradigms." *Media, Culture, and Society* 2, no. 1 (January 1980): 57-82.

Hamilton, Charles. *The Black Preacher in America*. New York: Morrow, 1972.

Harris, Paisley. "Gatekeeping and Remaking: The Politics of Respectability in African American Women's History and Black Feminism." *Journal of Women's History* 15, no. l (Spring 2003): 212-20.

Harris-Lacewell, Melissa. "From Liberation to Mutual Fund: Political Consequences of Differing Conceptions of Christ in the African American Church." In *From Pews to Polling Places: Faith and Politics in the American Religious Mosaic*, edited by J. Matthew Wilson, 131-60. Washington, D.C.: Georgetown University Press, 2007.

Harrison, Milmon F. *Righteous Riches: The Word of Faith Movement in Contemporary African American Religion*. New York: Oxford University Press, 2005.

Haskins, Jim, and Kathleen Benson, *African American Religious Leaders*. San Francisco: Jossey-Bass, 2008.

Hasu, Paivi. "World Bank & Heavenly Bank in Poverty & Prosperity: The Case of Tanzanian Faith Gospel." *Review of African Political Economy* 33, no. 110 (September 2006): 679-92.

Hellstern, Mark. "The 'Me' Gospel: An Examination of the Historical Roots of the Prosperity Emphasis within Current

Charismatic Theology." *Fides et Historia* 21, no. 3 (October 1989): 78-90.

Henry, Kaylois. "Bishop Jakes Is Ready Are You? The Nation's Hottest Preacher Brings His Message to Dallas." *Dallas Observer,* June 20, 1996.

Hewitt, Marsha Aileen. "Ideology Critique, Feminism, and the Study of Religion." *Method & Theory in the Study of Religion* 11, no. 1 (1999): 47-63.

Higginbotham, Evelyn Brooks. "African-American Women's History and the Metalanguage of Race." *Signs* 27, no. 2 (Winter 1992): 251-74.

————. *Righteous Discontent: The Women's Movement in the Black Baptist Church, 1880–1920.* Cambridge, MA: Harvard University Press, 1993.

Hill, Marc Lamont. "The Barbershop Notebooks: 'I Bling Because I'm Happy,'" August 5, 2005. http://www.popmatters.com.

Hill Collins, Patricia. *Black Feminist Thought: Knowledge, Consciousness, and the Politics of Empowerment.* New York: Routledge, 1991.

————. *Black Sexual Politics: African Americans, Gender, and the New Racism.* New York: Routledge, 2005.

Hodgson, Godfrey. *The Myth of American Exceptionalism.* New Haven, CT: Yale University Press, 2009.

hooks, bell. "Eating the Other." In *Black Looks: Race and Representation*, 21-40. Boston, MA: South End Press, 1992.

————. *Yearning: Race, Gender, and Cultural Politics.* Boston, MA: South End Press, 1990.

Hollinger, David. "Enjoying God Forever: A Historical/Sociological Profile of the Health and Wealth Gospel in the USA." In *Religion and Power, Decline and Growth: Sociological Analyses of Religion in Britain, Poland, and the Americas*, edited by Peter Gee and John Fulton, 53-66. Twickenham: British Sociological Association, Sociology of Religion Group, 1991.

Hoover, Stewart M. *Religion in the Media Age.* New York: Routledge, 2006.

Hopkins, Dwight N. *Shoes That Fit Our Feet: Sources for a Constructive Black Theology.* Maryknoll, NY: Orbis Books, 1993.

Hopkins, Dwight N., and Sheila Greeve Devaney, eds. *Changing Conversations: Religious Reflection and Cultural Analysis*. New York: Routledge, 1996.

Horsley, Richard A., ed. *In the Shadow of Empire: Reclaiming the Bible as a History of Faithful Resistance*. Louisville, KY: Westminster John Knox, 2008.

Howard, Ron R. "Gender and the Point of View in the Imagery of Preaching." *Homiletic* 24, no. 1 (Summer 1999).

Howard-Pitney, David. "'To Form a More Perfect Union': African Americans and American Civil Religion." In *New Day Begun: African American Churches and Civic Culture in Post-Civil Rights America*, edited by R. Drew Smith, 89-112. Durham, NC: Duke University Press, 2003.

Hubbard, Dolan. *The Sermon and the African American Literary Imagination*. Columbia, MO: University of Missouri Press, 1994, 4.

Hummel, George E. *The Prosperity Gospel: Health and Wealth and the Faith Movement*. Downers Grove, IL: InterVarsity Press, 1991.

Hunt, Stephen. "'Winning Ways': Globalisation and the Impact of the Health and Wealth Gospel." *Journal of Contemporary Religion* 15, no. 3 (2000): 331-47.

Isasi-Díaz, Ana María. *Mujerista Theology: A Theology for the Twenty-first Century*. Maryknoll, NY: Orbis Books, 1996.

Jackson, Martha. "Jakes Hiked Long Road to Success." *Charleston Daily Mail*, November 18, 1995.

Jackson, Robert. "Prosperity Theology and the Faith Movement." *Themelios* 15 (October 1989): 16-24.

Jakes, Jaqueline Yvonne. *God's Trophy Women: You Are Blessed and Highly Favored*. New York: Hachette Book Group, 2006.

Jakes, Sarah. *Colliding with Destiny: Finding Hope in the Legacy of Ruth*. Bloomington, MN: Bethany House Publishers, 2014.

Jakes, Serita. *The Princess Within: Restoring the Soul of a Woman*. Bloomington, MN: Bethany House Publishing, 2011

Jakes, T.D. *God's Leading Lady: Out of the Shadows and into the Light*. New York: G. P. Putnam's Sons, 2002.

―――. *The Great Investment: Faith, Family, and Finance.* New York: G. P. Putnam's Sons, 2000.

―――. *The Lady, Her Lover, Her Lord.* New York: Berkley Trade, 1998.

―――. *Lose That Man and Let Him Go.* Tulsa, OK: Albury Publishing, 1995.

―――. *Reposition Yourself: Living Life Without Limits.* New York: Atria Books, 2007.

―――. *Woman Thou Art Loosed: Healing the Wounds of the Past.* Shippensburg, PA: Treasure House, 1993.

Johansson, Erin. "Checking Out: The Rise of Wal-Mart and the Fall of Middle Class Retailing Jobs." *Connecticut Law Review* 39, no. 4 (May 2007), 1461-91.

Jones, Serene. *Feminist Theory and Christian Theology: Cartographies of Grace.* Minneapolis, MN: Fortress Press, 2000.

Kaufman, Gordon. *An Essay on Theological Method.* 3rd ed. Atlanta, GA: Scholars Press, 1995.

―――. *Systematic Theology: A Historicist Perspective.* New York: Charles Scribner's Sons, 1968.

Kelly, Robin D. "'We Are Not What We Seem': Rethinking Black Working-Class Opposition in the Jim Crow South." *Journal of American History* 80, no. 1 (June 1993): 75-112.

King, Deborah K. "Multiple Jeopardy, Multiple Consciousness: The Context of Black Feminist Ideology." *Signs* 14 no. 1 (1988): 42-72.

Koch, Bradley A. "The Prosperity Gospel and Economic Prosperity: Race, Giving, and Voting." Ph.D. diss., Indiana University, 2009.

Kort, Wesley A. *Bound to Differ: The Dynamics of Theological Discourses.* University Park, PA: Pennsylvania State University Press, 1992.

Kroll, Luisa. "Christian Capitalism: Megachurches, Megabusinesses." *Forbes,* September 17, 2003. http://www.forbes.com.

LaRue, Cleophus J. *The Heart of Black Preaching.* Louisville, KY: Westminster John Knox Press, 2000.

Lausanne Theology Working Group. "Statement on the Prosperity Gospel: From the Africa Chapter of the Lausanne Theology

Working Group at Its Consultation in Akripong, Ghana, 8-9 October, 2008 and 1-4 September 2009." *Evangelical Review of Theology* 34, no. 2 (April 2010): 99-102.

Lee, Shayne. *T.D. Jakes: America's New Preacher.* New York: New York University Press, 2005.

Lee, Shayne, and Phillip Luke Sinitiere. *Holy Mavericks: Evangelical Innovators and the Spiritual Marketplace.* New York: New York University Press, 2009.

Leffall, Dolores C. *The Black Church: An Annotated Bibliography.* Washington, DC: Minority Research Center, 1973.

Lippy, Charles H. *Being Religious American Style: A History of Popular Religiosity in the United States.* Westport, CT: Greenwood Press, 1994.

———. *Modern American Popular Religion: A Critical Assessment and Annotated Bibliography.* Westport, CT: Greenwood Press, 1996.

Lincoln, C. Eric. *The Black Church since Frazier.* New York: Schocken Books, 1974.

———, ed. *The Black Experience in Religion: A Book of Readings.* Garden City, NY: Anchor Books, 1974.

Lincoln, C. Eric, and Lawrence H. Mamiya. *The Black Church in the African American Experience.* Durham, NC: Duke University Press, 1990.

Long, Charles H. *Significations: Signs, Symbols, and Images in the Interpretation of Religion.* Aurora, CO: Davies Group Publishers, 1995.

Loy, David R. "The Religion of the Market." *Journal of the American Academy of Religion* 65, no. 2 (1997): 275-90.

Lyon, David. *Jesus in Disneyland: Religion in Postmodern Times.* Cambridge: Polity Press, 2000.

Machacek, David W. "Prosperity Theology." In *Contemporary American Religion.* Vol. 2, edited by Wade Clarke Roof. New York: Macmillian Reference USA, 1999.

Mamiya, Lawrence. *River of Struggle, River of Freedom: Trends among Black Churches and Black Pastoral Leadership: Pulpit and Pew Research on Pastoral Leadership Reports.* Durham, NC: Duke Divinity School, 2006.

Marable, Manning. *Beyond Black and White: Transforming African American Politics*. 2nd ed. New York: Verso, 2009.

———. *Blackwater: Historical Studies in Race, Class Consciousness, and Revolution*. Niwot, CO: University Press of Colorado, 1993.

Marshall, P. David. *Celebrity and Power: Fame in Contemporary Culture*. Minneapolis, MN: University of Minnesota Press, 1997.

Martin, William. "American Idol." *Texas Monthly* 34, no. 8 (August 2006): 122-214.

Marty, Martin E. *Righteous Empire: The Protestant Experience in America*. New York: Dial Press, 1970.

Mauss, Marcel. *The Gift: The Form and Reason for Exchange in Archaic Societies*, translated by W. D. Halls. New York: Routledge, 1990.

Mays, Benjamin, and Joseph Nicholson. *The Negro's Church*. New York: The Institute of Social and Religious Research, 1933.

McClendon, James William, Jr. *Biography as Theology: How Life Stories Can Remake Today's Theology*. Nashville, TN: Abingdon, 1974.

McCloud, Sean. *Divine Hierarchies: Class in American Religion and Religious Studies*. Chapel Hill, NC: University of North Carolina Press, 2007.

McConnell, Dan R. *A Different Gospel: Biblical and Historical Insights into the Word of Faith Movement*. Tulsa: Faith Library, 1980.

———. *A Different Gospel: Biblical and Historical Insights into the Word of Faith Movement*. Rev. ed. Peabody, MA: Hendrickson, 1995.

McGee, Paula L. "Pastor or CEO? The New Black Church Leaders," *NBV: The National Baptist Voice* 5, no. 3 (Summer 2006), 64-65.

———. "Feminist Theology, Identity, and Discourse: A Closer Look at the 'Coming Out' of Sheryl Swoopes." *Feminist Theology* 19, no. 1 (2005): 54-72.

———. "The Wal-Martization of African American Religion: T.D. Jakes and Woman Thou Art Loosed." 2012. CGU Thesis and Dissertations. Paper 70. http://scholarship.claremont.edu/cgu_etd/70.

MegaFest International. "Megafest Press Release," 2008. http://www.mega-fest.com.

Miles, Margaret R. *Seeing and Believing: Religion and Values in the Movies*. New York: Beacon Press, 1996.

Miller, Lisa. "Prophet Motives: Grammy Nomination, Book Deal, TV Spots—A Holy Empire Is Born." *Wall Street Journal,* August 21, 1998, eastern edition.

Miller, Vincent. *Consuming Religion: Christian Faith and Practice in a Consumer Culture*. New York: Continuum, 2004.

Mitchell, Henry H. *Black Preaching: The Recovery of a Powerful Art*. Nashville, TN: Abingdon Press, 1990.

Mitchem, Stephanie Y. *Name It and Claim It? Prosperity Preaching in the Black Church*. Cleveland, OH: Pilgrim Press, 2007.

Mizruchi, Susan L., ed. *Religion and Cultural Studies*. Princeton, NJ: Princeton University Press, 2001.

Morgan, David, and Iain Wilkinson. "The Problem of Suffering and the Sociological Task of Theodicy." *European Journal of Social Theory* 4, no. 2 (2001): 199-214.

Morken, Hubert. "Bishop T.D. Jakes: A Ministry of Empowerment." In *Religious Leaders and Faith-Based Politics: Ten Profiles*, edited by Jo Renee Formicola and Hubert Morken, 25-52. Lanham, MD: Rowman & Littlefield, 2001.

Morris, Aldon D. *The Origins of the Civil Rights Movement: Black Communities Organizing for Change*. New York: Free Press, 1984.

Moyd, Olin P. *The Sacred Art: Preaching and Theology in the African American Tradition*. Valley Forge, PA: Judson Press, 1995.

Mumford, Debra. *Exploring Prosperity Preaching: Biblical Health, Wealth & Wisdom*. Valley Forge, PA: Judson Press, 2012.

Muskus, Eddy. "Liberation Theology: Its Origins and Early Development." Affinity Archives. Foundations 29 (Autumn 1992): 31-41. http://www.affinity.org.

Nelsen, Hart, and Anne Nelsen. *The Black Church in the Sixties*. Lexington, KY: University of Kentucky Press, 1975.

Muniz, A. M., and T. C. Guinn. "Brand Community." *Journal of Consumer Research* 27, no. 4 (March 2001): 412-42.

Nelson, Janet R. "Walter Rauschenbusch and the Social Gospel: A Hopeful Theology for the Twenty-First Century Economy." *Crosscurrents* 59, no. 4 (December 2009): 442-56.

Niebuhr, Gustav. "Where Religion Gets a Big Dose of Shopping-Mall Culture." *New York Times*, April 16, 1995.

Ortega, Bob. *In Sam We Trust; The Untold Story of Sam Walton and How Wal-Mart Is Devouring America.* New York: Time Business Random House, 1998.

Pappu, Sridhar. "The Preacher." *Atlantic Monthly* 297, no. 2 (March 2006): 92-103.

Paris, Peter J. "African American Religion and Public Life: An Assessment." *Cross Currents* 58, no. 3 (Fall 2008): 475-94.

———. *The Social Teaching of the Black Churches.* Philadelphia: Fortress Press, 1985.

Pattillo-McCoy, Mary. "Church Culture as a Strategy of Action in the Black Community." *American Sociological Association* 63, no. 6 (December 1998): 767-84.

Perriman, Andrew, ed. *Faith, Health and Prosperity: A Report on "Word of Faith" and "Positive Confession" Theologies by ACUTE (Evangelical Alliance Commission on Unity and Truth among Evangelicals).* Carlisle: Cumbria UK: Paternoster Press, 2003.

Pew Forum on Religion and Public Life. *Spirit and Power: A 10-Country Survey of Pentecostals,* October 6, 2006. Washington, DC: The Pew Forum on Religion and Public Life. http://www.pewforum.org.

Phillips, Kevin. *The Politics of Rich and Poor: Wealth and the American Electorate in the Regan Aftermath.* New York: Random House, 1990.

Pinn, Anthony. *The Black Church in the Post-Civil Rights Era.* Maryknoll, NY: Orbis Books, 2002.

———. "Jesus and Justice: An Outline of Liberation Theology within Black Churches." *Crosscurrents* 57, no. 2 (Summer 2007): 218-26.

———.ed., *Moral Evil and Redemptive Suffering: A History of Theodicy in African-American Religious Thought.* Gainesville, FL: University of Florida Press, 2002.

Poole, Sheila M., Megan Matteucci, and Katie Leslie. "Lawsuits

Accuse Bishop Long of Sexual Coercion; Long 'Adamantly Denies.'" *Atlanta Journal-Constitution*, September 21, 2010. http://www.ajc.com.

Posner, Sarah. *God's Profits: Faith, Fraud, and the Republican Crusade for Values Voters.* Sausalito, CA: PoliPoint Press, 2008.

Potter Engel, Mary, and Susan Brooks Thistlethwaite. "Introduction: Making the Connections among Liberation Theologies Around the World." In *Lift Every Voice: Constructing Christian Theologies from the Underside*, edited by Mary Potter Engel and Susan Brooks Thistlethwaite, 1-18. Rev. and expanded ed. New York: Harper and Row, 1998.

Potter's House. "T.D. Jakes Biography." http://www.thepotters house.org.

"Prosperity Gospel." Episode no. 1051. *Religion and Ethics Newsweekly.* August 17, 2007. http://www.pbs.org.

Quinn, Christopher. "Megafest Takes an Indefinite Break." *Atlanta Journal-Constitution,* July 3, 2007. main edition.

Raboteau, Albert J. "African Americans, Exodus, and the American Israel." In *Fire in the Bones: Reflections on African American Religious History,* 17-36. Boston, MA: Beacon Press, 1995.

———. *Slave Religion: The "Invisible Institution" in the Antebellum South.* New York: Oxford University Press, 1978.

Richardson, Nicole Marie, Krissah Williams, and Hamil Harris. "The Business Faith." *Black Enterprise* 36 no. 10 (May 2006): 102-14.

Rieger, Joerg. *Christ and Empire: From Paul to Postcolonial Times.* Minneapolis, MN: Fortress Press, 2007.

Riggs, Marcia. *Plenty Good Room: Women versus Male Power in the Black Church.* Cleveland, OH: Pilgrim Press, 2003.

Ritzer, George. *The McDonaldization of Society.* Thousand Oaks, CA: Pine Forge Press, 2004.

Roberts, J. Deotis. *Bonhoeffer and King: Speaking Truth to Power.* Louisville, KY: Westminster John Knox Press, 2005.

Roberts, Oral. *How I Learned Jesus Was Not Poor.* Altamonte Springs, FL: Creation House, 1989.

———. *Miracle of Seed Faith.* Tulsa, OK: Oral Roberts Evangelistic Association, 1970.

Roof, Wade Clark. *The Spiritual Marketplace: Baby Boomers and the Remaking of American Religion*. Princeton, NJ: Princeton University Press, 1999.

Ruether, Rosemary Radford. "Religion and Society: Sacred Canopy vs. Prophetic Critique." In *The Future of Liberation Theology: Essays in Honor of Gustavo Gutiérrez*, edited by Marc H. Ellis and Otto Maduro, 172-76. Maryknoll, NY: Orbis Books, 1989.

————. *Sexism and God-Talk: Toward a Feminist Theology*. 2nd ed. Boston: Beacon Press, 1993.

Sarles, Ken L. "A Theological Evaluation of the Prosperity Gospel." *Bibliotheca Sacra* 143, no. 572 (October–December 1986): 329-52.

Saroyan, Strawberry. "Christianity, the Brand." *New York Times Magazine*, April 16, 2006: 46-51.

Savage, Barbara Dianne. *Your Spirits Walk beside Us: The Politics of Black Religion*. Cambridge, MA: Belknap Press of Harvard University Press, 2008.

Scharen, Christian. "Ideology, Ritual, and Christian Subjectivity." *Worship* 70, no. 5 (Summer 1996): 406-22.

Schmidt, Eric Leigh. "Practices of Exchange: From Market Culture to Gift Economy in the Interpretation of American Religion." In *Lived Religion in America: Toward a History of Practice*, edited by David D. Hall, 69-91. Princeton, NJ: Princeton University Press, 1997.

Schreiter, Robert J. *Constructing Local Theologies*. Maryknoll, NY: Orbis Books, 1985.

Schultze, Quentin J. *Televangelism and American Culture: The Business of Popular Religion*. Grand Rapids, MI: Baker Book House, 1991.

————. "Television Drama as a Sacred Text." In *Channels of Belief: Religion and American Commercial Television*, edited by John P. Ferre, 3-28. Ames, IA: Iowa State University.

Schüssler Fiorenza, Elisabeth. "Method in Women's Studies in Religion: A Critical Feminist Hermeneutics." In *Methodology in Religious Studies: The Interface with Women's Studies*, edited by Arvind Sharma, 207-42. New York: State University of New York Press, 2002.

———. *The Power of the Word: Scripture and the Rhetoric of Empire.* Minneapolis, MN: Fortress Press, 2007.

———. *Rhetoric and Ethic: The Politics of Biblical Studies.* Minneapolis, MN: Fortress Press, 1999.

Schutte, Flip. "Myth as Paradigm to Read a Text." In *Psalms and Mythology,* edited by Dirk J. Human, 1-8. New York: T & T Clark, 2007.

Scott, Bernard Brandon. *Hollywood Dreams and Biblical Stories.* Minneapolis, MN: Fortress Press, 1994.

Scott, James C. *Domination and the Arts of Resistance.* New Haven, CT: Yale University Press, 1990.

Sedmak, Clemens. *Doing Local Theology: A Guide for Artisans of a New Humanity.* Maryknoll, NY: Orbis Books, 2002.

Segovia, Fernando F. *Decolonizing Biblical Studies: A View from the Margins.* Maryknoll, NY: Orbis Books, 2000.

———. "Toward a Hermeneutics of Diaspora: A Hermeneutics of Otherness and Engagement." In *Reading from This Place.* Vol. 1, *Social Location and Biblical Interpretation in the United States,* edited by Fernando F. Segovia and Mary Ann Tolbert, 57-74. Minneapolis, MN: Fortress Press, 1991.

Siegel, Tatiana. "Author Jakes Lands Inspiring Deal with SPE," *Hollywood Reporter* 394, no. 1 (April 18, 2006): 4.

Slagle, Dana. "The Personal Side of T.D. Jakes." *Jet,* July 2007, 8-60.

Smith, Archie, Jr. *The Relational Self: Ethics & Therapy from a Black Church Perspective.* Nashville, TN: Abingdon Press, 1982.

Smith, Theophus. "Ethnography-as-Theology: Inscribing the African American Sacred Story." In *Theology Without Foundations: Religious Practice and the Future of Theological Truth,* edited by Stanley Hauerwas, Nancey Murphy, and Mark Nation, 117-39. Nashville, TN: Abingdon Press, 1994.

Spivak, Gayatri Chakravorty. "Can the Subaltern Speak?" In *Marxism and the Interpretation of Cultures,* edited by Cary Nelson and Lawrence Grossberg, 271-316. London: Routledge, 1988.

Starling, Kelly. "Why People, Especially Women, Are Talking about Bishop T.D. Jakes." *Ebony* 56, no. 3 (January 2001): 108-14.

Stephanson, Anders. *Manifest Destiny: American Exceptionalism and the Empire of Right.* New York: Hill and Wang, 1995.

Stenger, Mary Ann. "Paul Tillich's Theory of Theological Norms and the Problems of Relativism and Subjectivism." *Journal of Religion* 62, no. 4 (October 1982): 359-75.

Stievermann, Jan, Phillip Goff, and Detlef Junker, eds. *Religion and the Marketplace in the United States.* New York: Oxford University Press, 2014.

Storbakken, Jason. "God Is in the T-Bills." *Forbes* 179, no. 12 (June 2007): 58.

Stuart, Elisabeth, Tim Morrison, and John McMahon. *Religion Is a Queer Thing: A Guide to the Christian Faith for Lesbian, Gay, Bisexual and Transgendered People.* Cleveland, OH: Pilgrim Press, 1997.

Swanson, Douglass J. "The Beginning of the End of Robert H. Schuller's Crystal Cathedral Ministry: A Towering Failure in Crisis Management as Reflected Through Media Narratives of Financial Crisis, Family Conflict, and Follower Dissent." *Social Science Journal* 49, no. 4 (December 2012): 485-93.

Synan, Vinson. "Word of Faith Movement Has Deep Roots in American History." http://www.believersstandunited.com.

Tanner, Kathryn. "Theology and Popular Culture." In *Changing Conversations: Religious Reflections & Cultural Analysis*, edited by Dwight N. Hopkins and Sheila Greeve Davaney, 101-22. New York: Routledge, 1996.

Taylor, Mark Lewis. *Religion, Politics, and the Christian Right: Post 9/11 Powers and American Empire.* Minneapolis, MN: Fortress Press, 2005.

Terrie, Martha E. "Social Constructions and Cultural Contradictions: A Look at a Christian Perspective on Economics." *Journal of American Culture* 17, no. 3 (September 1994): 55-63.

Tillich, Paul. "Problem of Theological Method II." *Journal of Religion* 27, no. 1 (January 1947): 16-26.

———. *Systematic Theology.* Vol. 1. Chicago: University of Chicago Press, 1971.

Trim, Cindy. *The 40 Day Soul Fast: Journey to Authentic Living.* Shippensburg, PA: Destiny Image, 2011.

Trimiew, Darryl M., and Michael Greene. "How We Got Over: The Moral Teachings of the African-American Church on Business Ethics." *Business Ethics Quarterly* 7, no. 2 (1997): 133-48.

Trulear, Harold Dean. "The Lord Will Make a Way Somehow: Black Worship and the Afro-American Story." *Journal of the Interdenominational Theological Center* 13, no. 1 (Fall 1985): 87-104.

Tucker-Worgs, Tamelyn. *The Black Megachurch: Theology, Gender, and the Politics of Public Engagement.* Waco, TX: Baylor University Press, 2011.

Twitchell, James B. *Branded Nation: The Marketing of Megachurch, College, Inc., and Museumworld.* New York: Simon & Schuster, 2005.

————.*Shopping for God: How Christianity Went from in Your Heart to in Your Face.* New York: Simon & Schuster, 2007.

Ukah, Asonzeh. *A New Paradigm of Pentecostal Power: A Study of the Redeemed Christian Church of God in Nigeria.* Trenton, NJ: Africa Word Press, 2008.

United Automobile Workers. "UAW History." http://www.uaw.org.

Van Biema, David. "Spirit Raiser: America's Best." *Time,* September 17, 2001, 52.

————, and Jeff Chu. "Does God Want You to Be Rich?" *Time,* September 18, 2006, 48–56.

Wallis, Jim. *God's Politics: Why the Right Gets It Wrong and the Left Doesn't Get It.* New York: HarperSanFrancisco, 2005.

Walton, Jonathan L. "A Cultural Analysis of the Black Electronic Church Phenomenon." Ph.D. diss., Princeton Theological Seminary, 2006.

————. "Empowered: The Entrepreneurial Ministry of T.D. Jakes." *Christian Century* 124 no. 14 (July 10, 2007): 25-28.

———. *Watch This: The Ethics and Aesthetics of Black Televangelism.* New York: New York University Press, 2009.

Ward, Ken, Jr. "Successful Books, TV Exposure Allow Kanwaha Minister to Live in Style." *Charleston Gazette*, April 5, 1995.

Warner, Stephen R. "Work in Progress Toward a New Paradigm for the Sociological Study of Religion in the United States." *American Journal of Sociology* 98, no. 5 (March 1993): 1044-93.

Warren, Rick. *The Purpose-Driven Church: Growth Without Compromising Your Message and Your Mission*. Grand Rapids, MI: Zondervan, 1995.

———. *The Purpose-Driven Life*. Grand Rapids, MI: Zondervan, 2002.

Watkins, Justin R. "Always Low Prices, Always at a Cost: A Call to Arms Against the Wal-Martization of America." *John Marshall Law School Review* 40 (2006–7): 267-309.

Watts, Benjamin K. "Social Justice and Church Growth in the African-American Church." In *Why Liberal Churches Are Growing*, edited by Martyn Percy and Ian Markham, 87-99. New York: T & T Clark International, 2006.

Weedon, Chris. *Identity and Culture*. New York: Open University, 2004.

Weekley, Ayana. "Why Can't We Flip the Script: The Politics of Respectability in Pearl Cleage's What Looks Like Crazy on an Ordinary Day." *Michigan Feminist Studies* 21, no. 1 (Fall 2008): 24-42.

Weiss, Richard. *The American Myth of Success from Horatio Alger to Norman Vincent Peale*. New York: Basic Books, 1969.

West, Cornel. "Black Theology and Marxist Thought." In *African American Religious Thought: An Anthology*, edited by Cornel West and Eddie S. Glaude, Jr., 874-92. Louisville, KY: Westminster John Knox, 2003.

———. *Democracy Matters: Winning the Fight Against Imperialism*. New York: Penguin Press, 2004.

———. *Prophecy Deliverance!: An Afro-American Revolutionary Christianity*. Philadelphia: Westminister Press, 1982.

———. *Prophetic Fragments*. Grand Rapids, MI: William B. Eerdmans, 1988.

———. *Race Matters*. New York: Vantage Books, 1994.

Whitford, David. "So Shall Ye Reap." *Fortune Small Business* 15, no. 8 (October 2005): 32.

Wiggins, Daphne. *Righteous Content: Black Women's Perspectives of Church and Faith*. New York: New York University Press, 2005.

Williams, Chad, and Kidada E. Williams, and Keisha N. Blain, eds. *Charleston Syllabus: Readings on Race, Racism, and Racial Violence*. Athens, GA: University Georgia Press, 2016.

Williams, Delores. *Sisters in the Wilderness: The Challenge of Womanist God-Talk.* Maryknoll, NY: Orbis Books, 1993.

Williams Crenshaw, Kimberlé. "Mapping the Margins: Intersectionality, Identity Politics, and Violence Against Women of Color." *Stanford Law Review* 43, no. 6 (July 1991): 1241-99.

Wilmore, Gayraud S. *Black Religion and Black Radicalism: An Interpretation of the Religious History of Afro-American People.* 2nd ed. Maryknoll, NY: Orbis Books, 1983.

————. *Pragmatic Spirituality: The Christian Faith through an Africentric Lens.* New York: New York University Press, 2004.

Wilson Bridges, Flora. *Resurrection Song: African American Spirituality.* Maryknoll, NY: Orbis Books, 2001.

Winner, Lauren. "T.D. Jakes Feels Your Pain." *Christianity Today* 44, no. 2 (February 7, 2000): 53-59.

Wolcott, Victoria W. *Remaking Respectability: African American Women in Interwar.* Chapel Hill: University of North Carolina Press, 2001.

Woman Thou Art Loosed, special edition DVD, directed by Michael Schultz. Beverly Hills, CA: Twentieth Century Fox Home Entertainment, 2006.

Woman Thou Art Loosed: Live at Azusa, VHS. Dallas, TX: T.D. Jakes Ministries, 1993.

Woman Thou Art Loosed: Thankful Women, CD. Dallas, TX: T.D. Jakes Ministries, 2009.

Woodson, Carter G. *The History of the Negro Church.* 3rd ed. Washington DC: Associated Publishers, 1972.

Wright, Melanie J. *Religion and Film: An Introduction.* New York: I. B. Tauris, 2007.

Wuthnow, Robert. *After Heaven: Spirituality in America since the 1950s.* Berkeley, CA: University of California Press, 1998.

Young, Iris Marion. *Justice and the Politics of Difference.* Princeton, NJ: Princeton University Press, 1990.

Young, Richard. *The Journey of T.D. Jakes: Living a Life of Faith, Blessing, and Favor.* New Kensington, PA: Whitaker House, 2008.

Index